D1878992

EDUCATIONAL PLANNING

EDUCATIONAL PLANNING

Prof. Shri Prakash

GYAN

GYAN PUBLISHING HOUSE

NEW DELHI-110002

EDUCATIONAL PLANNING

(Education)

ISBN: 81-212-0603-0

Reprinted in 2011 in India by
Gyan Publishing House
23, Main Ansari Road, Daryaganj,
New Delhi - 110002
Phone : 23282060, 23261060
Fax : (011) 23285914
E-mail : books@gyanbooks.com
website: gyanbooks.com

Printed at: G. Print Process, Delhi

Contents

Preface

Education has always been and still remains an essential part of socio-economic milieu. Education not only conditions and governs social transformation but it also contributes both directly and indirectly to the growth of the economy. At the same time, it furnishes an instrument of conditioning the thought processes and behavioural propensities of individuals. Hence, it acts as an agent of socio-economic change. It also offers a potent weapon to the rulers for brain-washing, if they so choose to use education for narrow and selfish purposes. But the educational system draws its sustenance from the economy, social system, institutional structure and the overall intellectual environment. On the other hand, education also contributes both directly and indirectly to economic growth, psychological change and institutional restructuring. Above all, education is the single largest source of inventions, innovations, and hence, technological developments. Education is the largest employer of educated manpower. Such a complex web of multi-dimensional relationships naturally necessitates intricate developmental planning, comprehensive and all encompassing policy framework.

Though education has always been planned at the institutional level by academic administrators and at individual level by teachers, parents and students, planning of education at the societal level had emerged much later, when it was felt that the development and maintenance of educational system at any given level requires huge amounts of resources, vast network of administrative support base and the common pool of wisdom for the management of educational system. These resources and competencies are difficult to be mobilised by individual parents and individual institutions. Therefore, public interventions, partial or complete state ownership and planning of educational system emerged gradually in the evolutionary process.

In the pre-industrial societies, where all socio-economic operations are undertaken on small scales by autonomous individuals and institutions, education has also remained autarchic, by and large. But the industrial revolution transformed the system. It transferred education from the individual to social domain. It transformed education from an instrument of value inculcation and personality development into the means of producing human capital or manpower on large scale to meet the human resource needs of the centralised large scale commodity production system of the industrial economy. It necessitated centralised large scale production of education to match the centralised large scale commodity production system of the economy. It naturally created the need for educational planning, which received great stimulus in the post Second World War period when the need for economic planning was accepted almost universally.

Almost all the countries of the world had been practising educational planning of one type or the other and the need for and the philosophy of educational planning has been almost universally accepted, yet there do not exist very many books that adequately deal with the intricate and highly specialised subject of educational planning. Hence, I have dared to undertake this venture to write this book on educational planning that attempts to deal with this intricate subject in its complex relationships with economic planning. One view is that educational planning is older than economic planning. But then it is also recognised that, what educational planners are doing today, it had been done by economic planners decades ago, highlighting the twin facets of educational planning that (a) educational planning depends a great deal on the concepts, theoretical paradigms, techniques and methods of analysis developed by economists in general and economic planners in particular, and (b) knowledgewise, educational planning lags behind economic planning. Naturally, the educational planner owes a great deal of intellectual debt to the fraternity of economic planners and economists. These twin facets have created some chasm between the borrowed analytical and theoretical apparatus and the practical needs of the policy makers and practitioners of educational planning. Then there is the neglect of adaptation and modification of the borrowed concepts and theories to suit the needs of educational planning. Besides, those planners who had no background in economics and training in quantitative methods find it difficult to perform efficiently the task of educational planning. In fact, it is much more difficult to be an educational planner than to be an economic planner. An educational planner has to keep abreast of the developments in economic analysis, economic planning and the methodology of economics and economic planning on the one hand, and the emerging trends, problems, needs and complexities of educational planning on the other. I am lucky to have received my possible quota of (i) learning of economics, (ii) acquisition of specialisation in quantitative economics, and (iii) research in educational economics. This has endowed me with requisite skills needed for educational planning. This prompted me to make a modest attempt to fill up the observed gaps in the area of educational planning. Unfortunately, there are not many books available to meet the demanding needs, specially the needs of those who receive and/or impart training in the educational planning to academic or non-academic administrators.

During all these years of my stay at NIEPA, I felt an urgent need for a treatise on educational planning which may simultaneously be used as a training module, a textbook to teach postgraduate students of educational planning and still facilitate the work of those who are actively engaged in empirical research in educational planning. After great deal of hesitation over a period of nearly one decade, I decided to accept the task of writing this book with a view to meet the above types of needs of the scholars, policy makers, trainers and researchers. Only they can tell me the inadequacies of the end-output of my endeavours.

I am heartily thankful to Mrs. Sharda Sharma and my daughter, Ms. Shikha Sharma for reading the proofs of the final drafts of the manuscript. I am also thankful to the Gyan Publishing House to accept the task of publishing this work.

Shri Prakash

V/3, NIEPA Quarters,
17-B, Sri Aurobindo Marg,
New Delhi 110016.

1

Philosophical and Conceptual Base of Planning

Alternative Views and Theories of Operational Systems

The real operational systems may be viewed from several alternative angles. Main schools and streams of thought are: (1) deterministic; (2) naturalistic; and (3) non-deterministic or interventionistic. The differences among the alternative view-points are derived (a) partially from the differential concepts and precepts of the state's roles and functions and their scope in the socio-economic affairs; (b) partly from the assumption of the futility or the efficacy and the desirability of attempts to change the natural course of events, and hence, the conditions of the society, including economy and its constituents; and (c) partially from the differences between the cosmic views and the importance attached to the world within and without.

Deterministic View

Deterministic and non-deterministic views of the functioning of the material world and the outcomes of its operations have the origins in different streams and schools of philosophical thought. The Marxian view is based on historical determinism. Marxism envisages capitalism to carry its own seeds of destruction. Ultimately, according to Marxian prediction, anarchy will prevail under which individuals shall totally be free and autonomous but self-disciplined, when the institution of state itself would have withered away. The state, in fact, shall cease to exist and there will be no need for it to exist.

The deterministic view may itself be based either on the (a) Marxian Concept of Historical Determinism, based on the assumption of the supremacy of economic over all other interests and aspects of life and inevitability of the class conflict leading to the destruction of capitalism. But it is obvious that economic factors alone may not be sufficient to determine the ultimate outcomes. Political supremacy or the access to administrative power are often required for the fulfilment of economic objectives, though the die-hard Marxists may not be ready to concede this: although academic circles unwilling to break with those self-serving aspects of the Marxists' legacy legitimising them as higher moral agents insist on reducing all conflicts to their more 'real economic parameters', it is obvious that nowadays economic relations are far from being the only source of social conflict.

'The privileged status of economic conflictuality as an explanatory model within the social sciences de-emphasises the growing relevance of the cultural-political split between the managerial elite entrusted with cultural and political administration and the increasingly clientised mass of the rest of the people'. This has resulted in 'practically universal acceptance of a one-sided vision of history as an unrelenting class struggle between labourers and capitalists, while intellectuals as the agents of an equally divisive and destructive cultural-political domination generating similar conflicts have managed to conceal their role, thus legitimising themselves as the new secular priesthood; the disinterested brain and conscience of an allegedly self-determining polity' (Paul Picone, quoted from M.L. Sondhi). The Marxian determinism has been questioned by Eugen Loeble from the angle of optimising the whole economy as an organised and integrated system: "...the question whether our society and economy are our creations or part of the determined universe is not a mere search for truth. It is far more a philosophy which will guide our action. If we accept the philosophy of determinism, then our society will be governed by determined phenomena. On the other hand, if we view society as our creation, then we will be able to control and create the future instead of only predicting it"(quoted from Sondhi). It is this perspective of Marxian determinism which is important from the viewpoint of planning; or (b) Hindu Philosophical Concept of Determinism of 'Ultimately the Inevitable Occurring Eventually';or (c) Early Western Philosophy of Naturalism which envisaged that social phenomena, institutional structures, organisational forms and the laws governing the behaviour of the socio-politico-economic systems and the interrelations between the different socio-economic phenomena are patterned on nature and natural laws. Just as natural phenomena traverse their predestined course regularly, systematically and autonomously in accordance with Nature's own endogeneous laws, similarly, the socio-politico-economic phenomena should follow the definite and systematic course in accordance with the social laws, framed and patterned on the basis of the laws of Nature. None of the above viewpoints leaves any scope for planning and state's policy interventions in socio-economic affairs at the macro level.

Non-Deterministic View

The interventionistic or non-deterministic view of social phenomena has been evolved gradually along with the development of culture and civilisation. The growth of knowledge and the accumulated experiences have also contributed to the evolution of the interventionistic view of the material world. This view has, however, culminated finally in the realisation that the state can and should play a definitive role in the socio-economic transformation through planning and policy. But first the concept of the Welfare State has been evolved and operationalised. Under the welfare state, the government was obliged to intervene in the decisions and the resultant operations of the freely acting individuals and the freely working autonomous market forces so as to initiate both the positive and punitive measures to correct the distortions created by the autonomous forces of the market and also to promote socio-economic development, and hence, social welfare through policy interventions. This view gradually led to the development of the concepts and the theories of planning and policy and the methods of state interventions through the instruments of policy and planning on a much wider canvas and much larger scale than what were originally envisaged. The accumulation of experience through the practice of planning and policy interventions, especially during the (a) great depression of the late twenties and early thirties, (b) the management of wartime needs of the economy through controls during the Second World War period, and the success of the Keynesian policy prescriptions of state intervention for the stabilisation and immunisation of the economy from the destabilising effects of the cyclical fluctuations furnished the testimony of the efficacy of planning and policy. The enlargement of the power of the state functionaries to control the socio-economic processes, in turn, propelled the state functionaries to raise the roles and functions of the state in the socio-economic affairs manyfold. Naturally, this has consistently been widening the roles and functions of the state, while the horizons of the theory and practice of the policy of state interventions and planning have been gradually raised.

Marxian Determinism

According to the Marxian concept of historical determinism, the organisation, nature, working and its evolving patterns and the resultant orderings of the socio-economic systems and outcomes of their functioning are conditioned, regulated, guided and determined by the historical processes operating incessantly but imperceptibly through time. Hence, the form and structure, the nature and level of development of society, including economy, is more or less predetermined, marginal adjustments and alterations in the material conditions of the society and its members resulting from human endeavours, planning, policies and state interventions notwithstanding. Man, under this philosophical conceptualisation, emerges as the taker rather than the maker of the decisions and the resulting events and their outcomes. It implies the futility of planning, policy and state or individual interventions in the natural course of events associated with the scaffolding of the social and economic phenomena under the impact of the historical forces at work. The concept of historical determinism also limits the roles and functions of the state in the socio-economic affairs. All the same, the theory and practice of planning has been evolved and perfected by the socialist rulers and the followers of the Marxian ideology. It is thus paradoxical that the philosophy, theory and practice of planning for socio-economic transformation emanated from the socialist countries of the world in general and the former USSR in particular.

Marxism perceives that capitalism carries within itself the seeds of its own disintegration and destruction. It is, however, ironical that it is communism/socialism which has disintegrated and disappeared under the capitalist onslaught on the mind-set and the culture of the people of the second and third worlds. The impact of the capitalist culture is reflected by the behavioural patterns of the people, imitating US consumerism and the distortions of the culture and values across the globe. Marxism also envisions and predicts the eventual emergence of anarchism just as the mature stage of culture, civilisation and socio-politico and economic development dawns, when the institution of the state itself would have withered away, leaving the individuals completely free and autonomous but responsible and self-disciplined. There will be no exploitation of man by man under this dispensation. Then, there shall neither be any need nor shall there be any scope for the state and its interventions in socio-economic affairs if such mature stage of development or evolution has been reached. The state shall cease to exist and there will be no need for it to exist. Naturally, there shall neither be any need for planning, nor shall there be any scope for policy interventions at macro level.

Hindu Philosophy of Determinism

According to the Hindu/Oriental philosophical determinism,the course of events both in the lives of individuals and societies is *predetermined, as if it were ordained by the will of God.* Consequently, neither human actions can change the given status of individuals nor can these actions alter the outcomes of their endeavours, nor the actions and policies of the states can alter the ordering and the outcomes of the autonomous operations of the socio-economic systems and their processes, and the institutions, which are only the small parts of the systems, nor the conditions of the individuals, who have to bear the brunt of the outcomes of their own acts of omissions and commission, can be changed by the state: *Hoga wahi jo Ram rachi rakha, ko kari tark badabe sakha.* Only God's will shall prevail, why then anyone should argue or dispute or interfere with the natural course of events. Philosophical speculations and religious explorations of the East and their resultant concepts and approaches to life and society have emphasised the autonomy and complete freedom of the individuals whose actions are supposed to be governed by the social ethics, religious ethos and moral laws that are evolved from within rather than being imposed from without or above with force or coercion. Values or 'Sanskars' are imbibed and cultivated through the proper upbringing of the children rather than these being taught or imposed by the force of legal, social or moral laws. The basic values of life get autonomously internalised by the individuals in childhood itself.

> *The Oriental philosophy of the East bases its world-view on individuals' autonomy which is generally guided by social ethics, religious ethos and moral laws, embodied within rather than being imposed from without or above through coercion or force. But it envisages God, the Lord of the Universe, to be the sole Karta/actor and the human beings as being only the puppets in His Hands. The human beings are, at best, the agents who execute God's will.*

Thus, the Indian philosophical viewpoint of the material world is radically different from the Western philosophy. According to Western philosophy, each individual should be left free to pursue his/her own self-interest, while the self-interest is also defined narrowly in material terms. It is implicitly assumed that the private interests do not diverge from the social interests, and that there is no clash between the interests of different individuals or groups which may pull them in different directions. The fact that the social interests may diverge from the interests of the state under the despotic, autocratic or dictatorial rulers is also overlooked. As against this Western philosophy, Indian philosophy advocates a finely tuned balance among the material, emotional, physical and the spiritual aspects of human life: *Dharma* (righteousness, duty), *Artha* (wealth), *Kama* (love, desire), *Moksha* (process of gaining spiritual freedom). These four goals are, in fact, sought to be pursued in an integrated but balanced manner both by the individuals and the societies. Besides, the duties of each individual to self, family, neighbours, group/caste/community, society and the nation to which he/she belongs are well defined. The emphasis is on promotion of social harmony, fellow feelings, common good and weal, the voluntary sharing of the available resources, and the individual advancement through cooperation rather than by the pursuit of self-interest single mindedly through competition or conflict, irrespective of its adverse effects on other individuals, community/society or the country.

Another variant of the philosophy perceives the current status of an individual and outcomes of his efforts to be predetermined and preordained by the acts of omission and commission in his/her previous birth. So the current status is nothing but the retribution for the misdeeds or the reward for the good deeds performed in the previous birth. In practice, the belief and faith in this philosophy have often verged almost on the threshold of fatalism and even passivism: *Karma gati tare nahin tari,* leading the individuals to remain resigned to the current status or destiny, which may generally impair their initiatives and enterprise.

One of the interpretations of the Indian philosophy postulates that God alone is the Karta/actor; while the mortal human beings are pawns in his hands. He takes care of every aspect of life of every living being. One should, therefore, not worry about anything pertaining either to the present or to the future because whatever happens, it happens according to the wishes of God for the good of all. Hence, the occurrences, events and their outcomes will eventually be beneficial for all. But this philosophy does not advocate the type of the passivistic approach as is typified in the following expression: *Ajgar kare na chakri, panchhi kare na kam, Sant Maluka kah gaye, sabke data Ram.* All the same, it will be wrong to infer from this poetic expression that the Hindu philosophy advocates inactivity or passivism. The birds have to fly in search of food and *ajgar* (python) also has to hunt its prey; even though God is supposed to make provision for every living being. The correct meaning and the message of the Hindu philosophy is that each individual should play his/her part actively to perform the roles and functions assigned to him/her by the virtue of his/her position in the family, society and the country; while God will take care of the results of the actions of all individuals and their well-being. It may be inferred from this view of human life and the material world that there is neither any need nor is there any scope for either the individuals or for the state policy interventions for improving the socio-economic conditions of the people and/or to raise the level and the stage of development of the economy and society; since the results or the outcomes of the individual and the collective actions are predestined and a priori determined. It almost verges on the blind faith in God's will and/or one's own destiny.

The Oriental philosophy also suggests that the individuals should continually cast glances at their innerselves in order to improve the world within, on the one hand, and all individuals should act correctly in order to better their future prospects,that is, the life after life, on the other. Thus, there is an emphasis on correct individual behaviour and guidance of the private decisions not only by the immediate material gains but also by the considerations of the moral values, social ethics and spiritual gains. It implies an optimistic view of the future and a certain element of non-determinism in the sense that all individuals have the freedom as well as the opportunities to shape and determine their distant, if not immediate, future through their own acts of commission and omission. Thus, the Eastern philosophy is neither passivistic nor is it pessimistic. It is rather eternally optimistic and activistic. It perpetually impels, propels and inspires man to perform his Dharma or duty, that is, all the activities that men undertake in the usual or ordinary course of life have the material-social-ethical motivating forces underlying behind these as the chief propellants. Man is, therefore, not as helpless as it may appear at the superficial view of the philosophy, and/or its particular understanding and interpretation. The Indian philosophy and Hinduism do not propagate fatalism or passivism. In fact, the philosophy of *Karmayoga* has virtually activism as the cardinal principle of human life and individual behaviour.

Philosophy of Karmayoga

Lord Krishna propounded the philosophy of three distinct types of *Yogas: Jyanayoga, Bhaktiyoga* and *Karmayoga*. According to him, Karmayoga is the least difficult to understand and practise, while Jyanayoga is the most difficult to understand and even more difficult to practise. Practical being as He is therefore, commended Karmayoga to Arjun most emphatically. Interrelations among *Karan-Karya-Karmafal,* that is, *cause-action-effect* are the base of the cardinal principle of Karmayoga. *Karan* or *cause* is the fountain from which all *Karmas* or *actions* flow. It implies that the cause is the eternal motivating force of human action and behaviour. Karan or cause provides the impetus, kindles the desire or want for the performance of the action. Behind every human endeavour or activity, there has to be some 'hetu' or cause to motivate and inspire the human action. But the concept of motivation is wider and inclusive of 'Want' that economists consider to be the fountain-head of all human actions. Action, in its turn, leads to the definite consequences or karmafal. Cause-action-effect are bound together by the inevitable interrelationships among themselves. The laws or the principles governing human behaviour, are the embodiment of these interrelations among cause-action-effect. The subtle nature of the relationship among cause-action-effect is highlighted by the saying *jo jaisa boega, voh vaisa hi katega* (as you sow, so shall you reap). The results or the outcomes obviously depend upon the nature, intensity and mode of the performance of the activity and the cardinal relationship between the cause and effect that underlie the given act.

Traditional Interpretation

The commonly accepted interpretation of karmayoga is that one should perform actions with mental detachment so as to be indifferent towards the rewards or the fear of loss/failure or punishment. All actions should be undertaken as Dharma or duty. Karmaphal should then be accepted, as it were, the gift of 'the Lord,' that is, God without any rancour, pain/disappointment or elation, irrespective of its agreeable or disagreeable nature and the success or the failure of the action undertaken. This interpretation of Karmayoga, in our opinion, makes Karmayoga not only the most difficult yoga to practise but it also runs counter to the basic philosophy underlying the Karmayoga's principle of cause, action and their effect(s) being inevitably interrelated. One is bound to hope for the reaping of the rewards/retribution in accordance with the nature of the relationship between the action— its cause and their effects or the consequences of the operation of the law(s) based on these interrelations between the causes and effects.

Nature of the causes or ends itself determines the nature and the strength of the motives which prompt, inspire and induce the actions to be undertaken for the realisation of the given end(s). But the nature of the causes that motivate a person to perform the acts he does, itself depends upon the kind of ideas one has and the ideals one subscribes to and holds dear to his/her heart. The ideas and the ideals of a person depend a great deal upon the kind of food one eats and the lifestyle one maintains, while the language one uses in the interpersonal interactions depends upon the kind of water one drinks: *Admi jaisa dhan khata hai, vaisi hi uski budhi aur achar-vichar hote hain, aur woh jaisa pani peeta hai, vaisi hi uski vani hoti hai.* The ideas govern and shape the cause or causes one upholds and lead to the actions for the realisation of these causes; while the ideas and ideals are formed by the type of food one eats and the lifestyle one leads.

The complex interrelations among karya-karan-karmafal and the motivating forces underlying the human actions prompted Lord Krishna to distinguish *tamswik ann* (food) and *tamswik karma* (activities) from *satwik ann* (food) and *satwik karma* (activities). This implies that the nature of the end(s) or cause(s), the want of which motivates a person to undertake a variety of actions, is as important as the nature of the act(s) itself. Besides, the nature of the means adopted or used to realise the given end is as important as the nature of the end itself. Pious ends should be realised through pious means alone.

The upholding of the cause or the ideal both in thoughts and deeds implies the impossibility of indifference towards the consequences or the karmafal that flows from human actions. As against the common belief that Karmayoga is the performance of activities as *Dharma or duty* without the *expectation of any reward*; what Lord Krishna advocated is that the outcome of any act or the karmafal should be accepted without being ruffled or elated, without rancour or grudge, as it were the will of God, irrespective of the karmafal being agreeable or disagreeable. The individual human beings have the option to choose from a large variety of actions. They also have the choice to perform or not to perform any given act. They can exercise choice between different options according to their preferences. But once an act has been performed, the role of the performer is over, since the performer of the act has no control over the outcomes. The outcome(s) depends rather on the exogeneous forces or factors in operation and/or the will of the God. The individuals have neither control over the God's will nor have they any control over the exogeneous forces at work. Just as we accept the *prasada* (offerings made to a god) from the priest, after the prayer has been completed, without bothering whether it is just tulsi leaves, sugar bubbles or other sweets, similarly karmafal should also be accepted as it has unfolded, notwithstanding the success or failure of the act. One should not be elated at success and become despondent at failure. What is implied is that the results depend upon the karma/ action and the strength of its motivating force(s). There is an objective but scientific relationship between the karma and its fal or outcome. There are objective laws that govern the outcomes of each activity. An individual has control over his own actions, while he hardly has any say or influence on the actions undertaken by others, or the exogeneous forces that influence the outcomes of these actions. So it is futile to cry foul at disagreeable results or failures. One cannot change the nature of the objective and scientific laws, and hence,the results should be accepted as these are. The Lord alone is the Karta or the doer and we mortals are only the agents of his wishes. So whatever results flow from our activities are, in fact, the consequences of the act of God and His will which should be accepted without any pleasure or pain as something which is inevitable to materialise.

New Interpretation

Karmafal does not depend upon the performance of the karma or act alone. The following factors have to be considered in relation to the outcomes of the given action(s), as all of these have a direct bearing upon the results of human decisions and actions: (a) timing of the act, (b) circumstances under which the act has been performed, (c) the mode and method of its performance, (d) the nature and direction of the natural relationship between the given act and the consequences or effect of the given decisions and actions, and (e) above all, the *Daivayoga,* that is, the wishes of God which, in modern scientific language, may be called the random factors in operation at the given moment of time. All the above factors together determine the outcomes or the results of human decisions and actions, that is, the karmafal. Hence, after the completion of each act, one should reflect on the outcomes, or the results of one's activities in relation to all these factors in order to identify the causes or factors determining the nature of the outcomes or the results, that is, the factors leading to the complete or partial success or the failure with a view to perform one's acts better in future. It does not imply that one should not desire fruits or results from one's own actions. This is not humanly possible.

Lord Krishna did not advocate such an attitude towards human activities and their outcomes. The performance of any act without the desire for the fal or results leads to the weakening of the motive to do that act or the performance of the given task, while the weakening of the motive to realise the chosen goals and the objectives weaken the intensity, strength and the momentum of action(s). With the weak motivation neither the lofty ideals and objectives can be realised, nor the duty or dharma can be performed with commitment and conviction. Naturally, the outcomes of actions performed with weak motivation will not be in accordance with the desires, objectives, ideals and the goals. Obviously, the outcomes are as important as the actions. This is amply clear from the fact that, when Arjun expressed the desire that he will prefer to go without the kingdom rather than to fight the war and kill his own kith and kin for the sake of kingdom, Lord Krishna told Arjun that fighting the war was his dharma or duty and that if he won the war, he along with his brothers and the family will enjoy the fruits of victory, that is, the joys and pleasures of the kingdom, while his death in war will bring him glory as the brave *yodha* (warrior), the hero to be remembered by posterity with respect as one who laid down his life for duty. If, however, he refused to fight the war, he will be remembered as someone who flinched from his duty and shall be dubbed as a coward, and *kleeve*. Thus, Lord Krishna explained to Arjun the nature of the karmafal of both types of his decisions and actions. He highlighted the danger of the damage to Arjun's reputation as the consequence of his refusal to fight the war and the pleasant reward of the kingdom as the consequence of his winning the war, waging of which was his duty; or the glory in death in case he died fighting his enemies in the war. Allurement of kingdom on winning the war, or the glory of the death of a hero as the reward in the event of even losing the war, and the shame and ill-fame for not fighting the war were dangled before the mental eyes of Arjun as the likely karmafal of both types of his decisions regarding the war with his cousins. The message about the attitude to be cultivated towards karmafal is crystal clear.

There is no question of one being indifferent to the results of one's own actions, or the cultivation of an attitude of mental detachment from or negligence of the likely karmafal of one's actions, which are inspired by the lofty causes or ideals one upholds, or the duty that one has to perform in order to discharge his/her obligation to the self, family, society, and/or the country one belongs to.

Social Order and Natural Laws of Society

Early philosophical thought has envisaged that the socio-economic conditions will remain either stationary or these will evolve under the influence of the natural forces. Socio-economic systems and their structures will approximate the natural system and its structures. Consequently, Nature's laws will also govern, guide, regulate, and even determine the primary functions and operations of the socio-economic systems which may, therefore, be patterned on Nature's structures and functions. So the early philosophers hypothesised that the socio-economic systems may be governed and guided by the same laws as govern the working of Nature. Therefore, social laws may generally be patterned on natural laws.

> *Western philosophers perceived social laws to be patterned on and guided by the laws that govern and guide the natural order and its functioning. Thus, natural laws tended to determine the nature, expanse and contents of social laws that were supposed to prevail then. Faith in the efficacy of natural laws or the pursuit of the self-interest by individuals as the guiding principle of socio-economic systems and Smith's dictum of laissez-faire seem to have flowed from each other as natural corollaries.*

As against the natural school of thought and the stream of philosophy, Adam Smith seems to have been inspired by the concept of *individuals' autonomy* as the *guiding principle* to propound the *theory of the free working of the invisible hand* for having the best outcomes for individuals and the society. The invisible hand operates through the freely working competitive market. Smith's approach to the theory of the state was the minimalist's approach, which envisages the state to undertake the responsibility for only such functions as the defence of the country against external aggression, the maintenance of the internal law and order, administration of justice, such public works as the construction and maintenance of roads and railways, parks, sanitation, etc. The state should leave the economy and the society autonomous and free (Prakash and Chowdhury, 1994, 1997). As against the Eastern view that social ethics and moral laws should govern individual actions, Smith envisaged the *pursuit of the self-interest* as the *guiding principle* of human decisions and behaviour. The socio-economic policy of *laissez-faire* or the pursuit of *non-interventionism* by the state in the autonomous working of the economy and the society in order to leave them to be guided by the natural pursuit of self-interest, governing the operational mechanism of the market forces, and the faith in the natural laws as the governors of socio-economic systems seem to have flowed automatically from each other as the natural corollaries. Adam Smith did not perceive and foresee any dissonance or conflict between the interests of different groups of individuals, or any dissonance between private and social interests, or the discrepancy between the social interests and the interests of the state, especially under the despotic, autocratic and/or the dictatorial rulers. He rather implicitly assumed these diverse interests to converge.

It is interesting that such diverse views and philosophical thoughts as the Indian and Western ones about the material reality and the individuals' autonomy embody the same or similar notions about the roles and functions of the state in the socio-politico-economic affairs and their policy prescriptions, or implications. Both the Eastern and Western views and the philosophy of determinism about the material reality, that is, the world around us, embody the implication that the material world around us may be accepted as it is and as it has emerged, and/or it emerges from the scaffolding of the operational socio-economic forces and the resultant operational processes and their consequences for the society and its individual members. However, the logic, assumptions and the basic principles relating causes to their effects, that is, the thoughts and the basic philosophies of these two schools radically differ from each other.

Non-Determinism and Planning

Non-deterministic or interventionistic view of the socio-economic systems is neither pessimistic nor fatalistic, nor passivistic. This view is rather interventionistic and activistic. The philosophy underlying non-determinism does not approve the notion of limiting the roles and functions of the state in socio-economic affairs to the minimal level. It is the maximalist rather than the minimalist approach to the theory of the state's responsibilities and the roles in socio-economic affairs, since this stream of thought does not advocate the assigning of the minimal role either to the state or to the individuals in the socio-economic affairs. It is based on the assumption that neither man nor the state is completely helpless in relation to the natural, social, political and economic forces that operate upon the material world, or the surroundings in which men live and the society or the economy operates. Non-deterministic world-view takes man and his society and the state as the *Karta,* the Doer, the Performer rather than being an agent of God's will, the Omnipotent Being, the *Sole Karta* or the only Performer. Man is thus rather conceived to be the master of his own destiny. The socio-economic status and the living conditions of men depend upon what men and their societies do individually and collectively. The stage of development of the economy and the living conditions of the people depend upon the personal efforts of the individuals and policy framework in general and the legal structure of the state in particular under which the individuals and socio-politico-educational and economic systems have to operate, and the degree of success of the state's policies and individual efforts. People's own decisions and actions and the state's policies thus play the pivotal role in the process of socio-economic transformation. Hence, man can do what he wishes to, and he can attain what he desires to, while the state has to play the triple— promotional, prescriptive and proscriptive— roles within the broad contours and the framework of the state's policies and legal structure, devised to give the direction, thrust and momentum to the individual initiatives and enterprise so as to maximise the gains both to the individuals and society. Thus, the state as well as the individuals can realise their *a priori* determined goals and objectives through the implementation of their own decisions that they usually make in the discharge of the routine functions and duties on the one hand, and to achieve the personally well cherished career goals and loftier ideals and the objectives of life, and the societal/state's objective of the maximum good of the maximum number of persons on the other.

The individual as well as the collective decisions are implemented as a part of the execution of the consciously devised plan and deliberately designed implementation strategy or the agenda/programme of action with a view to realise the objectives and goals adopted both at the micro and macro levels.

Man first started intervening in the natural order, then subsequently he started designing and devising his own life-style, social order, institutional and organisational structures. Experiences gained and the successes achieved by such interventions furnished the empirical basis of the philosophy of interventionism. This stream of philosophical thought conceives man as rational in approach, decisive in action and interventionistic in nature, while the state is assumed to furnish an appropriate operational framework for the individual initiatives and enterprise. These concepts of man and the role of the state are based on the observation of man and his behaviour over long periods of the history of the civilisational and cultural evolution.

It will be in consonance with the reality to assume that several decisions and actions undertaken for their implementation are inevitably random or unplanned in nature; while it will also not be unrealistic to assume, to conceive and perceive that most of the decisions and actions emanating from these individual and collective decisions are the consequences of one or the other type of planning done in advance. While a large number of individual and social or collective actions are undertaken in accordance with the deliberately and consciously devised and designed strategy to implement plan(s), planned programmes and actions with a view to realise *a priori determined* goals and objectives, some decisions and actions may just be random or unplanned. The concept, theory, practice and policy of planning have obviously been derived from this alternative conceptualisation of human life, man and his behavioural propensities, the human society and the state. In other words, the above views pertain to the materialistic world in general and the economic and educational systems of the nations in particular. Interventionism is neither fatalism, nor is it passivism or pessimism. Interventionism bases itself on a belief that Man is the Master of his own Destiny.

> *Policy of state's active role in socio-economic process, or interventionistic view of the socio-economic systems is neither pessimistic nor fatalistic nor passivistic. It is rather the philosophy of active state intervention in the socio-economic affairs and the incessant efforts by individuals to improve their own conditions. Interventionism bases itself on the belief that 'Man is the Master of his own Destiny,' while the state has to play the role of the supporter and sustainer of the individual initiatives and enterprise and the promoter of the social well-being.*

The non-deterministic view is neither passivistic nor pessimistic nor fatalistic. It is rather based on the assumption that man is not completely helpless in relation to the natural, social, political and economic forces that operate in the material world, and those which regulate and guide the outcomes of their working. Man is, therefore, conceived as the Master of his own life. Consequently, he can do what he wishes to, and he can attain what he deserves, desires and aspires for. He can realise his *a priori* determined goals and objectives through the implementation of the deliberately and consciously devised and designed plan and the strategy or the agenda/programme of action(s) for the implementation of the plan. Man is conceived as rational in approach, decisive in action and interventionist in nature.

Whatever is true for individuals holds true for the society or the community as well. If, however, society follows the rational approach of intervening in the natural operations of the socio-economic processes, the approach may be called planning. 'Planning, in all its manifestations, is essentially rationalist in approach, interventionist in design, and decisive in effect or conclusions' (Myrdal, p. 175). The philosophy and the ideology of planning are inevitably rooted in the belief that it is possible as well as desirable that the socio-economic systems should be under the active guidance and the control of the state so as to move them into the desired directions through consciously and deliberately conceived, rationally designed and coordinatedly implemented policies (Cf. Myrdal, 1973). It is the rational nature of planning that prompts Erich Fromm to consider planning as essential for society: "The irrational and planless character of society must be replaced by a planned economy".

> *Planning is rational in approach and interventionist in nature and design. Planning requires deliberate and conscious decisions for integrated formulation and coordinated implementation of the chosen policy to bring consonance between the individual self-interests and the community aspirations and social objectives.*

The concept, theory, ideology and policy of planning have obviously been derived from this alternative view of the ordering and functioning of the material world in general and the social and the educational systems and the economies of the nations in particular. The philosophy of planning is thus based on a highly specialised 'Concept and Theory of the State'. This theory of the state is based on the premise that the autonomously operating individuals, guided as they are by the desire to promote their self-interests, and the market mechanism reflecting the effects of such atomistic decisions of the self-seeking individuals lead to such consequences as may either be socially irrational, harmful, and hence, undesirable in nature for the society, or these may promote social conflict and disharmony, or even, these may lower the social welfare and eventually retard the economic growth. Alternatively, these may even run counter to the social objectives and goals of the public policy.

Competition is the essence of the free market economy. Competition can prevail in the market only when the following conditions are satisfied: homogeneity of products; such a large number of consumers and producers as renders it impossible for any one of them to influence the price; free entry into and exit of the firms from the industry; perfect knowledge and perfect mobility of the consumers among the producers and vice versa as well as various lines of productions; unbiased behaviour to facilitate transactions to be guided only by the considerations of price. Under these conditions, only one single price can prevail in the market. Violation of even one of these conditions will render the competition imperfect. But the freedom to operate unhindered by state interventions is no guarantee for the existence of competition in real life. As Streeten (1992) highlights "there is nothing in the nature of the free markets that either establishes or maintains competition though the efficiency and success of the market in promoting growth warrants the existence of competition." Even Smith, the most ardent advocate of the minimal scope for state interventions and maximum freedom to the individuals and private enterprises, recognised the *capacity of the free markets to conspire against public interest* through *'businessmen's 'contrivance to raise prices'*; while the *'landlords' and other 'rentier classes love to reap where they never sowed.'* The modern markets lead to the concentration of power in a few hands of dominant firms of the industry to influence the market leading to the emergence of the cartelisation, oligopolisation and even monopolisation which facilitate 'the acquisition and the exercise of control by the transnational corporations not only over the national but multinational markets also. (Cf. Shapiro and Taylor, 1980).

> *Planning is based on the assumption that the free market is not capable of safeguarding the social interest as internal contradictions and structural limitations of the unregulated market operations permit the manipulation of the system by the vested interests. Business and other rentier classes reap through the manipulation of the system where they have not sown.*

Experiences with the autonomously functioning market mechanism have exposed the internal contradictions inherent in the structure of the free market. The tendencies towards secular stagnation due to the inadequacy of investment and the consequent deficiency or the excess of savings, unemployment and inflation, the emergence of periodic recession even in the midst of inflation and other market imperfections, distortions and maladjustments on gigantic scales (Prakash, 1992) have led to the thesis that the 'market can do nothing much right'. This is in contradistinction to the thesis that 'whatever the state can do, the market can do better.' Exaggerations in both these theses notwithstanding, the new 'concept of the state' has emerged. The 'state is benign, idealistic, competent, well-informed and Platonic-like Guardian or Fabian style Bureaucratic.' Such states have the capacity to ' run normally above the individual conflicts to promote the common weal, the general good, and social welfare.' The modern states have "the will, resources and the power to initiate, subsequently nurture and accelerate the economic growth" (Prakash, 1992). The above concept of the state has been accepted widely. This concept of the state has furnished the theoretical base for 'State Interventionism'. Dissonance between the private gains and the social benefits, and private goals and social objectives also warrant state interventions and the adoption of planning as the appropriate approach to socio-economic development : 'Society is no longer content to passively evolve, it wants to develop. Planning is thus purposive adaptation of resources to social ends' (Planning Commission, p. 8, 1951).

Competition is the essence of the free market mechanism. But there is an inherent tendency in the modern markets towards the concentration of power, cartelisation, oligopolisation and even monopolisation for exercising control not only over national but multinational markets also. Imperfections and internal contradictions, secular stagnation, unemployment and perpetual existence of recession in the midst of inflation are such failures of the market as lend credance to the thesis that markets can do nothing much right or better than what the state can do.

The efficacy and effectiveness of planning as an instrument of accelerated growth has already been established by the spectacular success of the former USSR. Soviet Russia demonstrated the efficacy and effectiveness of planning as an instrument of accelerated growth to accomplish that quantum of growth in a period of about three decades only which the market economies like those of US and Western Europe took more than two centuries to attain. In 1913, Lenin declared that he would transform the backward agrarian economy of USSR into highly industrialised, developed and modern economy if he were provided with electricity and education. Interestingly, Soviet agriculture was much more backward than the Indian agriculture at that point of time. The Soviets launched their economy onto the planned growth path in 1922-23. In a period of only about three decades, USSR emerged as highly industrially and economically developed space power of the world in the early fifties, leaving even US trailing behind. USSR achieved that level of economic development through the instrument of planning in a period of few decades which the Western countries had taken a couple of centuries to accomplish through the free market mechanism. Of course, the market mechanism was not as free even there as the Western world will like us to believe. Western economies do not allow free competition even today as they have developed a variety of means and instruments to discourage competitive imports from the rest of the world, especially the countries of the Third World. Listian protectionism was evolved and practised on a large scale both by the US and Germany for a pretty long time in the early stages of their economic development, while the UK not only directly exploited the resources of its colonies for sustaining its own development but it also forced the system of imperial preferences in the trading relations with its dependencies. These facts and practices furnished the basis of the Naorojian Drain Theory of Underdevelopment of the countries like India in the nineteenth century. Even now the Western economies do not rely completely on the markets and use several policy props to boost their economies. Dumping into the sea or the burning of the excessive agricultural output by US in order to prevent the prices from falling and the adoption of the policies of subsidisation of agriculture, animal husbandry and dairy sectors through the minimum support price system have been evolved and practised in US and Western Europe during the fifties and sixties. They protect such sectors as textiles against the imports from the Third World in the name of the protection of domestic jobs even today. While the Western countries are coercing the countries of the Third World through the international agencies to open their markets for goods, capital and technology imports from the West, the labour markets of the Western countries are protected through intricate mechanisms against the migrants from the Third World. The size, role and scope of the public sector in US during the sixties was much larger than the corresponding size of public sector in planned developing countries like India. US, Japan and West European countries restrict imports from the developing countries on such flimsy grounds as International Labour Standard and Environmental Protection; though US derived considerable benefits from slavery in the early stages of its development and it is the developed West which had inflicted maximum damage to the environment. The damage caused by the developed countries to the environment is much greater than what is warranted by their population or per capita incomes. Japan subsidises its exports in an extremely subtle manner by determining the prices of its products for the domestic market on the basis of the average cost, while the exports are priced according to the marginal cost of production. Thus, both the imperfections and the failures of the market and the success of planning in the countries of the Soviet bloc made planning intellectually quite attractive and appealing to the Third World during the fifties and sixties. Even the war-ravaged and damaged economies of Western Europe and Japan were provided development aid by US under the 'Marshall Plan'. Practically every country accepted and practised one or other type and form of planning during the fifties and sixties.

The premises that the state can remain above the individual self-interests and it can act as platonic-like guardian in safeguarding the social interest, and the spectacular success of planning in USSR have strengthened the case for planning; while the internal contradictions, inherent in the market mechanism, and their distorting effects on the economy, the resultant failures of the markets and the practical experience of the Third World countries with the free markets debilitating their growth in the colonial era weaken the case of the free market operations.

Factors Facilitating Popularisation of Planning

Planning has become almost ubiquitous and universally popular, gaining the approbation of decision makers, enthusiastic and spontaneous approval and support of the analysts and academicians and the unequivocal support of the masses. The third quarter of the twentieth century has dawned really as an era of the dominance of the theory, practice and the policy of planning. Emergence of planning, especially centralised planning, in the Rip Van Winkle world drowsy with slumber, perpetuated for centuries, has been a unique phenomenon of the second half of the twentieth century (Cf. Myrdal, 1973).

Several factors have facilitated the popularisation, enhancement of the intellectual appeal and the spread of the principle, practice and policy of planning as an instrument of accelerated development both among the developed and the developing economies of the world during the post Second World War period. The following are some of the important factors that have popularised planning both among the academicians and the policy makers.

The transition from the concept of the ruling and oppressive to the welfare state, the demonstrated success, effectiveness and efficacy of the interventionist policies, derived from the Keynesian propositions and the stabilisation policy formulations in mitigating the adverse effects of the depression of the thirties and the subsequent containment of unemployment thereafter, widespread acceptance of Keynesian policy prescriptions in the post Second World War period, successful operation of the regimes of controls and regulations for managing the wartime shortages in the Western countries, the emergence of independent India and People's Republic of China with the declared objective of improving the living conditions of the masses through planning and, above all, the spectacular success achieved by the former USSR in telescoping that quantum and quality of development in only a few decades, which the market economies of the developed West took a few centuries to accomplish, have demonstrated the efficacy and effectiveness of planning as an instrument of accelerated development, especially that of the newly independent countries of the Third

World, having under-developed economies dominated by backward agrarian structures like the former Soviet Union one up to the first two decades of the twentieth century.

> *Emergence of planning in the Rip Van Winkle world, drowsy with slumber of centuries, has been the unique phenomenon during the second half of the twentieth century. Transition from the ruling to the welfare state, popular appeal of the Keynesian policy prescriptions, success of wartime controls and spectacular success of USSR in accelerating development through planning have facilitated the rising popularisation, enhancement of the intellectual appeal and spread of the principle and policy of planning as an instrument of accelerated development.*

Thus, the speedy achievement of goals, especially the goal of social transformation and economic development, has been the essence of planning as an alternative approach to rapid economic development and transformation of social structures. Emphasizing the need for speedy development, Jawaharlal Nehru observed: "We are not going to spend the next hundred years in arriving gradually, step by step, at that stage of development which the developed countries have reached today. Our pace and tempo of progress has to be much faster. (1956, ECAFE). He has expressed this concern and need for the accelerated development not for India alone but for the developing world as a whole. Almost all the developing countries have undergone a revolution of rising expectations even before they had achieved the political independence from the colonial rule. Therefore, they looked forward for the political independence as effective means to realise the objective of the rapid socio-economic transformation in the shortest possible time. They neither have had the time nor have they had the patience to wait for the initiation of the development process and proceed slowly along the path of development at leisurely pace, as has been the case with the unplanned market based capitalist economies of the West: "We have been in a hurry...

we have waited for a long time and feel we must accomplish a great deal in a short time". (Quoted from Tinker, p. 382)

> *Speedy achievement of goals is the essence of planning. Intellectual appeal, popular approval and the decision makers' approbation of planning has been evoked by its promise of success to mitigate the inequalities of incomes and wealth and the provision of equal opportunities to the masses for the upward social and economic movement. Wartime success of controls in the management of shortages, efficacy of Keynesian interventionist stabilisation policies and the intensity and urgency of the desire for the accelerated development of the Third World have facilitated the rapid development of the theories and the spread of the varied practices of planning.*

The intellectual appeal, popular approval and policy makers' approbation, evoked by planning, have been derived from the promised success in the containment of the inequalities of incomes and wealth within the well-defined limits and the provision of equal opportunities to all for the upward social and economic movement through direct mitigation of the poverty, unemployment, misery, destitution and deprivation of the masses. Equalisation of the opportunities for education and employment was naturally very high in the order of preferences and priorities of the planned development, since education empowers its recipients to have an access to high occupations, requiring the high level of skills, training and knowledge as the prerequisites for entry, while employment at adequate wages/ salaries directly mitigates the poverty and enhances the socio-economic status of the poor, especially of those from the weaker and backward sections of the society.

Long experience with the limitations of the institutional structure, resource constraints and the internal contradictions of the operations of the free markets, periodic emergence of recession and unemployment in the midst of inflation and relative stagnation and/or the slow growth of the market based economies over prolonged periods have persuaded the United

Kingdom to experiment with its own brand of planning and socialism based on the nationalisation of the private enterprises in such core sectors as steel and the sustained but planned public investment in infrastructural and social sectors. France has also evolved the mechanism of the market oriented indicative planning. Interpersonal, intercommunity and regional differences, resulting from the free market operations in countries like the US and Germany, have persuaded the political leadership to opt for the planned state interventions in these bastions of free enterprise and competition. Such market-oriented economies as Japan and South Korea, as Bhagwati (1988) aptly observes, follow the "prescriptive rather than the proscriptive policies" of the state interventions in the market operations under the different types of planning regimes. The accumulated experiences of the developed West have also highlighted the limitations and the shortcomings of the autonomously functioning market mechanism in these very respects, buttressing the case for planning. Influence of Keynes, failures of the free market operations experienced during the interwar period, especially the disastrous consequences of the depression and the emergence of the concept of the welfare state, necessitating public provision of such merit goods as health and education, the urgency of the need for accelerating development, warranting public investment in the socio-economic infrastructure as the guiding principles of public decisions, have induced the policy makers in the West to opt for one or the other form and some degree of state interventions either as the policies of stabilisation or the planning for the reconstruction and development of the economies damaged during the war.

Indicative planning for the guidance of the market mechanism in France, nationalisation of the core sectors like steel, and the nurturing of public investment in merit goods and infrastructure in Britain, the direct state interventions to mitigate the interpersonal, interregional and intercommunity differentials of incomes, wealth and education in US, and the regionalisation of the growth in Germany have furnished varied models of planning in the West, while the pursuance of the prescriptive rather than proscriptive policies in South Korea and Japan have provided different modes and models of planning in the market-based Asian economies.

The adoption of the policy of import substitution has been the expression of the objective of the national economic independence for the achievement of the self-sufficient, self-reliant and self-sustained growth of the mixed indian economy in which both the private and public sectors were envisaged to play complementary rather than competitive roles, necessitating the acceptance of planning as the state policy. Scarcity of industrial enterprise and capital, on the one hand, and the historical conditions of poverty and underdevelopment of the economies of South and South-East Asia, based largely on primary production, made the adoption of planning as an instrument of accelerating growth and ensuring social justice and equity inevitable.

The demonstration effect of the spectacular success of planning in USSR, the historically inherited socio-economic conditions of underdevelopment, backwardness, poverty of the masses and the urgency of the desire to catch up with the developed West in the shortest possible time are some of the factors that have prompted the policy makers to adopt the planning as the state policy by almost all the countries of the Third World during the post Second World War period. Lenin declared to his countrymen in 1913 that, if he were given the two Es, that is, education and electricity, he could transform the backward, agrarian and underdeveloped economy of USSR into an industrially developed and modern economy. But the planning in USSR for development could be launched only in 1922-23. Naturally, a very high priority had been assigned to the development of education and electricity in the programmes of development, incorporated in the Soviet plans of development. This led to the emergence of the USSR as the second most industrialised, developed and modern nation and the first *Space Power of the world* in early fifties. Thus, USSR achieved only in three decades that level and quantum of social, economic, educational and technological development through planning which the market oriented West could achieve in a couple of centuries. This spectacular success story not only established the efficacy of planning as an instrument of rapid economic growth and social transformation but it also stimulated and encouraged other countries to opt for planning as an instrument and strategy of breaking the economic stagnation and initiating the process of rapid growth and social transformation similar to that of USSR. Even US adopted and implemented the Marshall Plan to facilitate the rapid development of the war ravaged and damaged economies of Japan and Western Europe.

The limitations and the failures of the market mechanism and the demonstrated success of the planned state interventions as the policies of stabilisation, the public provision of such social services and merit goods as health and education, and the public investment in economic infrastructure have necessitated the adoption of one or the other form of planning during the post Second World War period even in the capitalist market economies of the West.

The urgency of the need for socio-economic reconstruction and the lifting of the poor from their shoestrings have been an essential component of the Indian struggle for the political independence (Prakash, 1977). Neo-nationalism during the colonial era itself has included state planning for socio-economic development as an essential element of the struggle for independence and the political programmes, imparting an emotional thrust to the principle and policy of planning. Political independence, in fact, was viewed only as an instrument and the means to economic independence and rapid growth with a view to ameliorate the living conditions of the masses. Acceptance of the ideology of planning might have been a form of protest against the particular brand of *laissez-faire* practised by the colonial regimes. *Laissez-faire* has, in fact, been viewed as an instrument of the colonial exploitation, leading to the de-industrialisation and the movement towards backwardness and underdevelopoment of the Third World. Naoroji's drain theory was developed on such observed facts of colonial exploitation and the underdevelopment of the Indian economy in the nineteenth century as has been noted above. The drain theory also lends testimony to this thesis (Prakash, 1997). Planning furnished the instrument to link the nationalism to social objectives and democratic ideals for economic transformation. Boycott of the foreign goods, the launching of the Swadeshi Movement, and the appointment of the Planning Committee in the thirties by AICC have been the essential components of the Indian national movement for the political independence (Prakash, 1977; Prakash and Chowdhury, 1994, 1997).

Several plans for the social and economic development of India have been prepared even during the British rule. Mahatma Gandhi's views inspired the formulation of the Wardha Plan, while the industrialists prepared the Bombay Plan and People's Plan was authored by the Communist Party of India. Thus, there was a plethora of planning exercises even in pre-independent India. The strategy of import substitution by domestic production has naturally been only an extension of the Swadeshi Movement which has been an inseparable element of the struggle for freedom during the British rule and that has constituted an essential part of the planned industrialisation and economic development of the Indian, Pakistani, Sri Lankan and other Asian and South Asian economies with the possible exceptions of Malaysia, Thailand and Philippines after the attainment of political freedom.

Reluctance of Malaysia, Thailand and the Philippines to adopt planning and the spontaneous acceptance of the same by the countries of South Asia might have resulted from the adequacy or inadequacy of the differential endowments of these two respective sets of the economies with physical capital, natural resources, competent bureaucratic infrastructure and other forms of human capital. Private enterprise and capital have been furnished in such countries as Singapore, Indonesia and Malaysia by the large number of immigrants from China and the Indian subcontinent during the colonial era itself. Rapid commercialisation has also led to the large scale monetisation and the widespread development of the market. As against this, numerous segments and sectors of the Indian economy remained beyond the reach of the market during the colonial era, in spite of the intensification of the twin processes of monetisation and commercialisation of the economy. But the bureaucratic structure and the administrative set-up have been developed much better in the Indian subcontinent than in the rest of the British colonies. These factor endowments made the adoption of planning feasible as well as advantageous for the countries of South Asia. Mahatma Gandhi has very aptly formulated the issue as follows : "Real planning consisted in the best utilisation of the whole manpower of India and the distribution of the raw products of India in her numerous villages instead of sending them outside and re-buying finished articles at fabulous prices" (*Harijan,* p. 79, March 23, 1947).

The urgency of the need for planning in Third World arose from the existent socio-economic conditions inherited from the colonial regimes. These socio-economic conditions have resulted from the policies and the decisions of the colonial rulers over which the national leaders have had no control. Intervention by the state becomes inevitable under such circumstances. Highlighting this, Higgins (1959, p. 435) opines that "no government can launch economic growth where it does not exist without interfering in the market in a sense quite different from the intervention involved in the nostrum of welfare economies. We have seen that launching a take-off is not merely 'patching the market". Even raising the ratio of effective savings and investment to national income to finance a 'minimum effort' involves an element of intervention, it would not occur through market forces alone'. Under the historically given conditions in these countries, economic development would have never occurred by itself automatically. Consequently, the socio-economic development has to be planned (Cf. Lange, p. 10, 1961).

Then, India, Pakistan, and Sri Lanka have been better endowed with bureaucracy and other manpower, administrative structures and institutional support base than with entrepreneurial talents and skills and physical capital. Besides, the economies of these countries have been monetised only partially, while the large chunks of areas of the country and the sectors of the economy remained not only unmonetised but also in the trap of production for low level self-consumption. But Malaysia, Thailand and Philippines probably have had private enterprise in relative abundance with the scanty administrative support base. The abundance of private enterprise and physical capital in these countries might have been due to the large number of migrants from China and the Indian subcontinent, who had settled down there in business and industries with their own capital and enterprise. Such factor endowments made the adoption of the capitalistic market oriented mode of development feasible for these countries. This probably made Malaysia, Philippines and Thailand tilt towards the market rather than the policy of planning and state oriented strategy of growth, even though the successive political regimes in Thailand have had almost continuous state interventions without the benefits of planning (Myrdal, Chapter 9).

Centuries of economic stagnation under the so-called *laissez-faire* regimes of the colonial rule of the alien political powers and the seeming perpetuation of the poverty and misery of the masses, on the one hand, and the revolution of the rising expectations of the people from the national rulers about the improvement in their socio-economic conditions in independent era, on the other, imparted urgency to the need for the rapid development of the Third World, whereas the rapid development, in its turn, warranted the interventions by the state within the policy and planning framework. The dominance of the economic structure of the developing world by the primary production, based on the low technologies of different vintages, warranted rapid industrialisation and the upgradation of the technological base of production in other sectors. Industrialisation as the prime mover of the development of the developing world has been repeatedly emphasized by UN studies, undertaken by such eminent economists as Singer and Prebisch. Their thesis has been supported by such eminent economists as Kuznets, Myrdal, Nurkse, Lewis and Rosenstein-Rodan. Neither private capital nor enterprise were available indigenously on scales warranted by the varied goals of rapid development through massive industrialisation. Capital and technology imports warranted carefully planned negotiations, which the state alone could undertake. Modern technology and research and development efforts, needed for its development, require ever rising public investment and super specialisations and expertise in multiple disciplines to be possessed by manpower. The private sector was neither willing to undertake nor was it in a position to afford the investment in physical and human capital on such large scales as is required by R & D for the development of modern technology. Limited degree of industrial base, from which the developing economies have to start with, implied that the early pioneers of industrialisation in the private sector would be able to acquire the monopolistic or oligopolistic control over the market right at the entry point, which might have obstructed rather than facilitated subsequent development of the economy, on the one hand, and the realisation of the goal of rapid growth with equity and social justice, on the other. Mason has designated this facet as the need for planning by default: "Government has to dominate through planning almost by default" (1958, p. 57).

Economic integration and even distribution of growth over space, time and sectors through planning might have also been envisaged as an instrument of political integration and the provision of economic infrastructure in areas widely scattered over space, particularly in the large countries, having in-built tendencies of disintegration due to intercommunity and inter-regional rivalries and feuds. The twin processes of commercialisation and monetisation, unleashed with the initiation of the process of development of the economy and the radical transformation of the society, were expected to lead to the emergence of the organically integrated national market for goods, factors and technology in the course of development while the market was hypothesised to contain the tendency towards political and social fragmentation. Then, the attainment of political independence made it imperative for the national leaders to achieve the national policy goals of social transformation and economic development as rapidly as possible in the shortest possible period through planning, which they had been talking almost incessantly during the freedom struggle, since the colonial rulers could no more be blamed for the social ills, and economic and political failures. Removal of interpersonal and interregional inequalities of distribution of incomes and wealth was another objective which warranted the adoption of the policy of planning. Planning has thus emerged almost universally acceptable as the policy and instrument of rapid growth, equity and justice.

So far as the Indian subcontinent is concerned, it faced very special problems immediately after the attainment of the political independence. The country has not only been partitioned geographically into two independent and sovereign nations, but there has been a deep, wide and unbridgeable psychological divide between the people on the basis of religion. This resulted in widespread communal riots, arson, rape, loot and murders, leading to the exodus of the millions of people as refugees from one part to another of undivided India. They have lost their homes and hearths and their near and dear ones. Besides, they have been converted into panpers, necessitating their permanent rehabilitation in their adopted countries. This task could not have been achieved by the market economy.

Then, the geographical partition of the country was economically irrational and illogical. Nearly 98 per cent of the jute mills were located in India, whereas the areas suitable for the cultivation of jute and mesta were confined largely in to then East Pakistan or the present-day Bangladesh. Similarly, the areas endowed with appropriate agroclimatic conditions for the production of large and medium staple varieties of cotton were located in West Pakistan, whereas large proportion of cotton textile mills were located in India. Consequently, the problem of shortages of raw materials faced by Indian industries was extremely acute. The management of the shortages of these raw materials was made even more difficult by the political intransigence of the producing/exporting country, forcing India to import the erstwhile indigenous raw materials from such far off countries as Egypt and Sudan against hard currency payments. Thus, not only the exports of the erstwhile surpluses of these raw materials was eliminated by the partition of the country, but this also forced India to import its erstwhile exports from other countries against payments in hard currency. This constituted a heavy drain on the foreign exchange reserves of the country on the one hand, and a continuous drain on the balance of trade and balance of payments on the other. The country would have not been able to regain self sufficiency in the production of these raw materials if the farmers' decision to allocate cultivable area among different crops was not tampered by incentives and inducements offered through public policy and if such decisions were to be left totally to the free operations of the market. Then, the basic infrastructural facilities like assured irrigation, high-yielding seeds suited to the agroclimatic conditions of the country, and other essential inputs for the cultivation of such crops could be provided only through public investment under the planning regimes. Planning was made essential by this contingency again.

Areas best suited for the cultivation of wheat have also gone to Pakistan. Consequently, the food scarcity became much more pronounced than before. It may be noted that even before the attainment of the political independence, India had emerged as food deficit country under the colonial rule after the separation of Burma. This was partly due to the diversion of nearly 20 per cent of the total cultivated area under foodgrains to the cultivation of cash crops. The output of these cash crops was being exported as raw materials to be used by British industries for which the colonial rulers provided encouragement and incentives to the Indian producers and suppliers of the raw materials. Shrinkage in the area under foodgrains, without there being any countervailing gains in yields, led to shortages of foodgrains. The shortages of foodgrains were further accentuated by frequent crop failures. At one time, these shortages were so severe that India had to live from the ship to mouth. Consequently, rationing regimes over prolonged periods had even led to subtle changes in the composition of the staple diets of the Indian people, especially in the rice eating areas, since wheat alone could be imported at concessional prices from US under PL 480 on deferred payment basis, while rice had to be imported from Burma and other countries against cash payments in hard currency. The food imports had constituted a severe strain on the foreign exchange reserves of India till the late sixties when the Green Revolution occurred. The policies of the minimum support price and the assurance to the farmers that their surpluses sold to the open market will be procured at remunerative prices by the government even when supplies far exceeded the demand, heavy investment in research for the evolution of high-yielding varieties of seeds and better cultivation practices, provision of fertilisers, water, electricity, diesel and pesticides at reasonable and affordable prices to the farmers could have been formulated and implemented only under the planning regimes. It may be noted that even the capitalist US was either burning its standing crops in the fields or sinking the surpluses into the sea or selling the same to countries like India at concessional rates on deferred payment basis to maintain the price stability in its agricultural markets so as to leave enough incentives for the farmers to produce more. Similarly, when rivers of milk started flowing and the mountains of butter started piling up in Western Europe, they had to adopt the planning of prices of these goods. Under the garb of foreign aid, millions of tons of milk and butter were dumped by these countries in the markets of the Third World during the fifties and sixties.

Then, the Indian industries had overused their plants and machinery during the war in order to take advantage of the unprecedented boom in the export demand for their products. This had resulted in large-scale wear and tear of the plants and machinery which were not repaired for fear of interruption in the production schedules. This necessitated the large scale replacement investment in the plants and machinery on the one hand, and investment in the upgradation of the technological base of production on the other. The private sector needed state's help even to meet these investment requirements. The decision to opt for massive industrialisation with basic and heavy goods industries as the pivots of development necessitated such massive scales of investment as the private sector was not in a position to mobilise and invest. Long gestation periods and low returns on investment in heavy and basic goods industries made such investment in these industries even more unattractive to the private enterprise which, in any case, was limited to the couple of such business houses as those of Birlas, Dalmias, Tatas, Sahus and Jains. Today's giants, such as Modis, Godrejs, etc., were still the pygmies in their infancy on the then Indian industrial scene. Above all these, Jawaharlal Nehru, the first Prime Minister of Independent India, was committed to the ideology and the philosophy of planning and the socialistic pattern of society. All these factors made the adoption of planning as the state policy inevitable.

> *Planning in the developing economies is essential almost by default. The inadequate development of the market mechanism, scarcity of capital and enterprise and the need for rapid industrialisation make planning inevitable.*

But the planning for economic development encompassed social transformation also and education is considered to be the most potent instrument and the catalytic agent of social change (Prakash, 1977). Hence, planning could not and should not remain confined only to the planning of the development of the economy. Development planning invariably involves the planning of education and employment, that is, manpower planning. Then education is only one among many sectors of the economy competing for the allocation of the scarce available resources. Naturally, it needs the fusion and the synthesis of educational and manpower planning into economic planning as an organic and inseparable part. Meanwhile the introduction of the concept of human capital into economic analysis in order to find answers to the many riddles and puzzles of growth economics has revolutionised economics. The subjects of economic, educational and manpower planning have naturally emerged as the important disciplines which have attracted attention of researchers, policy makers and academicians alike. Lot of research has already been done and the literature has greatly been enriched since the sixties. Many universities have set up full-fledged departments of planning, while numerous others have instituted the teaching of such subjects as educational economics, economics, economics of human resources, economics of health, manpower, and economic planning as separate papers at the postgraduate level in the departments of commerce, economics, education and management. However, the books, having comprehensive material to subserve the needs of servicing such courses by teachers and to meet the learning needs of the students are not readily available. Most of the material is scattered either over professional journals or edited books that contain articles on diverse subjects. The matching of the theories and the methodology with the relevant empirical facts is also missing to make learning contextually relevant to the students. This study is an attempt to fill up this gap in the existing literature, though it may be pointed out that it is not a textbook in the general sense of the term as it incorporates the research findings of the author, which themselves are scattered in several national and international journals and edited books.

But the same material has been presented here in a coordinated, coherent and systematic manner sequentially. Besides, the earlier material has been radically updated in the light of the author's own subsequent research findings, better understanding made possible by greater maturity and the proliferation of new knowledge generated during the last one and a half decades.

The broad outlines of the study are as follows: Second chapter deals with the origin, concepts, inputs, products and processes of economic and educational planning. Third chapter discusses the different approaches and strategies of planning, while the fourth chapter outlines the types and varieties of planning. Fourth chapter is devoted to a detailed discussion of the institutional planning and the methods and the models of school mapping and institutional location. Fifth chapter focuses on the policies and problems of educational planning in India. The last chapter contains the resume and conclusions.

References

Bhagwati, Jagdish, N. (1988), *Protectionism,* MIT Press, Masachusetts.

Bhagwati, Jagdish, N., Development Theory and Strategy. Published in Grossman, G. (Editor) *Wealth and Poverty: Essays in Development Economics*, Oxford University Press, Delhi.

Fromm, Erich (1949), "Psychoanalytic Characterology and its Applications to the Understanding of Culture": Published in Sargent, S.S. and Smith, M.W. (Editors) *Culture and Personality,* The Viking Fund, New York.

Gandhi, M.K. (1947), *Harijan*, March.

Higgins, B. (1956), 'The Dualistic Theory of Underdeveloped Areas'. Published in *Economic Development and Cultural Change*, Vol. IV, January.

Keynes, J.M. (1936), *The General Theory of Employment, Interest and Money*, Macmillan, London.

Kindleberger, Charles, P. (1958), *Economic Development,* McGraw Hill.

Kuznets, Simon (1966), *Modern Economic Growth: Rate, Structure and Spread,* Yale University Press, Connecticut.

Lange, Oskar (1958), *The Political Economy of Socialism,* Van Keullen Publishers, Hague.

Lange, Oskar (1967), *Essays on Economic Planning,* Statistical Publishing Society, Calcutta.

Lewis, Arthur (1955), *The Theory of Economic Growth,* George Allen and Unwin, London.

Myrdal, Gunnar (1970), *Asian Drama— An Inquiry Into Poverty of Nations,* Vols. I-III, New York, Pantheon.

Myrdal, Gunnar (1953), *Economic Theory and Underdeveloped Regions,* Vora & Co., Bombay.

Nehru, J.L. (1947), *ECAFE,* Annual Meeting.

Nurkse, Ragnar (1953), *Problems of Capital Formation in Underdeveloped Countries,* Oxford University Press.

Planning Commission, Govt. of India (1951), *First Five Year Plan,* New Delhi.

Prakash, Shri (1976), Input Output Models of Educational Planning with Applications to Indian Data. Published in Mathur, P.N. (Editor) *Economic Analysis in Input Output Framework,* Vol. III, Input Output Research Association (India).

Prakash, Shri (1977), *Educational System of India—An Econometric Study,* Concept Publishing Company, New Delhi.

Prakash, Shri (1992), Theoretical and Methodological Base of Education—Economy Nexus. Paper presented to *Xth International Conference on Input Output Techniques,* Seville (Spain).

Prakash, Shri (1994), Liberalisation of Indian Economy and Relevance of Nehru-Mahalanobis Strategy of Growth. Published in Sinha, Ajit Kumar (Editors) *New Economic Policy of India,* Deep & Deep, New Delhi.

Prakash, Shri (1997), *Essays in Honour of Prof. V.N. Kothari—A Review Article. Journal of Educational Planning & Administration.*

Prakash, S. and Chowdhury, S. (1994, 1997), *Expenditure on Education: Theory, Models and Growth,* NIEPA Publications, New Delhi.

Prebisch, Raul (1953), *A Study of Terms of Trade Between Latin America and Europe,* U.N., Geneva.

Prebisch, Raul (1955), *Processes and Problems of Industrialisation in Underdeveloped Countries,* U.N., New York.

Rosentein-Rodan, P.N. (1943), 'Problems of Industrialisation of Eastern Europe.' Published in *Economic Journal,* June-September.

Sondhi, M.L.(1997), Uniting Centrist Forces, *The Hindustan Times,* Nov. 25.

Shapiro, Helen and Taylor, Lance (1990), The State and the Industrial Strategy. Published in *World Development,* Vol., XVIII, No. 6, June.

Singer, H.S. (1962), *Problems of Industrialisation in Underdeveloped Countries.*

Smith, Adam (1776), *An Inquiry into Nature and Causes of Wealth of Nations.*

Streeten, Paul (1992), Markets and States : Against Minimalism. Published in *Political Economy Journal of India,* Vol. II, Nos. 3-4, July-December, Chandigarh.

2

Historical Origins and Experiences of Planning

Need for Dating the Origin of Planning

Along with such disciplines as 'Statistics', 'Political Economy' or 'Economics' and 'Political Science', which came into existence almost along with the birth of the 'institution, science and craft of the state', science and the art of planning also came into vogue almost along with the birth of the state. The coming of state into being initiated the process of centralisation of power in the hands of state and its functionaries as well as the devolution of responsibilities upon the state and its agencies and assumption of duties by it towards its citizens. For smooth conduct of the affairs of state, the efficient discharge of its duties and responsibilities towards its citizens and the exercise of its powers over its subjects, the theory of state has to be developed to furnish the conceptual basis of state policies and actions, and also to clearly demarcate, delineate and distinguish between the spaces and zones of duties, roles and functions of individuals and state. But the theory of the state has to be multidisciplinary by its very nature, since the roles and functions of the state touch almost every sphere of human life and all aspects of society, its polity and economy. The state has to incur expenses on its own maintenance and expansion and also for the discharging of its responsibilities and the performance of its duties towards its citizens, organisations and institutions. The choice of *political institutions, mode of governance,* and above all, *political system* required political theory for guidance. The political theory itself must have led to the determination of the roles, functions and powers of the state, its government and their spheres of influence.

For performing its duties and obligations and the discharging of its duties, the state needs resources. For the meeting of its expenditure requirements, the state has to raise revenues. Naturally, economic theory in general and theory of public finance or public economics in particular was needed to guide the state's decisions and policies of public expenditure and revenue. For the performance of all such comprehensive and encompassing tasks and the discharging of honorous and extensive duties, a sound conceptual framework, elaborate theory, policy and practice of planning, and logically consistent strategies for their implementation were needed. Enormous information and data base would be the natural necessity for the formulation of policies and their implementation on the one hand, and for the monitoring and evaluation of the progress and impacts of public policy and planning on the other. The political theory and sciences of 'Statistics' and 'Economics' were evolved originally to furnish precisely this kind of theoretical basis for the evolution of state policy and for the furnishing of an explanation of the conventions and practices of the state and the varied activities it performed.

The state, however, does not function either in a vacuum or randomly. The decisions and policies of the state and strategies of their implementation generally emanate from well conceived and properly chosen goals and objectives. The plans, programmes and projects are designed under planning of various sectoral and macro activities of the state for the realisation of these cherished and carefully chosen goals and objectives. Therefore, the history of planning may be as old as the institution of the state itself. The origin of planning may thus be traced to the origin of the state and to the operationalisation of its various systems and the subsystems such as the economic and educational systems. The modern planning has, however, been developed to deal with the priori determination of objectives, principles, priorities, methodology of growth and the guidance for the functioning of organisations and institutions, associated with various state systems and subsystems, the polity and economy of the nations, which are owned and operated by the state.

The dating of the origin of the given concepts, disciplines, systems and policies is considered essential for the tracing of their historical evolution. This is different from the process and the need for dating of the core variables of a dynamic or non-dating of a static system for purposes of analysis, explanation and forecasting. Dating of variables of a dynamic system is essential, whereas the variables of a static or stationary system require no dating. The variables of static systems/ tend to remain invariant through time and over space, while the dynamic systems, and hence, their core variables tend to change through time and over space. Dating of the variables thus plays a pivotal role in the analytical framework. But the dating of the origin of particular concepts, systems and disciplines is required for the tracing of their historical development and the evolution of their forms, structures, nature and the changes in the scope during the different phases and stages of development. This process of dating of the origin of particular disciplines has, in fact, resulted in the birth and subsequent enrichment of such disciplines as 'Political History','Social History', 'History of Science', 'History of Literature', and 'Economic History'. The dating of the origin of planning in general and educational planning in particular is not an exception to this general rule. Incidentally, educational planning has invariably been an inseparable and essential part of economic planning. So the dating of economic planning will facilitate a great deal in the dating of the origin of educational planning.

Historical Perspectives of Planning

Almost all the countries of developed West have had adopted the policies of state intervention in economic activities under the planning regimes of various shades, hues and varieties for the development of their respective economies even in the Middle Ages. The economists of Mercantilist Schools of early and late Middle Ages recognised precious metals like gold as the only form of wealth. They propounded the thesis that the wealth of nations can be increased only through international trade. Obviously, national wealth could have been raised through trade only if a country had a favourable balance of trade and positive balance of payments. Hence, Mercantilists propounded the principle that the state should intervene in international trade with a view to promote exports and restrict imports. Naturally, export promotion and import restriction required not only an elaborate state apparatus to guide the direction and composition of foreign trade but it also needed an intricate and elaborate policy framework and detailed planning to achieve the desired goals and targets of trading with each trade partner separately. It shall, therefore, be wrong to identify the origin of planning with any date that succeeds the Mercantilist era.

Listian theory of protection of the domestic industries against competitive imports was only a variant of the Mercantilist doctrine of the guided trade. Listian protectionism postulated protection of the infant, nurturing of the adolescent and leaving the mature and developed industries to compete with the export industries of other countries both in the domestic and foreign markets. An extended version of the Listian theory of protection would have allowed even this competition to be restricted to remain operative only among equally developed trade partners and even among equally developed industries of the trading partners. Formulation and implementation of such policies of protection could not have been done without industry and countrywise elaborate planning.

Physiocrats recognised agriculture as the only sector capable of generating the 'net produce'. They probably were the first ever economists to have analysed the intricate web of interrelations between the activities of different agents and the wide network of the linkage mechanisms through which the distribution of income and wealth, intermediate and final goods between different sectors and agents operating in the economy was effected. Quesany's *Tableau Economique* furnished to the analysts an indispensable but a powerful tool of comprehensive national income accounting and planning. Exclusive emphasis on agriculture as the only real producer of income implied that the policy had been focused on the objective of agricultural development. The realisation of this objective would have not fructified without the state's guidance and planning.

Adam Smith advocated *laissez-faire* as state's policy in reaction to the Mercantilists' overemphasis on the multifarious roles and functions of the state and its virtual empowerment to intervene in each and every economic operation of individual agents and the functioning of economic system. Besides, the experience accumulated over the years had already established that excessive state interventions not only retarded the pace of growth but these had also distorted economic structure in the long run. Under the pervasive influence of Smith on the thinking of his contemporary economists on the one hand, and the philosophy, analysis and economic thought of his successors on the other, the philosophy of *laissez-faire* got widely spread through time and over space, leading to the adoption of the *Minimalist Approach* to the theory of state in general and its roles and functions in socio-economic affairs in particular. This minimalist approach to roles and functions of the state reduced the scope of state interventions almost to the minimum. But even these minimum roles and functions of state would have not been performed randomly, since these had to be planned, and hence, the planning could have not been eliminated altogether even under such *laissez-faire* regimes.

However, the resources of the Third World had been fully exploited by western colonial rulers systematically through well-designed plans and programmes for facilitating the rapid growth of their own economies at the cost of development of the economies of the countries of the Third World even under the Smithian *laissez-faire* regimes then in prevalence in the home countries of the rulers. This could have not been done so successfully without planning. Naorojian Drain Theory had been formulated to explain the exploitative nature of the then international economic order, leading to stagnation of the most and even development of the economies of many of the colonies due to the draining of their resources through trade and other devices used by the imperial rulers. Imperial trading preferences in the trading relations of the colonies of British Commonwealth with Britain, imposed upon the colonies by alien rulers, is just an illustration of the subtle and intricate planning involved in such exercises. Thus, these developed countries advocated and probably practised a certain degree of *laissez-faire* internally, while they used the state apparatus fully to throttle the development of the Third World in order to use the natural resources, labour, commodity and capital markets of underdeveloped countries to further their own economic growth. Thus, Western countries did not practise the policy of *laissez-faire* themselves which they preached to others and which their analysts, economists and philosophers like Smith, Ricardo and Mill showed to do the maximum good of the maximum numbers across the geographical boundaries of the globe. The policies and approaches of Western countries were thus dichotomous. This hypocrisy has been in operation since then till date. But this was the period when education was considered to be a private and non-merit good, and hence, it was left solely to the parental choices and their own capacities to pay for the education of their children. This controverts Blaug's thesis that educational planning may be older than economic planning.

The brief description of historical perspective of planning may support Blaug's view that educational planning is as old as the state system of education. This may, however, be true about economic planning also. In fact, economic planning may be considered to be as old as the state ownership of (i) means of production, (ii) production units, and (iii) state policy of intervention in the economy. Even if this view is accepted, precise dating of the origin of either economic or educational planning may be difficult.

Planning in Third World during Colonial Era

Several developing countries accepted the principle of planning even before they had achieved political freedom and before they could have had an opportunity to translate their plans into action. Once these countries became politically free, they adopted and implemented the policy of planning of development of the economy and the transformation of society. The practical experiences of the developed West showed that education had been (i) an instrument of social change and structural transformation, (ii) an agent of changes in psychological motivations, attitudinal and behavioural propensities of individuals, (iii) a source of human capital formation, and hence, a supplier of manpower for meeting skills and knowledge requirements of growth, and (iv) both direct and indirect promoter of economic growth and employment (Prakash, 1976, 1977; Prakash and Buragohain, 1992). Since education has come to be considered as an instrument of social transformation and as the factor of economic development, educational planning has invariably been an essential part of economic planning. India provided the lead to the Third World by formulating its development plans even before the attainment of its political freedom. Bombay Plan, Wardha Plan or Gandhian Plan and People's Plan had been prepared in the late thirties and early forties for the development of Indian economy, while Congress Party appointed the Planning Committee in late thirties. These illustrations support the above thesis. It may also be noted that Indian planners even at that point of time treated educational planning to be inseparable from economic planning (Prakash, 1977).

Gandhiji considered Western education too costly to be affordable to a poor country like India and too elitist in orientation to be of any help or practical use for the masses. He thought that the British system of education linked it only to the white-collar jobs in the government sector to the almost complete exclusion of blue-collar jobs accessible to the general mass of the people. Naturally, education came to be looked upon as a licence for entry into salaried jobs in the government or its agencies. Such jobs commanded higher prestige and incomes. But both the direct and indirect costs of Western education were so high as made it unaffordable to the poor, and hence, inaccessible to the masses. This imparted an elitist bias to Western education in India. But the elitist approach to education was deliberately adopted to: (i) reduce the cost of Western education to British administration in India, (ii) to propagate and popularise Western education among the elite of the society to (a) change public opinion in favour of new system of education, (b) to establish the superiority of the British relative to the indigenous system of education, and (iii) to leave the job of modelling and patterning the indigenous educational system according to the British pattern of education to social leaders of India. This served the intent and purpose of the introduction of Western education in India by the British rulers. It led to the lowering of the dignity of labour as blue-collar jobs, involving physical labour, commanded lower incomes and prestige.

Treatment of Western education as the direct means of entry into government service, commanding higher incomes and having greater prestige, and conferment of status of partners of the ruling elites in British administration upon the government servants, though of inferior and subordinate category, made British education emerge as superior to the indigenous system of education in the eyes of the masses. As the white-collar jobs were extremely limited in number, spread of education led to the emergence of unemployment among the educated. Hence, Mahatma Gandhi formulated Buniyadi Shiksha/Talim Yojana for the masses, which attempted to bridge the gap between formal learning and occupational and vocational training. It mainly focused on the bridging of the gap between education and employment outside the tertiary sector by the incorporation of the learning of crafts and trades in educational curricula. Gandhiji also emphasized the need for an alternative educational system to be cheaper than the British education so as to make it affordable, and hence, accessible to Indian masses. Dr Zakir Hussain formulated an exhaustive, comprehensive and detailed plan for the introduction of Buniyadi Talim in India. Buniyadi Talim scheme was naturally developed according to the views of Mahatma Gandhi.

Experiences of Planning in Different Countries

The need for planning in Western economies has stemmed from the logical and practical needs of the formulation and implementation of social welfare programmes and the techno-economic feasibility plans of projects which had to be minutely planned and their effects on the economy required careful evaluation and assessment before implementation. Thus, their need for planning was economic rather than ideological predelictions of policy formulation. But the developing world opted for planning partly to meet the needs of speedy development and partly due to ideological influences, emanating from both the socialist and capitalist blocks of the erstwhile polarised world. The historical origins of modern planning may, therefore, be traced to two major sources: socialist planning in USSR, on the one hand, and macro-policies of stabilisation of Western economies and the success of development and welfare planning in such major Western economic powers as the US, the U.K, France and Japan, on the other.

War ravaged and damaged economies of Japan and Western Europe were not only reconstructed and revived but these countries were also enabled by the Marshall Plan to develop rapidly to almost match collectively the US development and economic might during the post Second World War period. Eastern Europe also developed rapidly though relatively at lower rates than those of Japan and Western Europe under Soviet type of planning. This demonstrated the efficacy and superiority of planning over autonomously operating market mechanism as an instrument of accelerating development. The demonstration effect of the success of planning on policy makers of newly independent countries of the Third World persuaded the decision makers to readily accept planning. Consequently, planning came to be accepted by one country after another in quick succession. India, China and erstwhile Yugoslavia have had experimented with planning models which were different in orientation from the ones emanating from the original sources. For example, India opted for the mixed economic structure with public sector in centre-stage of the economy, while the communist planning of China and Yugoslavia were basically different from that of USSR in numerous respects.

Planning in USSR

Soviet planning has been formed largely by ideological needs of social restructuring of the inherited feudalistic socio-economic structures and the imperatives of rapid development rather than by the needs of macro stabilisation and/or social welfare approach of the West. Socio-cultural and institutional structures, required for the operation of centralised planning processes, had been evolved in due course in the process of development planning itself. Soviet planning had been guided mainly by the objective of transforming a feudalistic backward agrarian economy into a highly industrialised and socialist modern economy within a period of only a few decades so that it could match the military and economic might of the developed West in general and the US in particular. The objective of Soviet planning was socialistic and industrial transformation of the backward and feudalistic agrarian economic structure. The urgency of socio-economic transformation and under-development of the Soviet economy may be considered to have prompted the leaders, who came into power after the Bolshevik Revolution of 1917, to opt for planning as an alternative method to the market mechanism and an instrument of rapid development.

The ideological inspiration for planning in USSR-emanated from Marxism. It warranted the complete public ownership of the means of production so as to transform the feudalism oriented capitalistic economic structure into socialistic state capitalistic structure. Soviet planning has, therefore, been designed to guide and regulate the production processes of all sectors and enterprises within the sectors with a view to facilitate the maximum growth of output and to move the economy simultaneously along the socialistic path of development. Maximal growth has been the primary objective of development planning in USSR. In order to mobilise the maximum surplus for investment so as to maximise growth, individual consumption and income levels had been kept deliberately low. Priority to the development of heavy and basic goods industries had also facilitated the mobilisation of surpluses of material resources for growth rather than consumption. Naturally, detailed plans, consisting of the projects and programmes of development of such diverse units as range from individual farms and factories, hospitals and schools to the aggregative sectors, and from individual sectors to the economy as a whole, have to be prepared in an integrated and consistent framework of planned growth of production.

When the Bolsheviks had taken over from the feudalistic lords, there existed neither the theory, nor the method, nor the practice, nor the policy, nor the institutional support base for planning. All five of these have been evolved step by step through practical experimentation and learning by doing or on the job training of the planners and policy makers (Cf. Tinbergen, p. 5). Consequently, trial and error method had to be pushed into the centre-stage of planning in USSR. As Soviet planning aimed at radical transformation of political, social and economic structure in the shortest possible planning horizon, planning in USSR was comprehensive and all encompassing. Education and electricity were considered to be the essential instruments of this transformation. Lenin, in fact, declared in 1913, "Give me two E's, and I shall transform the backward agrarian Soviet economy into an industrialised, modern and developed one." Obviously, these two E's stood for education and electricity. Educational planning was naturally an important and inseparable part of comprehensive and centralised Soviet planning for rapid economic development and complete socialistic transformation of the feudalistic socio-political structure. That is why Sylvian Lurie opines that 'the expression educational planning' originated in `USSR at the beginning of the nineteen-twenties'. Of course, his assertion is based on the fact that the comprehensive centralised planning for development, as we understand it today, was initiated in USSR with the launching of its first seven-year plan in early twenties and educational planning was an integral part of this plan. Projects and programmes of educational development had obviously been formulated, dovetailed and integrated into the plan of economic development. This could have been achieved only through detailed educational planning which was guided and regulated by development needs on the one hand, and the affordability of educational investment to the economy at macro level at that stage of development of the Soviet economy, on the other (Cf. Komarov, 1964.).

But the dating of educational planning by Lurie is not correct, since educational planning has come into vogue even earlier than the advent of Soviet economic planning. Lurie's view is also at variance with the facts and views of other experts. For example, Mark Blaug avers that 'educational planning is much older than economic planning,' and that 'educational planning is as old as the state system of education itself.' This is, however, a very clever but a vague manner of dating of the origin of educational planning. If we wish to date educational planning according to Blaug's criterion, then we should first date the origin of the state system of education itself. This, in turn, may necessitate the dating of the origin of (i) state and, (ii) the beginning of the system of state ownership of various systems and subsystems of the society and the economy. Blaug, however, does not commit any error by not associating the origin of educational planning with any particular country or any specific date.

Psacharopoulos differs both from Blaug and Lurie. He opines that educational planning was formally introduced in late fifties as a spin-off of the Keynesian interventionist policies on the one hand, and the main concern of that era with the economic planning for development, when almost all the developing and most of the developed countries supported planning enthusiastically on the other. Thus, Psacharopoulos, like Lurie, associates the origin of educational planning with the advent of economic planning. But unlike Blaug, Psacharopoulos does not associate educational planning with the state ownership of educational system. All the same, his dating of the advent of educational planning to late fifties is incorrect. Tanzania incorporated educational programmes and projects in its ten-year plan of development in 1948, though it could develop the full conceptual framework, methods and criteria for the determination of priorities of educational development towards the beginning of sixties (Cf. Mwingira & Pratt, 1965). But Lurie is decidedly nearer the truth than Psacharopoulos. It is an established fact that USSR did introduce educational planning along with economic planning in early twenties. Obviously, educational planning has come into vogue much earlier than the second half of the twentieth century, which controverts Psacharopoulos's thesis. Lurie's view is, however, also not corroborated by facts.

Educational Planning in Japan

During the Meiji Restoration in Japan, sweeping and wide ranging changes had been introduced in social structure, including education, which swamped the indigenous educational system of Japan of those days. The changes focused on reforming the fairly developed education system that was inherited from the Edo period at that time. In the closing stages of Edo period, preceding the Meiji Restoration, no modern system of schooling had existed in Japan, though educational development had reached a fairly high level in that pre-modernisation era. But the term modernization may be defined by two factors: "One is the tendency of individual persons to take a reasonable and secular attitude toward the surrounding environment as progress is made in scientific knowledge. The other factor is a trend among the component members of society to participate and become involved in political, economic, social and cultural processes, both extensively and independently" (Aso and Amano, Preface, 1972). Thus, the objective of the new system of education was (i) to develop rational attitude and scientific temper among the masses, and (ii) to facilitate transition from the feudalistic towards the democratic structure of the polity through the instrumentation of the mass orientation of education.

In the pre-Meiji Restoration era, the Tokugawa Shogunate Government (Tokyo) has a higher educational institution under its control, while each feudal clan vied with others in setting up schools of its own. At the lowest level, numerous elementary educational institutions existed for the general public, which were widely spread all over Japan. Each school consisted of one teacher and 30 pupils and maintained itself by meagre tuition fees collected from students. Naturally, the then educational system was characterised by inadequacy of resources in general and instructional and infrastructural facilities in particular. These schools for general public provided elementary education in 3 R's and moral values. But the schools had already started introducing Western sciences, mainly medical and military sciences, even before the dawn of the era of Meiji restoration.

Japan's modern educational system inherited substantial educational legacy in a large measure. This made the introduction of wide ranging and sweeping reforms and changes in educational system in 1872 somewhat smooth though, in effect, it was almost complete substitution of one by another system of education. Japan's modern system of education originated from ***Fundamental Educational Code***, which was promulgated by the government in 1872. Like various other socio-economic systems and subsystems introduced in those early days of Meiji Restoration, new educational system was 'also patterned after those of the United States and the countries of Europe'(Aso and Amano, p.1,1972). The Western system of education was introduced and then prevalent Japanese indigenous system of education was totally discarded. This switchover from indigenous to the Western system of education was not confined to either the form or pattern of education alone. The contents of learning and teaching were also directly imported from Europe and US. This created mismatch between the knowledge imparted through new educational system and the knowledge required to face the problems of life both at the societal and individual levels. Consequently, people resisted and opposed the new educational system which had to be revised and modified subsequently to bring it into tune with reality at the grassroots. The failure of Western education due to this reason had happened in Manipur also, a state of India, when Western education was introduced there for the first time.

Even before the British occupation of Manipur, British political agents imported Western education into Manipur in the belief that it would eventually lead to better administration of justice and a gradual sweeping away of abuses (Johnstone, 1971). Captain Gordon established an English school in Manipur during his political agency from 1835 to 1841 and he also pursuaded the then Maharaja of Manipur to establish another English school, which was eventually converted into Johnstone Middle School in 1885. At the instance of another political agent, W.F. Nuthel, an English school was opened in 1872 (Roy,1973). But none of these schools survived mainly because the new educational system did not meet either the societal or individual needs of Manipuris, who needed physical education and training in martial arts rather than literary education to cope up with the inter-tribal and intercommunal feuds, on the one hand, and aggressions from such neighbouring countries as Burma and China during those days (Lokendra, 1988). So the initial failure or relative lack of success of Western education in Japan in the early phase of its development was neither unique nor was it the result of its inherent weaknesses. But both these instances of the failure of Western education in Asia in the initial years of its introduction highlight the need for adaptation and modification of any imported system according to the local needs and conditions of the times on the one hand, and adequate preparatory groundwork to be completed before the effective introduction of any new system of education, the success of which depends a great deal on the objective and material conditions of the society on the one hand, and receptivity and acceptance of the system by the people, on the other.

The Education Code, a comprehensive plan for the establishment of 1953,760 primary schools throughout Japan to give modern compulsory elementary education to all children aged between 6 to 14 years and the creation of 256 middle schools and eight universities was carefully prepared and vigorously implemented. Along with the establishment of new institutions, existing ones were restructured in order to enable them to switch over to the new system of education. Naturally, an extremely large number of educational institutions had to be established to confer the benefits of modern education over the entire population and all the regions of the country. This is in sharp contrast to the introduction of Western education by colonial rulers in India, Nigeria and Tanzania for the classes rather the masses. Obviously, establishment of such large number of institutions and nurturing them for imparting education by the government of Japan would have not been possible without large scale educational planning.

However, the following factors constrained and limited the success of new educational system in the initial years of its operation: (i) government during the Meiji Restoration did not possess sufficient financial and real resources to undertake and finance educational investment on the scale warranted by the establishment and operation of the desired or projected modern system of education at one stroke. Financial stringency and real resource constraints made adequate supplies of not only infrastructural facilities and equipment, but also proper teaching materials and able teachers unaffordable to the government of those days. This facet of Japanese educational planning and development lend support to Gandhiji's view that Western education is too costly to be affordable to the less developed countries and too alien in nature to be of practical use to the people; (ii) inadequacy of public investment in education had to be supplemented by private educational investment by the residents of the areas where schools were located and the parents of students lived. But the low level of economic development limited their capacity to invest adequately in education; (iii) Western system of education, imposed by the then rulers on the people from above almost in its totality upon the then Japanese society, entrapped in the feudalistic modes of thought and behaviour and upon the underdeveloped economy had no relevance to the socio-economic conditions of the society and the problems of daily life of the people at large, leading to strong resistance from the masses to the enforcement of education code and their reluctance to invest in this irrelevant education; and (iv) cost of school education was extremely high relative to the level of incomes and wealth of the people and the stage of development of the Japanese economy. Naturally, the initially introduced educational system had to be modified in the light of experience gained through its operation for more than a decade. The new system of education had, therefore, to be adapted and modified to meet the Japan's socio-economic needs and people's aspirations by the rectification of its operational shortcomings. This is in sharp contrast to the planning and development of education in India, where Western system of education had hardly been changed that too only cosmetically even during the post-Independence period.

The *Centralised educational system* could actually be established in Japan in 1886: "That is to say, this period of confusion from the start of the Education Code to the establishment of a 'centralised educational system' in 1886 with the promulgation of various ordinances concerning schools corresponded to the stage in which Japanese education was to prepare for its next step forward or to use W. Rostow's expression, a period in which to prepare the 'pre-conditions for take off'." Educational legacies from the latter part of Edo period (1603-1867) and the new Western influences were attempted to be integrated in new educational system (Aso and Amano, p. 2, 1972), whereas new system of education itself was adapted continuously to the emerging development needs of Japan.

Before the promulgation of Education Code, the ministry of education under the newly introduced cabinet system was established. Tokyo Kaisei School and Tokyo Igakko (medical school) were merged into Tokyo Imperial University. Education Ordinance replaced the education code in September, 1879 and 'educational principles' were published under this ordinance for guiding the day-to-day functioning of the system. In 1880, education ordinance was further revised and the ministry of education itself was reorganised in 1885 under the revised cabinet system of government. After the initial fumblings and experimentation with the Western educational system, Japan had very successfully transformed and adapted its educational system not only to expand it phenomenally but education has also played the pivotal role in the modernisation and industrialisation of the Japanese economy. In 1880, when Japan's modern educational system was in its infancy, school enrollees constituted 41.1 per cent for elementary education, and merely 1 and 0.3 per cent respectively for secondary and higher education. But 90 years after the introduction of Western education in Japan, enrolment ratio was 99.8 per cent for elementary education and 82 per cent for secondary education, while the ratio for higher education rose to 17 per cent in 1970. This astonishing growth of education has matched Japan's spectacular economic growth. This brief sketch has been drawn to highlight the fact that the last quarter of the nineteenth century had witnessed large scale transformation of the Japanese system of education under a continuous process of planning. But educational planning was itself marked by the method of trial and error.

Educational Planning in Nigeria

Introduction of the Western system of education in Japan in the early seventies of the nineteenth century does not mean that Japan was the first country either to develop the theory and methods or adoption of the policy of educational planning. Nigeria introduced Western education even before Japan, where 'First schools to impart modern Western education were established around 1850's by the Christian missionaries. Large number of such schools could have not been started randomly without any planning, patronage and the support of the colonial rulers to the efforts of missionaries. This has also been the Indian experience. British rulers kept the policy of *laissez-faire,* and hence, non-interference in socio-economic affairs only as their frontal face and the mask to disguise the real intents and purposes of colonial rule. Realisation of the true objectives of the rulers were entrusted to the churches and their missionaries, who promoted state's interests through the extension of pecuniary benefits, health care and education. But the government did extend financial support and political and administrative backing to the activities of churches and their missions. As the 'educational facilities continued to expand rapidly' thereafter, 'the governments gradually came forward to shoulder ever rising responsibilities of planning, financing and administration of education' in Nigeria for transforming it from the education of the classes into the education of the masses (Cf. Callaway & Musone, 1968).

Educational Planning in India

Indigenous system of education had practically disappeared from India at the dawn of twentieth century. But the twin processes of disintegration of the indigenous system and its replacement by Western system of education in India had started in the first half of nineteenth century itself. For example, after the annexation of Matak Territory of Assam in 1839, Western education was introduced there almost immediately after the annexation. Capt. Vetch, Political Agent, located at Dibrugarh, wrote to Capt. Jenkins, Agent to the Governor General, North East Frontier, that out of an estimated population of 5000, only 3 persons were somehow found to be fit for government jobs. In the entire territory, not a single person was available for the job of a teacher who could attract students to attend school. It is to be noted that the 'British government realised the political need for taking measures to educate the Matak people to make them fit for government jobs in their own place, thus leaving lesser scope of heart-burning afterwards.'

It was recommended that the 'Political Agent be authorised to spend a sum not exceeding Rs.68 a month for the establishment of a Bengalee and an Assamese school at Dibrugarh for the instruction of the children of the principal Muttuck in common reading and writing to qualify them for holding situations in our judicial and revenue establishments' (S. Dutta, 1988). It clearly establishes that the colonial rulers adopted (i) manpower requirements, and (ii) elite or class rather than the mass-oriented approaches to educational planning in India. But education was designed mainly to produce manpower for the British administration in India on the one hand, and to brainwash the educated Indians to support the British rule in the country on the other. The educated were also expected to mould public opinion in favour of the British. So education was an instrument of colonialism: 'Education as one of the most powerful agents of British colonialism' began to be used with the advent of the 'Christian missionaries', and '...from the very beginning of their contact with the Nagas, the British officers perceived the necessity of introducing *Christianity and Education* among the Naga tribes, for they considered education as the best agency for reclaiming the rugged Nagas to order and civilisation' (Sema, Piketo, 1988). Civilisation, education and order were nothing but the Western civilisation, Western education and order of the British rule. 'With this viewpoint, the Colonial Education Policy was mainly directed to the extension of pecuniary grants to the Christian Mission in Naga Hills' (Sema,1988). This is explained best in the words of Vatican II, "School is one of the explanations for our missionaries' existence before the non-Christian world. The influence of the Church in the field of education is shown in a special manner by the Catholic school."

The main objective of Christian missionaries in India, as in other countries, was to convert Hindus into Christianity.

Conversion into Christianity was used not only to spread this religion but also to facilitate the infusion of denationalism into the hearts and minds of the converts. Despite the fight for supremacy between the Church and State in Britain, the churches always cooperated and helped the Christian government in the extension and maintenance of the colonial rule in the colonies. The British government collected secret information about the colonial societies through the churches. The British derived advantages from the contacts forged by the churches and their missionaries with the local people. The missionaries put on the frontal face and mask of service of mankind through health care, education and even by conferring direct pecuniary benefits on the needy and the poor. These were the instruments for penetrating into non-Christian societies. Some knowledge of medicine and/or eligibility for entering into teaching as a profession were almost essential qualifications for becoming a missionary. The missionaries had been sent even to the remotest and the most isolated areas, which were totally untouched by development. The operations of missionaries used not only financial and other material resources received from European countries but health care and Western education in general and English language and English literature were also used quite effectively. Widespread and concerted efforts to spread Western education were a part of cultural imperialism, which not only alienated the recipients of Western education from their culture, language, literature, tradition, customs and values but it also instigated them to oppose their own societies. Mission schools and colleges played the pivotal role in this process. Macaulay, in one of his letters, informed his father that 'every Brahmin youth, who comes to study geography in our schools and colleges, starts ridiculing Vedic Hindu values and philosophy of life...Every Hindu, who studies English, is alienated from his religion.' Similarly, Charles Travillion, Finance Member of Governor's Council, observed, "anyone, who studied English literature, stops considering us foreigners. He, like us, starts considering our (English) great men as his own. After becoming educated like us, he develops the same mentality and thoughts as we cherish and he develops an attraction to our things and thoughts. Just as Italians appeared more Romans than Italians, similarly Hindus looked more English than Hindus."

Christian missionaries had started schools to impart Western education in different parts of India in early nineteenth century. Some mission schools were operating in some parts of India even in 1820s and 1830s. The objective was to influence the masses in favour of the British rule through the provision of pecuniary benefits, health care and education for which the good offices of the church and their missionaries were used. Hence, the churches and the missions had been fully supported financially, politically and administratively both overtly and covertly by the colonial rulers. The support extended to missionaries was neither haphazard nor was it designed as a charity. This was the result of careful and elaborate planning for the strengthening of British rule at the grassroots. Christian missionaries had systematically started schools for the imparting of Western education in Nagaland, Mizoram, Manipur, Meghalaya, Assam, and other parts of North-East India during the second half of the nineteenth century, since they had succeeded in extending the British rule in these parts of the country quite late. Late start of Western education in North-East India is accounted mainly by the delayed extension of British rule over these parts of the country. But the sporadic and isolated attempts to introduce Western education in North-Eastern and other parts of India had been made much earlier by missionaries than this. Missionaries had the full political support of the alien rulers and European churches had been providing full financial backing to such schools, though there may be no trace of explicit operation of the policy of educational planning for the simple reason that the direct intervention by government in social afffairs was considered to be undesirable under the *laissez-faire* regime of those days. Hence, missionaries were used as the frontal faces to mask and disguise direct intervention by the government in order to further their interests and realise the objectives of colonial rule in India.

The first war for liberation in 1857 had forced the British to introduce many reforms in administrative structures. They were under ever increasing pressure from Indian leaders and freedom fighters; so they wanted to display that British rule was actually beneficial to India. Several Indian leaders and scholars, like Naoroji and Ranade, had undertaken detailed theoretical and empirical studies to show the nature, degree and direction of exploitation by the British rulers to the detriment of development of the Indian economy. Studies have also been undertaken to establish the degree and nature of Indian poverty and underdevelopment; and these were directly attributed to the British rule in India. Dadabhai Naoroji, in fact, developed his full-fledged theory of underdevelopment of the Indian economy due to the draining of Indian resources by the un-British rule of the British in India (Prakash, Forthcoming). He even estimated the per capita income of the then Indian economy to lend empirical support to his thesis that the draining of resources by the British rulers was thwarting the development of the Indian economy. Full scale introduction of British system of health and education in India under well chalked out plans and projects constituted an essential component of epochal changes in nineteenth century Indian society to win the public support and sympathy for the colonial rule. Thus, the colonial rulers attempted to mute the criticism and prevent the recurrence of 1857 war of liberation through education, health care and pecuniary benefits to selected individuals, since the 1857 war had proved not only to be highly costly to the British in terms of the loss of men and materials but it had also shook the very roots and foundations of the British empire in India.

Educational System in Ancient India

Ancient educational system was well developed much before the advent of the Muslim or British rule in India. Gurukuls were the pivot of ancient Indian educational system. Each gurukul was centred and structured around the learning and specialisation of a distinguished Rishi or the learned and erudite guru. These were mostly single teacher schools which functioned rather informally. As the term guru-kul means the family of teacher, students were considered to be the part of teacher's family for all intents and purposes. The ancient system was comprehensive though informal in nature. The reputation of the particular teachers attracted disciples to their institutions. But both the teachers and students lived as a community away from the society. The teachers and their students were supported by the community in meeting their day-to-day needs so as to keep them free from mundane worries of daily life and to enable them to concentrate whole heartedly on learning and teaching.

Education was extensive in coverage, balanced in nature, and practical in orientation, though ethics, philosophy and religion constituted its core. Inculcation and the imbibing of higher values of life were given great importance in the process of learning and teaching. The values were to be imbibed and inculcated through the living of a rigorously disciplined, spartan and simple life, revolving around righteous conduct. Thus, there was no gap between precept and practice as both the teacher and the taught patterned their thoughts and actions around these values. Knowledge (Gyan) of *Tatava* (material related) and the knowledge of *Atman* (spiritualism related) were to be properly balanced through the learning of 14 *Vidyas, Kalas, Shilpa,* including *Shastras (scriptures) and Shustras* (weaponry). Learning and teaching were based on an integrated system of Dharma (religion-cum-duty), Darshan (philosophy), and Niti (ethics). Oral tradition of learning and teaching dominated the educational system. But the contents of learning and teaching were exhaustive and encompassed all aspects of both theoretical and practical knowledge, including science, technology, medicine, arts and architecture. Education was not totally detached from employment, though it was encompassed largely by religion, ethics, morality, philosophy and culture. For example, the learning of the state-craft and the conduct of warfare were an essential part of education of the princes and princesses, who were expected to practise these in their practical life. Dedication, meditation, abstinence (Brahmacharya) and discipline were greatly emphasised as the essential elements of learning. The learning of Sanskrit, the language of Shastras, had prime importance. Society in general and state in particular fulfilled the material and financial needs of education. The need for educational planning at macro level was probably not felt a great deal, though the establishment of individual gurus' gurukuls could have not materialised and these gurukuls could have not operated without micro educational planning and the support of society and the state. Financial support by the state would have certainly involved planning exercises in resource allocation, howsoever crude and tentative the exercise might have been.

Occupational and vocational training was mainly the responsibility of the family, where each individual was expected to follow the vocation or occupation of his/her forefathers. But the pursuit of any specific vocation was not rigidly controlled, leaving some space and freedom to individuals for occupational choices, though the choice was exercised only exceptionally. Thus, vocational and occupational training was much more directly related to employment than the formal system of education.

Flexibility, Adaptability and Transitional Modifications

The system served both societal and individual needs rather well due to the flexibility and mouldability of the system to meet the felt needs of both individuals and society. The organisational forms, institutional structures, and even more important than this, the range, quality and contents of learning and teaching evolved continually in response to the changing needs of the times. The emergence of maths, vihars and pathshalas in successive time periods reflects that (i) the system remained flexible, vibrant and responsive to the changes in societal and individual needs through time, and (ii) the system had maintained certain level of continuity through its adaptability to the changing nature of social and individual needs without completely rupturing its linkages with the traditions and customs, though customs and traditions were themselves changing gradually (Cf. Prakash, 1989). The adaptations and modifications of the inherited educational system was guided not only by emergent needs and aspirations for the future, but it was regulated also by the heritage and customs of the country. The acceptance of new goals and objectives of life led to the changes in social needs and individual aspirations. These necessitated the evaluation of the suitability and relevance of the inherited customs and traditions for the changing needs of the society and its individual members. Whenever a hiatus between the needs and customs and traditions was found to exist, or these were discovered to obstruct development, during each stage of societal evolution, new customs, traditions, values, systems, institutions and behavioural modes were evolved to suit the felt needs. Consequently, educational system was also swamped by radical changes.

The evolving Indian society approved not only the modifications in existing educational system with a view to afford equality of accessibility to education to the masses but it also accepted the need for such system of education as is capable of preparing highly duty conscious, liberal and secular minded and ever willing to learn individuals. Yet the evolving system has never lost its traditionality. Under this traditional system, there sprouted an extremely large number of educational institutions, spread widely over the entire length and breadth of the country. The gurukuls lost the race to these maths, vihars, pathshalas, maktabs and madrasas which were attached to the temples, mosques and even panchayats. Naturally, the movement had been from the education of selected few to the education of the masses. Consequently, pre-British India was much more and much better educated and literate than Europeans and Americans of those ages.

Education during Muslim Rule

Drastic changes had continued to affect education during the Muslim rule, which not only necessitated but also triggered the process of reorganisation of the educational system to meet the changing societal and individual needs to meet challenges of the times. Sanskrit and Prakrit lost official patronage, though Sanskrit continued to be taught and learnt as a result of the private interest and initiative. Official patronage was now extended to the learning of Persian and Arabic. This evoked great deal of response from the people also, since the knowledge of Persian and Arabic emerged as an instrument of access to the privileges of the ruling elites. Naturally, both these languages had to be incorporated into the curricula as new subjects of learning. But the changes in contents of education were not confined to the learning and teaching of languages and literature alone. New rulers of India have also brought with them new forms of art, crafts, architecture, system of philosophy, astronomy, medicine and all of these were very subtly integrated in the existing stock of knowledge inherited from the past.

Muslim system of education was introduced in India sometimes in the twelfth century. Qutabuddin Aibak established numerous mosques and attached madrasas to them. The madrasas imparted both spiritual and material education (N. Law, 1910). Education continued to expand during the rule of the Slave Dynasty. The Khiljees also attached great importance to education because of which Delhi emerged as an important centre of education and become a seat of learning. Numerous madrasas, schools and colleges also came into existence as a result of the private initiatives. According to one view, schools and colleges existed and operated practically in every part of the country even before the advent of the Mughal empire in India (S.M. Zafar, 1973).

Changing trends in education in Europe and US also started percolating into India and these were incorporated in the educational contents. The observatories constructed by Raja Sawai Mansingh at Jaipur, Delhi, Ujjain, Benaras and Mathura, and historical monuments like Jama Masjid, Qutab Minar, Taj Mahal and Red Forts of Delhi and Agra furnish the testimony to the level of development of such subjects as architecture, mathematics and astronomy. Mansingh had gathered the imported tables from Portuguese king Emanuel and found that those tables were erratic due to the use of instruments with shorter radius. Indian arts, architecture, mathematics and astronomy were much more and better developed than the development of these subjects in Europe. The subject of geometry was developed in India, Egypt and Lebnon. Mansingh was familiar with the use of log tables, horizontal and circular geometry and trignometry of Europe and he had also deeply studied the Greek treatises. Import of teachers by Tipu Sultan from France to impart training to his army, establishment of Jacobin Club by him, and appointment of both Indian and foreign instructors to train and impart other skills to his subjects are testimony to this thesis. It is thus obvious that the educational system of those days was extremely lively, vibrant and alive to the societal needs of the times. Naturally, new forms, organisational and structural patterns of educational institutions also emerged as maktabs and madrasas. Pandits and Moulvis emerged as the pivots of these pathshalas and madrasas.

Muslim rule in India not only diversified the then existing indigenous system of education but it also attached great importance to the provision of educational facilities so as to make it widely accessible to the vast majority of the people. Population growth had also imparted urgency to the expansion of existing facilities. Like pathshalas, maktabs and madrasas also sprang up like weeds. The resultant expansion of educational facilities ensured that there was hardly any mosque, temple or panchayat which had no pathshala or madrasa or maktab attached to itself.

But before the advent of British rule in India and with the beginning of the decline of Mughal empire, Indian society, economy, polity and education had started declining with the result that education was reduced to a ritual. Consequently, education could no more cope up with the dynamic changes which were engulfing the then Indian polity, economy and society, though the then prevalent education could suffice for the stagnant society and its needs. This trend could not be reversed even by the introduction of Western education, science and technology which, in any case, were not utilised for the benefit of Indian masses. In any case, the science and technology that reached India through the Britishers were the derivatives of commercial applications, and these were designed and devised to serve the British political interests. The British interests revolved round geographical and geological surveys for mining the precious mineral products and the exploitation of natural resources in general and raw materials in particular.

Rapid educational development is reflected in the observation of Thomas Munroe (1826) that there existed at least one pathshala per 1000 persons in Madras. This did not include those who received education at home, since data pertaining to persons being educated at home were not available. Similarly, Adam estimated that there were nearly 100,000 madrasas in

Bihar and Bengal alone in 1830. According to Lightner, every village in Punjab possessed one pathshala. According to Alexander Walker (1820), in a distant and remote place like Malabar, every village had its own pathshala. In fact, indigenous pathshalas at one time existed everywhere in India and no fees were charged for the education imparted in these abodes of learning. It will, however, be wrong to infer that madrasas, vihars, and pathshalas imparted religious and ethical education alone. There were any number of pathshalas and madrasas which admitted Hindus, Buddhists, Sikhs and Muslims as their students without any discrimination on religious grounds. These institutions imparted education that did not embody the teachings of any particular religion or faith. Education imparted by these institutions was secular in nature and socially relevant in orientation.

Large number of Sanskrit, Arabic and Persian schools operated, which imparted education up to the highest level not only in languages and literature but also in law, philosophy, logic, science, technology and medicine (Sharp and Richie, 1922). In most cases, education was free and there was no relationship whatsoever between the fees paid and education received by the pupils. The educational institutions were financially supported by the charitable endowments and/or incomes derived from rent free lands provided to such institutions, or lands granted for religious purposes to temples and mosques to which the educational institutions were attached. However, after the introduction of Western education in India, the then British rulers started gradually withdrawing these lands in order to starve the indigenous educational system of their financial support base so as to popularise and substitute the Western for Indian education.

It is the phenomenal expansion of education which made Indians not only literate but more and better educated than the Americans and Europeans towards the end of the eighteenth and the beginning of nineteenth century. This is supported by empirical evidence. Martin (1837) observes that one in five Indians used to be an educated person when only 1 was an educated person out of 15 in Britain, 17 in France, 11 in US and

15 in Australia. Education for the masses was initiated in 1801 in Travancore. In an isolated and remote area of Malabar, 'people eschewed all the feelings and considerations of wealth, family honour and caste so as to ensure the benefit of good and quality education for their children. They had an access to education from their own organisational system under which every village had one pathshala...pathshalas for providing free education used to be found all over India at one time (Quoted from Dharampal, 1983). Thus, education for the masses existed in India since long, while it started in Britain in only 1870 (Jawaharlal Nehru, 1951, p. 285). This is in contrast to the fact that only 5 per cent Indians were found to be literate by British rulers in the second census of India in 1901. This implies one of the following three things: (a) imposition of Western education in India deprived the masses of an access to education which they had earlier enjoyed, and (ii) conversion of such a large number of literates into illiterates could have been possible only because of the Western education, which revolved around the learning and teaching of English language. Besides, India had had an oral tradition with which Western system of education and its pedagogy did not match, and/or (iii) there was a deliberate and conscious undercounting of literate persons in 1901 census to put Indians in poor light by colonial rulers so as to enthuse the people to opt for British system of education.

But the vocational education continued to be imparted within the family itself, though there existed some formal arrangements for the development of skills and capabilities in the arts, commerce and trade and a wide variety of crafts through occupational guilds.

Formal Introduction of Western Education in India

sLord Macaulay had introduced British system of education in India much earlier than its introduction in Japan and other countries. But the approach to educational planning was (a) to focus on the preparation of manpower to meet the manpower needs, specially those of lower and middle order functionaries for British administration in India. Naturally, education was linked to the white rather than blue-collar jobs, (b) educational facilities were to be provided only on such limited scales as would restrict educational accessibility to the elites or classes rather than the masses, (c) contents of learning and teaching were designed to transform the uneducated and *uncivilised into educated and civilised* individuals to think and behave like the Britishers so as to alienate them from their indigenous cultural roots on the one hand, and which will leave the impression on the masses that the acquisition of English education was an instrument of transforming individuals from the ruled into the part of the rulers on the other, and (d) educated persons were expected to influence others in favour of not only Western education but also in favour of the British rule and British rulers. This is amply illustrated by Macaulay's declaration: "I feel...that it will be impossible for us with our limited means to attempt to educate the body of the people. We must at present do our best to form a class who may be interpreters between us and the millions whom we govern—class of persons Indian in blood and colour but English in tastes, in opinions, in morals and in intellect. To that class, we may leave it to refine the vernacular dialects of the country." Not only that, he seems to have adopted the manpower requirements approach to educational planning in India, though the plan was only to produce adequate manpower for white jobs in the government. The Western education introduced in India had naturally to be patterned on British model with modifications to suit the specific needs and purpose of its introduction in India.

Objectives of British Education in India and its Distorting Effects

It may, however, be noted that the industrial revolution had forced Britain to reorganise and revamp its educational system thoroughly. For this, the religious and philosophical base was replaced by the scientific base of education, where facts and the ability to link different factual information/phenomena in a causal framework in order to explain and interpret the observed reality rationally and scientifically emerged as the prime objective of education. Besides, it had to produce adequate manpower both in numbers and skills to meet the manpower needs of the industrial society. Such radical transformation could have not materialised without careful state intervention and the planning of education, even though education remained, by and large, the concern of parents in Britain of those days. Education was, in fact, meant to be imparted and acquired by elites rather than by masses in general and working classes of Britain of those days in particular. Macaulay imparted the 'same elitist' bias to education in India also by modelling it on the then British pattern of education. Thus, education was meant for the classes rather than the masses.

The educated persons, both individually and as a class were to comprise of the camp followers of the British (i) to mould public opinion in favour of the British rule, and facilitate the conduct of the administrative affairs of the British empire. In substance, the system was meant to produce the petty bourgeoisie, comprising mostly of clerks and other lower and middle order functionaries to carry out the orders and wishes of the rulers of those days: "In fact the study of English was emerging quickly as the means of earning high income, gain access to high status in society and entry into the black-coat occupation. It is, therefore, not surprising that many persons of that generation considered English education to hold the key to the solution of all problems" (Sayyad Nurulla). Similarly, Nazir Ahmed, in one of his novels, observed that "English education was not doing any good to the country, it was rather causing it serious harm. People wanted and opted to receive education so as to obtain a government job. Getting employment was the only objective of education for them. They were ready to accept only government service and the whole of their knowledge was just confined to that. Wherefrom so many jobs would be created...in fact, the education department was leaving a negative effect those days. Indians needed such education as might have promoted industry and crafts. However, the students were so moulded in thought as made them hate their parental occupations." Such observations as above not only substantiate our thesis but it also demonstrates the understanding of the real situation by the Indian nationalist intellectuals of those days also.

It is, therefore, amply clear that Macaulay's intents, purposes and policy to introduce Western education in India were well understood by national leaders like Mahatma Gandhi. The observations and declarations of the Britishers themselves and the practical experience furnished by educational development in India lent substance to Gandhiji's assertion that the British educational system was too costly to be affordable to a poor country like India and too elitist to cater to the needs of the masses. The mass orientation of education can be successful only if it is related directly to the concerns of the daily life of the people and the productive work they do. Gandhiji emphasised both these aspects of education. Another aspect of Macaulay's plan was to transform the mental modes of thinking processes, psychological motivations and propensities, mind-sets, and behavioural tendencies of educated Indians so as to make them conform to the British modes of thoughts and modes of behaviour, linguistic and cultural norms. In other words, education was to be used as an instrument of brain-washing, cultural hegemonism, political exploitation and linguistic anchorism. This was meant to keep the minds and souls of Indians enslaved for ever. The Indian system of Western education was a poor and third rate parody of the then British system of education. This fact shall be brought out clearly by what follows in the ensuing paragraphs. This digression will also highlight the shortcomings and limitations of the Western system of education in Britain itself during the first half of the nineteenth century.

British Education in Nineteenth Century Britain

The centralised factory system of large scale production of goods and commodities, based on an entirely new technology that embodied different skills and occupational components than the earlier technology in use, required the then existing system to be replaced by a new factory like centralised large scale system of educational production. Since the earlier system of formal education was controlled, owned, managed and operated by the churches, traditional education naturally focused mainly on religion, ethics, philosophy and moral values more than the practical problems of life, including employment. Vocational training, designed to endow the apprentices with skills and capabilities, that were required to perform the tasks associated with the jobs people aspired for and expected to join in local production establishments, was within the purview and domain of occupational guilds. Naturally, education-employment interface was conspicuously absent from the traditional formal system of education, whereas there was one to one correspondence between the guild-based vocational training and employment. The vocational training was consequently outside the conceptual circle and scope of formal system of education. But the guilds, like decentralised system of small scale production of goods, were widely scattered over space. They could naturally train only handful of persons at any given point of time and place. Naturally, vocational training imparted by the guilds focused on skills and capabilities needed to perform the locally available jobs, which were disappearing fast in the wake of industrial revolution. The existing occupations and their skill requirements were becoming obsolete and were being replaced by newly emerging occupations whose skill requirements were totally different from those of the traditional jobs. Consequently, these guilds could not meet the manpower requirements of the factory based large scale system of commodity production of the industrialised society.

The manpower requirements of centralised large-scale factory system of commodity production were so vast as required to be matched by factory like system of educational production both in terms of numbers and in skills and knowledge, otherwise the manpower shortages would have thwarted full utilisation of large-scale productive capacities installed to produce the goods and services in large-scale commodity factory production sector. Required manpower was to be produced on large-scale on the basis of factory like centralised large-scale system of educational production. Besides, skills and knowledge components of manpower supplied by new educational system had to be entirely different from those possessed by people who received education and training through the traditional educational system and the guilds. The new system of education and training had to match the manpower requirements of production based on the use of new techniques of production. The new system of education had, therefore, to embody and encompass only the perfunctory functions of earlier system of education on the one hand, while some of the functions of guilds had now to be performed by the formal system of education on the other. The nature and level of skills, training and knowledge to be imparted by the new educational system radically differed from those associated with guilds. Such drastic changes required complete overhaul or even the substitution of the existing by an entirely new system of education.

Factory like centralised large scale production design of the new educational system with entirely different subjects, methods of organisation, techniques of teaching and contents of learning ruptured the direct relationship between the teachers and the taught, just as the factory system of production of goods had disrupted the direct relationship between producers and consumers. Production, marketing, management, administration and the utilisation of output of the centralised educational system were now to be handled on a specialised basis separately by different agencies. Hence, education became much more impersonal but formalised than before. It had to lay emphasis on new subjects and facts for learning rather than exclusively concentrating on the transformation from a mere physical into a mental, rational and thinking man, endowed with proper ethical, moral and philosophical values. Facts, reality and practical problems became the main focus of new learning.

The new educational system had to be devised to prepare students to (i) think objectively and rationally so as to be able to relate the causes with their consequences or vice versa so as to be able to explain the observed phenomena, (ii) apply the knowledge imparted, received and absorbed through the processes of teaching and learning to solve of practical problems of life, specially those relating to the jobs expected to be available and to be taken up by the students in future, and (iii) make new discoveries and inventions so as to facilitate the upgradation of the techniques of production and to replace the existing with better and more efficient managerial, organisational and institutional structure through social engineering. However, actual system in operation got distorted by an overemphasis on some and neglect of other facets of new educational system mentioned above. This is especially so in regard to the memorization of facts and the learning of three R's. This is aptly reflected in Frederick Brereton's observation in the introduction to the Charles Dicken's novel, entitled *Hard Times*: "...progress during the past century has not been so considerable as one supposed. In education, for example, are not our schools still tainted by the Gradgrind insistence on the importance of Facts? Have we yet succeeded in changing the system which produced Mr. M'Choakumchild? He and some one hundred and forty other schoolmasters had been lately turned out at the same time, in the same factory, on the same principles, like so many pianoforte legs. He had been put through an immense variety of paces, and had answered volumes of head breaking questions...".

The points to be noted are that the, (i) number 140 of school teachers produced to run new educational system is extremely large relative to the total population of Britain of those days on the one hand, and in view of the fact that these 140 teachers were in addition to those who had already been there in the system on the other, (ii) 140 new or additional teachers should be taken as the annual outturn of institutions dealing with the teachers' education, (iii) it is important to note that one teacher could have a turnover of at least 30 students per year. Thus, total number of students trained by these new types of schools had been enormously large in those Victorian days, when population of Britain was much smaller than what it is today, and (iv) then, emphasis on the study of pure facts and reality to the exclusion of everything else, including religion, philosophy, ethics, languages, and literature from education represented a radical shift in emphasis and changes in the basic objectives, and hence, the contents of education of the children. It implied neglect of the higher values of life and almost an exclusive emphasis on the material uses of education.

The mid-nineteenth century England was in the throes of not only the metamorphosis of transition from an autocratic agrarian to a modernised democratic industrial society, but it was also in the process of transforming itself from a stagnant, traditional and feudalistic economy into a modern and rapidly growing economy. It was essentially a period when culture and ethical values were 'at a discount; when all that mattered was the insensate lust for wealth—and still more wealth'(Brereton, p. 11). The prevailing attitude is aptly captured by the phrase, 'The Good Samaritan was a bad economist,' when only a Charles Dickens could gather the courage to 'seize upon the all pervading ugliness of a Lancashire Cotton-town as a background for a penetrating study of the money grabbing industrialists who flourished under the beneficent influence of *laissez-faire.'* Education was just an instrument for preparing the manpower with requisite skills and knowledge, which could be bestowed upon the learners through the learning, understanding, explanation and analysis of facts and reality with a view to understand and explain the causal chains of inter relationships among the complex natural, social and economic phenomena: 'Now what I want is, Facts. Teach these boys and girls nothing but Facts. Facts alone are wanted in life. Plant nothing else, and root out everything else. You can only form the minds of reasoning animals upon Facts: nothing else will ever be of any service to them. This is the principle on which I bring up these children. Stick to Facts, Sir.' This declaration could have been in a classroom with the replacement of the word 'Sir' with the words 'boys and girls' *(Hard Times).*

A great deal of emphasis had been put on the study of such subjects as geography and geology. Study of facts pertaining to the geographical and geological phenomena/reality was needed to facilitate an access to the natural resources, especially minerals, and other raw materials of the world. Both the geographical and geological surveys were needed for identifying the resource bearing areas and the subsequent prospecting of the mineral and other natural resources. The delineation of the agroclimatic conditions to facilitate the determination of the cultivation of crops, suitable for local conditions of each area and which were needed for the operational needs of the British industries and even direct final consumption, needed geological and geographical surveys. Discovery and subsequent exploitation of mineral resources required the knowledge, both theoretical and practical, of conducting geological surveys for discovering and prospecting the mineral bearing areas.

Not only the emphasis of education had now shifted from ethics, philosophy and values to Facts and Reality and their analysis in a causal framework in order to develop the scientific temper of mind, but the educational system has also been transformed into a highly inequitous system. The then educational system of Britain reflected the inequitous social structure and high degree of inequalities of income and wealth between different groups and classes. The educational system operated where low wages for long hours of work and the system of child slavery and savagery for profits were the accepted norms. Dickens himself had to work at a blacking factory, where for 6 shillings a week, he had to stick labels on pots of paste blacking at a tender age of his early childhood. This long digression from a novel of the Victorian age is justified as it reflects not only the nature of educational system then in operation but also its operational socio-economic background, since 'in these latter novel...is not a novel but rather a thinly disguised treatise on psychology, sociology, or any other ology' (Brereton, p.11). This is also testified by Ruskin's observation that Hard Times should be studied with close and earnest care by persons interested in social questions' (p.15).

It is not surprising that the British rulers implanted a similar inequitous system of education, which emphasised learning of 3 R's by rote more than by understanding. But the difference was that the emphasis here was on the learning of three R's of English language. The learning of science and technology was neglected by and large. Introduction of Western education by the likes of Macaulay, for whom equity, justice, and welfare, and even a suggestion for the slightest improvement in the miserable conditions of the masses was 'sullen socialism', further accentuated the inherited ills of the system. The Indian Western system of education is, in fact, a poor and shoddy parody of the British system. Though the Britishers themselves had moved a great deal away from their nineteenth century system of education, India continues to struggle with the cosmetic reforms and modifications in the initially inherited system. But the above discussion makes it clear that India was probably the first country to introduce and practice educational planning with the limited purpose of producing manpower for the white jobs in the government sector(s).

References

Adam, William (1835), *State of Education in Bengal*, p. 6.

Ahmed, Nazir, *Ebul-Wakt.*

Aso, Makoto and Amano, Ikuo (1972), *Education and Japan's Modernization*, Ministry of Foreign Affairs, Tokyo.

Blaug, Mark (1967), Economics of Education and Educational Planning. Published in *Economic Journal.*

Brereton, Frederick (1854), Introduction to Charles Dickens' Novel: *Hard Times*, Roopa & Co., New Delhi, Reprint, 1991.

Callaway, A. and Musone, A. (1968), *Financing of Education in Nigeria,* UNESCO: I.I.E.P., Paris.

Dennison, E.F. (1961), *The Sources of Economic Growth in the U.S. and the Alternatives before US,* Supplementary Paper, Committee for Economic Development, NBER, New York.

Dickens, Charles (1854), *Hard Times*, Reprint, Roopa & Co., New Delhi, 1991.

Dutta, S. (1988), 'Post-Annexation British Policy in Matak'. Published by North East India History Association (1988), *Proceedings of Ninth Session, Gauhati* University, *Guwahati.*

Irene, Salam (1988), 'The Foundations of Catholic Mission Education in Manipur.' North East India History Association (1988), *Proceedings of Ninth Session, Gauhati* University, *Guwahati.*

Johnstone, James (1971), *Manipur and the Naga Hills,* p.144, New Delhi.

Khan, Mohamed Shamim (1990), *Education, Religion and Modern Age*, Ashish Publishing House, New Delhi.

Komarov, V. E. (1964), 'The Relationship between Economic Development and the Development of Education.' Published in Bowman, M.J. (Editor) *Readings in the Economics of Education*, UNESCO, Paris.

Lightner, G.W. (1833), *History of Education in Panjab since Annexation and in 1822*, Reprinted in 1973.

Lokendra, M. (1988), 'Education and Society in Manipur'. Published by North East India History Association (1988), *Proceedings of Ninth Session*, *Gauhati* University, *Guwahati.*

Lurie, Sylvian (1989), *Educational Planning*, Lecture Delivered to Participants of *'One Week Training Programme for I.A.S. Officers'*, NIEPA, Jan., 9-14.

Martin, R.M. (1837), *History of the Possessions of the Horrible*, Part II, p. 173, E.I.C., London.

Mwingira, A. C. and Pratt, Simon (1967), *The Process of Educational Planning in Tanzania*, UNESCO: I.I.E.P., Paris.

Nehru, J.L. (1951), *Discovery of India*, London.

Parnes, Herbert, S. (1964, Editor), *Forecasting Educational Needs for Social and Economic Development*, O.E.C.D., Paris.

Parnes, Herbert, S. (1964, Editor) *Planning Education for Social and Economic Development*, O.E.C.D., Paris.

Prakash, Shri (1976), 'Input Output Models of Education with Applications to Indian Data.' Published in Mathur, P. N. (Editor) *Economic Analysis in Input Output Framework*, Vol. III, Input Output Research Association, Bombay University.

Prakash, Shri (1977), *Educational System of India—An Econometric Study*, Concept, New Delhi.

Prakash, Shri (1989), *Analytical and Historical Perspectives of Educational Planning in India.* Included in the Proceedings of *Review Conference on Four Decades of Development*, Ministry of Human Resource Development and NIEPA, New Delhi.

Prakash, Shri and Buragohain, Tarujyoti (1993), *Theoretical and Methodological Base of Education—Economy Nexus and Economic Value of Education.* Presented at Plenary Session of *X International Conference on Input Output Techniques*, Seville, Spain.

Prakash, Shri and Chowdhury, S. (1994), *Expenditure on Education : Theory, Models and Growth*, NIEPA, New Delhi. Reprinted in 1996.

Prakash, Shri (1997), *Cost of Education: Theoretical Explorations and Empirical Prognostication*, Anamika, New Delhi.

Prakash, Shri (1998), *Economic Development, Methodology and Human Resources: A Review Article*, Forthcoming in *Journal of Educational Planning & Administration*, NIEPA.

Psacharopoulos, George (1985), *Planning of Education : Where Do We Stand?*, Discussion Paper, Education and Training Series, Report No. EDT. 4, World Bank, Washington.

Munroe, Thomas (Sir) (1826), *Minutes of Sir Thomas Munroe*, Fort St. George, Revenue Consultations.

Roy, J. (1973), *History of Manipur*, p. 167, Calcutta.

Sema, Piketo (1988),'Colonial Educational Policy in Nagaland' Published by North East India History Association (1988), *Proceedings of Ninth Session*, *Gauhati* University, *Guwahati.*

Sharp, H. and Richie, J.A.(1922), *Selections from Educational Records*, Part I: 1781-1839; II:1840-1859. Reprint, 1955, National Archives.

Sayyad Nurulla, Quoted from Shamim, Kaisher (1995), *Curriculam, Ideology and Education : Need for the Study of Madrasa Education.* Published in *Paripreksshaya*, Vol. II, No. 1 NIEPA's Journal

Travillion, Charles, *On the Education of the People of India.*

Tinbergen, Jan (1960), *Central Planning*, Minnesota.

Vatican II, *GRAVISSIMUM EDUCATIONIS 8*. Quoted from Irene, Salam (1988), *The Foundations of Catholic Mission Education in Manipur.* Published in *North East India History Association (1988): Proceedings of Ninth Session, Gauhati* University, *Guwahati.*

Walker, Alexander (1820), *Malabar Bibliography, Their Progress in Literature, Educational System Borrowed from it, Account of it from Peter Della Velle,* Quoted from Pal, Dharam (1993), *The Beautiful Tree,* New Delhi.

Zafar, S.M. (1973), *Education In Muslim India—1000-1800 A.D.*, Quoted from Zaidi, S.M.I.A. (1995), *Muslim Ideology and Education.* Published in *Paripreksshaya,* Vol. 2, No.1.

3

Concepts, Theoretical Paradigms, Procedure and Methods of Planning

Development and Planning as Focus of Theory and Policy

Like the concept of development, the concept of planning has also not been finally settled as yet. Just as the meaning, connotation, nature, scope and methodology of other 'terms' and 'concepts' tend to change from one context to another, the meanings and connotation of the concept of 'planning' have also been changing through time, over space, and between disciplines and socio-economic systems to which the concept is applied. The meaning or connotation, nature, scope and methods of planning may differ from one context to another. The contextual framework of planning is furnished by time, space, polity and economy to which it applies and within which it operates. Hence, the nature, methods and scope of planning differ from one country to another, from one time to another with changes in the pattern and stage of development and the structure of the economy to be planned. Consequently, the nature, scope and methods of planning are highly varied and greatly diversified. For example, the former USSR started with command based centralised planning, whereas the French patented and practised the incentive based and market oriented indicative planning. Whereas Britain alternated between nationalisation and denationalisation of the basic and core industries up to the end of the seventies, but the government had relied basically upon the market to a large extent. China and Yugoslavia offered alternative forms, patterns, structures and modes of socialist planning which differed radically from the Russian planning. India opted for the market based planning for a mixed economic structure, dominated by the public sector and its administered prices on the one hand, and dual pricing policies, including subsidization of essential and core commodities like foodgrains, cement, sugar, steel for the relatively weaker sections of society, leaving the affluents to purchase the same goods at higher prices from the open market, while the luxury goods, especially the durable consumer goods, were heavily taxed, on the other. Thus, the Indian planners used financial instruments in conjunction with physical controls and regulations of the private sector for the realisation of the accepted goals and objectives of planned development.

Different varieties, forms, patterns, structures and methods of planning do not offer a uniform concept, structure and method of planning to be encompassed within a single definition. It is, therefore, extremely difficult to encompass, cover, contain and incorporate all varieties and types of planning and their differential nature, scope, and methods in any one single definition. This may be kept in view in considering different definitions of planning that have been discussed in the chapter. There has, however, been a great deal of agreement about the desirability of planning, especially development planning in the underdeveloped countries, planning of social welfare measures and the measures of macro-economic stabilisation in the market based capitalist economies, the planning of rapid economic development through planned industrialisation of the economy and rapid structural transformation of institutions, organisations, society and the polity in the socialist countries of the world.

> *The nature, methods and scope of planning differ from one country to another, from one time period to another, since changes in the pattern and structure occur, when the economy to be planned moves from lower to higher*

stages of development. It is extremely difficult to encompass, cover, contain and incorporate all varieties and types of planning and their differential nature, scope, and methods in any one single definition of planning.

Planning is compatible with all types of economic systems, ranging from the market oriented, private capital and enterprise based pure capitalism to the socialistically oriented, public capital, and public enterprise based state capitalism. Between these two extreme poles of the spectrum, there exist several systems with differential degrees of combinations of public and private capital and enterprises, and market-based and socialistically oriented mixed economies, which operate through the market mechanism, and hence, incentives and inducements on the one hand, and the administrative orders and executive fiats, and administered prices for the realisation of the objectives, goals and targets of planning on the other. But planning is approved, adopted, and practised as the state policy in the mixed economies with a view to bring about structural transformation and diversification of the economy through planned and state sponsored industrialisation, conversion of obstructive into facilitating and enabling psychological attitudes, changes in social organisations and institutional set-up so as to maximise growth with the available investible resources within the given planning horizon.

Most of the underdeveloped countries preferred the Indian model of mixed economy of planned development rather than opting for the authoritarian Chinese model of socialistic planned development. Relevance and urgency of planning for the development of the underdeveloped countries and the compatibility of planning with different socio-economic systems are highlighted by the Machiavellian observation. Machiavelli, considering an underdeveloped country of the sixteenth century, exclaimed, "Behold her ready and willing to follow any standard if only there can be some one to raise it". (Griffin & Enos, p. 3). This aptly describes the urge and craze for development, which warranted planning in the underdeveloped countries even in Middle Ages. The receptivity of the masses to planned development had been capitalised by the rulers under different socio-political systems. First the kings and emperors seized the opportunity to unite the country politically and wield power as sovereigns. Armies were raised, administrative structures were erected, architecture, arts, crafts, science and technology, and commerce and trade were promoted for filling up their treasuries and enhancing their glory. But only a few were taught, though many were trained in the arts, crafts and vocations in recognition of the role of education in the maintenance of efficiency and the raising of productivity of the system. But these regimes were politically authoritarian, by and large. Maurya, Gupta, and Vardhan dynasties in ancient India and Khilji, Lodhi and Mughal empires during the Middle Ages furnish examples of this genre. All these monarchies needed and used planning of one type or other. For example, Todar Mal introduced land revenue system during the reign of Akbar, the implementation of which needed enormous information about land tenures and incomes of the land-holdings. The detailed planning of agricultural taxation had been undertaken on the basis of this information. But the socio-political structures and economic systems under the kings and emperors had, by and large, been inequitous both politically and economically.

> *Economic planning was originally an invention of the Bolshevik Revolution in Russia and socialistic transformation of the economies of Eastern Europe, following the lead furnished and the trail blazed by the USSR.*

French Revolution released such powerful socio-political forces of liberalism as ultimately engulfed the entire world. Consequently, authoritarian or autocratic monarchies came to be substituted by republican political systems, though kings and emperors remained at the helm of affairs in some countries. But these kings were now only figureheads, having no or only nominal authority and power. The U.K. and Japan are examples of such transformation. Elsewhere, the institution of royalty, and hence, the position of king and emperor was abolished and presidential or prime ministerial forms of democracy came to prevail as the order of the day. Under democracy, 'Liberty, Fraternity and Equality' emerged to dominate the functioning of the political systems in most parts of the world. Thus, autocratic and democratic regimes, under presidents and/or prime ministers, followed the authoritarian monarchical polities to provide popular and representative governance respectively. Rights and duties of the citizens were codified in the political constitution. Incidentally, democracy had been practised in India even in ancient times, when local kings were elected by the people. These democracies were eliminated partly by Maurya kings and partly by the kings of Gupta dynasty. These regimes had developed the concepts and techniques of planning in accordance with the needs of the times and the objectives of the individual empires/countries. But in the 'rural, agrarian, uncongested societies of the eighteenth and the nineteenth centuries, these political freedoms' were envisaged to be 'necessary for the welfare of the country and sufficient to secure its greatest prosperity' through development (Cf. Griffin & Enos, p. 3). These political systems represented much greater degree of people's participation in governance and much greater degree of political and administrative decentralisation under the rule of law.

The diffusion of political and administrative power was, however, not matched by an equitable diffusion of purchasing power, which remained concentrated in a few hands. This made economic system inegalitarian in nature. Thus, political democracy was not matched by economic democracy. Though theoretically each individual was free to choose to consume as much quantity of preferred goods as one liked or needed, produce what one preferred to produce, or pursue the occupation or profession of one's own liking and choice yet, in practice, the freedom to consume, produce and join occupations of one's liking and preference depended upon the purchasing power, capital and wealth that one possessed, and education and training one received. Freedom to consume was limited by income, whereas freedom to produce what one wanted to produce depended upon capital and wealth, and freedom of choice of occupations of one's liking and preference was restricted by unaffordable costs of education and training for the masses. The prestigious and most aspired for professions and occupations, carrying higher earnings, required for entry precisely the skills, training, and education that are inaccessible to the poor masses due to their inability to pay the high costs. Inequalities of income and wealth on the one hand, and unequal distribution of educational and occupational opportunities on the other, prevented political democracy from being transformed into economic democracy under *laissez-fairer, laissez-passer* that constituted the base of economic policy. The industrial revolution and imperialism, that accompanied it, 'by drawing men from agriculture, by conglomerating them in factories, by demanding new skills and adaptations, and by creating great wealth and then distributing the bulk of it to the owners of merely one of the agents of production, made insufficient the existence of political virtue' (Griffin & Enos, p. 3). Obviously, even the political virtue was meant probably only for citizens of the mother country rather than for the subjects of the colonies. The *laissez-fairer* of this period was merely the frontal face and mask of liberalism borne by the greedy and exploitative capitalists, and the nationalist selfish colonial rulers. The *laissez fairer* resulted in highly marked spatial inequalities of development on the one hand, and inequalities in the distribution of income and wealth among the people both within and between the countries on the other.

Underdevelopment of the countries of the Third World had been the result of the draining of their resources for nurturing and accelerating the development of the mother countries of the colonial rulers. Underdevelopment of the Third World was the direct consequence of the political imperialism and economic colonialism. *Initiation and nurturing of economic development of the underdeveloped countries devolved upon the twentieth century planners, who found the majority of the countries of the world at the end of the first half of the twentieth century to be where they or their colonial exploiters were probably at the end of the seventeenth century* (Cf. Myrdal, 1954, Cf. Griffin-Enos, 1967). Plan, the outcome of the endeavours of the planners and the process of planning, is like *an economic constitution, which guarantees economic democracy. But unlike the relative invariance of political constitution, the economic constitution tends to change periodically to adapt itself to the changing needs of the economy, rising expectations and changing aspirations of the people.* This highlights the dynamism of planning.

An important facet of modern planning is, however, that 'economic planning was originally an invention of the socialist economy'(Lange, 1967, p. 9). Socialist rulers of the centrally planned economies and the leaders of the newly independent countries of the Third World had realised that economic development does not occur spontaneously, such an envisagement in the classical model notwithstanding. Hence, state has to initiate, promote, nurture and guide development through direct policy and planning interventions on the one hand, and direct investment in socially desirable lines of production, especially economic infrastructure, social overheads and basic and heavy goods sectors of the economy on the other.

> *Planning is compatible with all types of economic systems, ranging from the market oriented, private capital and private enterprise based capitalism to the public enterprise and public capital based socialistically oriented state capitalism. Between these two extreme poles/ends of the spectrum, there exist several systems with differential degrees of combinations of public and private capital and enterprise, on the one hand, and market based and socialistically oriented mixed economies, where planning has been accepted as the state policy and is being practiced.*

The capitalist model of market based development could be replicated neither in the socialist states nor it could be applied to the newly independent countries of the Third World due mainly to the following factors:

(i) Development of the Western economies through the market mechanism had been extremely slow, though they had an access to the capital, cheap labour, natural resources as well as the factors and the commodity markets of the under-developed countries under the imperial control during the colonial era, and which they fully exploited to further their own development. Such an accessibility for exploitation of resources of others was neither available to the late starters in the development race, nor was it desirable to have such exploitation as the part of international political and economic order during the post Second World War era. The developed West had reached the given level of development in a couple of centuries. But the countries of both the Second and Third worlds were underdeveloped at the time of launching of their development planning, and they were not prepared to wait for centuries to reach the level of development achieved by the developed West, since the masses had already undergone the revolution of rising expectations from the new socio-economic-political order that had emerged in these countries;

(ii) Neither private capital nor the private industrial enterprise was available in adequate quantities to initiate, nurture and promote the market based development in these economies. This left the state no option but to undertake the responsibility of initiating, accelerating and guiding the rapid economic development through planned industrialisation;

> *Planning operates partly through the market mechanism, and hence, incentives and inducements, on the one hand, and partly through the administrative orders and administered prices for the realisation of the objectives, goals and targets of accepted and approved plans, on the other.*

(iii) The heavy and basic goods industries, chosen as the pivots of industrial and economic development, involved such long gestation periods, yielded such low profits and required such huge investment as made these beyond the economic reach and interest of the private entrepreneurs, who were then operating in these countries during those days;

(iv) Large-scale loans, imports of machinery, equipment, new technology and other inputs required for the newly established industries could have not been negotiated efficiently and effectively by the private entrepreneurs with the international agencies, governments of the developed countries and their MNCs;

(v) Socialist revolution started with the (a) nationalisation of the then existing capitalist industries, trade, finance, banking, insurance, communications and transport to replace these by the public sector, (b) agrarian reforms, abolishing feudal socio-economic relations in agriculture, had been implemented to confer the ownership rights of land on the actual tillers, (c) equitable allocation of land among the peasants had been effected and the cooperative and collective farming had been introduced, (d) mobilisation of investible resources and their deployment for rapidly developing prioritised sectors of the economy. These measures resulted in public ownership of means of production and production establishments on a large scale. The state had itself to initiate and promote the development of the economy and guide the private sector, if it existed at that time, along the planned growth path through planning and policy interventions in their operations.

The above facets of planned development are, in fact, the prerequisite for planning, adoption of the policies of effective state interventions, and hence, state guidance of the levels and patterns of production through planning: "Under conditions, where the major part of the means of production becomes publicly owned, it is only natural that the utilisation of these means and the process of production be subject to a general national economic plan" (Lange, 1967, p. 9). Thus, the state ownership of the factors of production and the consequent widespread existence of public enterprises, policy of state intervention in the socio-economic affairs, as against the tenets of *laissez fairer* and *laissez passer,* were considered to be the essential features of planning by Lange, though he also considered people's participation and decentralisation of planning as highly desirable.

> *Planning became an accepted instrument of rapid development in all countries of the world. A basic feature of actual economic development in the post Second World War era is the use of planning as the means to rapid development.*

After the Bolshevik Revolution in the USSR, planning had been adopted as an instrument of accelerated development, wherefrom it percolated to the countries which Lange (1967, p.9) called socialist revolutionary countries, and then to the countries of the Third World. Thereafter, the idea of planning began to penetrate into the old capitalist world also, though they had their own brand of planning for social welfare and macro stabilisation even earlier to that. The new patterns, forms and the desired rapidity and speed of development necessitated the development of the new technique of planning for development. Planning, in fact, became the universally accepted instrument of rapid development and a basic feature of actual economic development in the post Second World War era (Cf. Lange, 1967, p. 9).

Planning may be defined as a device and as an instrument of telescoping the entire developmental process, based on (a) persistent endeavours and hard work involved in the transformation of actual and potential surpluses into capital accumulation, (b) evolving of appropriate organisational forms and institutional structures, (c) development of ever newer technologies for converting the factor inputs into output, (d) the discovery and the productive use of new resources by the Western countries through the market mechanism over a period of centuries, (e) and the consequent achievement of high level of development into a much shorter period of few decades. Planning is a tool or the means of moving the economy from lower to each successive higher stage of development; it is the method to advance consciously and deliberately along the path of socio-economic development through the policy and practice of planning.

Emergence of the former USSR as the second strongest economic and military superpower of the world, its ideological challenge and political cold war with the West, and the felt need of the developing countries to achieve that level of development, which had been achieved by the Western countries in centuries through the market, made planning as an universally accepted and approved instrument of rapid development in the post Second World War period.

Three factors pushed economic development into the centre stage of economic analysis, and these very factors made it also the major concern of policy in the post Second World War period:

(Prakash, 1977a, 1977b, 1989, 1997; Prakash and Chowdhury, 1994, 1996):

(i) The emergence of the former USSR as the second super power of the world, almost equal to the US in economic development and military might, as a result of extremely rapid economic development in general and industrialisation in particular through the instrumentation of planning which assigned high priority to the growth of basic and heavy goods sectors. The technology acquired and/or developed for rapid industrialisation, based on heavy and basic goods sectors, served the threefold purposes of (a) generating high level of investible surpluses in the form of the output of the core, heavy and basic goods sectors, which could not be used for direct final consumption, (b) making the process of industrialisation self-sustained and self-sufficient over a period of time, and (c) furnishing dual purpose technology, which could also be used in defence industries for the production of modern weaponry and armaments. In fact, the USSR realised the level of economic development through planning in only a period of about four decades, which the US and other Western economies took one to two centuries to achieve through individual enterprise, private capital, operating through market mechanism, though they also had the advantage of exploiting the resources and the markets of the colonies to further their own economic development;

(ii) The trail of rapid development through planned heavy and basic goods based industrialisation, blazed by the USSR, was followed by the socialist countries of the Eastern Europe on the one hand, and India and China on the other, who launched their ambitious economic development through planned industrialisation. This inspired almost the entire Third World to accept and adopt planning as an instrument of telescoping that level of development, which the US and Western Europe achieved in centuries, in a short span of few decades;

(iii) Imergence of the USSR as the second super military and economic power of the world, rivalling the US, and its growing political and economic influence over the newly independent countries of the Third World, unleashed the political and ideological cold war among the Eastern and Western blocs of the countries. But the cold war was sought to be won by surpassing the achievements of the rivals in the development race among the comity of nations, including the Third World, Western economies, and the socialist countries. These factors forced both theorists and policy makers to focus on the problems of development in general and the development of the under-developed countries in particular (Cf. Lange, 1967, p. 1);

(iv) The international political climate and public opinion were highly favourable to assist the developing countries in their quest for development. Therefore, the world leaders attached great importance to the development of the underdevelopeo countries: 'The international importance of economic development of the countries of the Third World, which Lange called 'countries of national revolutions', 'became so great that the whole problem of underdeveloped countries, of their economic progress, became a major, I may say, the major international problem'. (Lange, 1967).

The accentuated focus on development brought planning also into the limelight, whereas the failures and the imperfections of the autonomously functioning market mechanism were not only recognised but also were accepted explicitly both in theory and policy to strengthen and buttress the need for planning. The strong case of planning was thus based partly on the limitations and the inadequacies of the market to cope with the problems and processes of rapid industrialisation based development, and partly on the demonstrated success of planning in accelerating not only the pace of development but also in drastic reduction of inequalities in the distribution of income and wealth.

Evolving and Varied Nature of Planning

Like the concept of development, the concept of planning has also been evolved through various phases and stages of the development of knowledge, intuitive insights gained from the conceptual and methodological developments, experiments made in the course of development planning itself, and the expansion of knowledge about the theory, policy, methodology and practices of planning that have been developed and/or accumulated over the years. This has led to the continuous revisions, modifications and adaptations of the concepts, processes and methods of planning, resulting in drastic changes in its nature and scope in economies of different types, having varied structures.

To start with, planning was confined to the government and its agencies. There was hardly any people's participation either in formulation, or in the implementation of national plans of development in the initial period of the planning era. Besides, the power to formulate the plans was concentrated and confined, by and large, to the Central agencies and their selected functionaries, though the responsibility of plan implementation devolved on the grass roots functionaries. While planning was meant to raise the standards of living of the people and solve their problems of daily life, people had no say or role in plan formulation and its implementation. The varied experiences and advances in knowledge suggested that planning would be made real only if persons outside the government and its agencies also participated in the conceptualisation and the formulation of the national/regional plans of development. Then 'planning' would have been transformed from 'planning by the government, planning of the government, and planning for the government' into 'planning by the people, planning of the people, and planning for the people': 'To make planning real, we must have thousands of people working at various levels who would know how to formulate, execute and assess a plan and what concrete studies and measures are required for this purpose of planning at technical, technological and professional levels' (Cf. Lange, p. vi). Then, the limitations of centralised planning were also exposed by the ever expanding size of the socio-economic systems under the impact of planned development itself, and the vast size and varied structures, differential development levels in countries like India. Thus, the growth of the socio-economic systems beyond a point, made them unmanageable centrally, while the varied, intricate and complex problems at the grass roots were continuously missed from being captured by centralised planning. The centralised planning had been rendered inappropriate by the very success of this type of planning, when the levels of development crossed the critical threshold, making the socio-economic systems too big and complex to be planned and managed centrally. Thus, the shortcomings of centralised planning came to the fore during the course of planned development towards the end of the sixties. The need for decentralisation of planning was realised towards the beginning of the seventies, when states/provinces emerged as the planning unit. But the planning had to be further decentralised in the eighties with the adoption of district as the basic planning unit.

> *Experiences accumulated from the plan formulation and their implementation over a period of time, the expansion in knowledge about the theory and practice of planning through the conceptual and methodological developments and the consequent intuitive insights gained from these, suggested the involvement of people both in formulation and implementation of planning, its decentralisation, and the use of new instruments, methods and techniques to plan economic development.*

The following factors also necessitated changes in the forms and methods of planning:

(i) Methods of planning have been diversified in each country according to the historically given material conditions of the economy and the level and patterns of its development at the given stage of planning. These changes have been facilitated by the developments in theory and methodology of planning during the intervening period;

(ii) Changes in the managerial techniques were introduced in the industrial enterprises. In the erstwhile Yugoslavia and India, the workers' participation in the management of public sector industries had been adopted to (a) ensure wider participation of the people, (b) make workers feel as partners in the national endeavours of development to enthuse them about it, and (c) thereby raise the efficiency and productivity of public enterprises. But in Poland, the adoption of the decentralised method of planning implied the limiting of the national targets to the basic macro objectives, while the details were to be worked out at the decentralised or even micro enterprise levels;

(iii) Strategy of implementation of the projects and the programmes of the plans, formulated for the realisation of the goals and objectives, had also been changed from executive fiats and administrative orders to be carried through coercion to incentives and inducements for efficient implementation.

For example, the family welfare programmes in India had undergone sea changes since 1977. Whereas the targets to be achieved by the grass roots workers for containing the population growth within each plan period used to be determined from above, while all the functionaries were made to apprehend punishment, if they failed to achieve the set targets. The programme is now totally revamped to generate micro level demand for small family norms. A variety of policy measures were evolved for this purpose;

> *More reliance is now placed on such financial instruments as prices, reduction in operational costs and enhancement of efficiency and productivity. Whereas the public enterprises were supposed to prompt, nurture and promote growth and welfare in the earlier stages of planned development even if it meant incurring of perpetual losses to the public enterprises, which are now required to earn profits for generating investible surpluses.*

(iv) More reliance is now placed on such financial instruments as prices, reduction in operational costs, and enhancement of efficiency and productivity. This shift has been caused partly by the change in the philosophy of public enterprise, and partly by the fact that many public sector undertakings have perpetually been incurring losses due mainly to inefficient management or improper personnel policies. The losses have to be compensated by the general budgetary support. Subsidization of public enterprises has thus emerged as a permanent need. Thus, the public sector not only failed to generate envisaged surpluses for reinvestment, but it also needed direct budgetary support for its own maintenance and operations. Whereas the public enterprises were supposed to prompt, nurture and promote growth and welfare in the earlier stages of planned development, even if it meant determining prices at levels lower than costs, and thus, resulting in perpetual losses to the public enterprises, which needed subsidisation. But no one questioned either the subsidization of losses of public sector or the subsidization of basic and essential goods in those euphoric days of planning. The same public enterprises are now expected to earn profits for generating investible surpluses (Prakash and Ghosh, 1978).

Now, the sole objective of economic policy in general and fiscal policy, in particular, seems to be the containment of fiscal deficit and curtailment of public sector activities under the new economic policy regime of 1991. This turn and twist in policy has taken place in total disregard of the fact that the development of Indian economy had been initiated, propelled and sustained by public expenditure in general and public investment in particular since the launching of India's First Five-Year Plan of development. (For details, See Prakash, 1982).

Formal Conceptualisation of Planning

Above facets of the evolving nature of the concepts, scope and the methods of planning notwithstanding, there exists a great deal of agreement among the theorists, policy makers and planners about the (i) need for development planning, and (ii) the essential and core elements of the concepts, approaches, strategies and the methods of planning. It, however, does not mean that all economists, planners and policy makers are unanimous about the meaning, nature, scope and the methods of planning. Different thinkers may view the concepts and methods of planning differently.

Griffin and Enos (1970) restrict the term 'Planning' to 'the construction and authorisation of economic, social and political programmes in the underdeveloped countries'. The construction consists of a 'determination of the *goals or aims of the programme, an enumeration of all the resources which are available for their attainment, a consideration of alternative policies governing the ways in which the resources may be used, perhaps a check for consistency to make sure that the goals can be achieved with the resources available, and finally, periodic revisions to allow for unexpected events'.*

The following important facets of this definition are noteworthy:

(i) It extends the concept of planning from economic to social and political programmes, and hence, the corresponding objectives and goals are much wider and more varied rather than being confined to the economy alone.

(ii) Planning is considered relevant only for underdeveloped countries and their socio-economic development, leaving the socialist and the capitalist countries beyond the domain of planning. This aspect of the definition is not only highly restrictive in nature and scope, but it is greatly unrealistic also.

(iii) It relates planning to the formulation of the projects and the programmes that constitute the plan, and hence, it treats planning as a process rather than being treated as one single stroke exercise.

(iv) It lays emphasis on the consistency of planning, which requires the use of such complex techniques as input-output and programming. This puts planning into the domain of the professionals, having requisite competence to do the job adequately, rather than leaving it to the care of the general administrators to convert the whole exercise into a bureaucratic mess.

(v) It makes a provision for the monitoring and evaluation of the progress of plan implementation. It provides for undertaking contingency planning, if the evaluation and monitoring exercises reveal encountering or discovering of unforeseen factors to obstruct the realisation of the major objectives and goals of planning.

(vi) It puts proper emphasis on the authorisation for the mobilisation of resources so as to match the available resources with resource requirements for planning. This leaves planning implicitly into the domain of the government and its agencies.

This is in contradistinction to the need for and the introduction of the process of professionalisation of planning, stated under (iv) above, unless only professionals are appointed and entrusted with the task of planning by the government.

> *The basic principle of planning is the state's active and decisive participation in the economy. The state initiates, spurs and steers economic development by its own acts of investment and enterprise, and its various controls-inducements and restrictions over the private sector. Measures of public policy are rationally coordinated, and the coordination is made explicit in an overall plan for a specified number of years ahead of the plan implementation.*

(vii) This definition emphasises the evaluation of alternative policies of resource mobilisation, but it neglects the evaluation of alternative patterns of resource allocation for growth maximisation. The definition also fails to indicate the importance of alternative approaches to the plan formulation.

(viii) The definition totally overlooks the need for defining the 'planning horizon' for the execution of the plan and attainment of accepted goals and objectives of planning within the given time frame. Thus, some of the facets of the above definition of planning are restrictive in scope, inadequate in coverage, and regressive in nature.

In view of these limitations of Griffin-Enos' definition of planning, Myrdal's definition is considered next.

Gunnar Myrdal (p. 709) defines the basic principle of planning as *'state's active and decisive participation in the economy: by its own acts of investment and enterprise, and its various controls, inducements and restrictions over the private sector, the state shall initiate, spur and steer economic development. These public policy measures shall be rationally coordinated, and the coordination be made explicit in an overall plan for a specified number of years ahead'.*

The following are the major attributes of this definition:

(i) The definition overemphasizes the functions of the state, and hence, it appears to be a bit narrow in scope. This definition, like that of Griffin-Enos', assigns the government a pivotal role in development planning.

(ii) Myrdal expects the state to (a) initiate, prompt and propel development through direct investment, (b) encourage private sector through incentives and inducements to participate in development on the one hand, and guide and regulate it to move into and operate in socially desirable directions of production, while curbing it through controls and regulations as well as through the use of fiscal instruments from undertaking investment and operations that may either be detrimental to the achievement of the accepted and approved goals and objectives of planning, or that may lower the growth of the economy.

(iii) Myrdal advocates the use of market mechanism selectively. But he suggests the use of both punitive and promotive measures to induce the private sector to propel the economy on to its planned growth path. Thus, the definition can capture and encompass actual planning in all three different types of economies much better than the earlier definition. It is because even the socialist countries have left some margin for private enterprise to operate, while the capitalist countries also have to make an allowance for public sector to operate in certain areas. In both these cases planning of one or the other type is involved.

(iv) He rightly emphasises the need for and role of rational coordination of the planned programmes of development so as to ensure the consistency between the targets of output for different sectors and requirements of their output as intermediate inputs in production, provision of public investment and investment requirements of both overall and sectoral growth, etc. But consistency is also required to be achieved between (a) resources required for the plan execution and the resources allocated and actually mobilised for the plan, and (b) chosen goals and targets and the actual achievements. Myrdal overlooks this.

(v) He rightly incorporates the concept of ***planning horizon*** in the definition of planning so as to facilitate the distinguishing between short and long run planning. This emphasises the need to make the programmes and projects included in the plan, time-bound so that time over-runs and consequent cost escalations involved in the time over-runs in completion of the projects/ programmes are avoided.

(vi) The definition overlooks the process and principles, and focuses almost exclusively on the instruments of planning.

We offer here a much wider and much more general definition of planning than the ones we have analysed earlier. Though the concepts and definitions of planning propounded by other economists and planners could have also been discussed, yet we have avoided it. Our objective is not to discuss all the definitions of planning that have been offered from time to time. We have attempted to highlight such aspects of the concept or definition of planning as focus on the operational aspects of planning in modern context. The focus has, naturally, been on the formulation of such a definition as is general in nature, comprehensive in scope and exhaustive in coverage rather than to consider all definitions and concepts of planning propounded in literature.

New Definition of Planning

Planning may formally be defined as the 'deliberate and conscious process of choices, exercised by planners, with a view to select (i) an ordered set from the (a) alternative but economically viable, and (b) technically feasible ordered sets of projects and programmes; (ii) appropriate strategies for plan implementation. This requires the execution of an agenda of action; (iii) strategies are expressed as policy packages; and each policy package is spelled out in hierarchical steps to be taken during implement action phase of the plan period; (iv) detailed and unambiguous description and prescription of the predetermined objectives and goals of planning; (v) specification of duration of time or planning horizon within which the plan is to be implemented and its goals, targets and objectives are to be realised (Cf. Prakash, 1960).

A careful examination of the above definition reveals that the planning refers to:

(i) Conscious and deliberate choices of projects/programmes of development. Under planning regimes, choices are made neither randomly nor are these left to be sorted out by the autonomously functioning market mechanism. Then, the choice making is a process rather than it being one single stroke exercise. The choice of projects/programmes is the positive as against the normative aspect of planning. These choices are based on an evaluation of (a) technological feasibility of different alternatives and options available to the planners. This evaluation includes not only an examination of alternative projects/ programmes to be included in the plan but it also involves the consideration of (1) modes and methods of implementation, (2) spatial location patterns of chosen activities, (3) economic viability in terms of costs and possible benefits, (4) suitability of selected projects/programmes for attaining both short and long term goals, targets and objectives of planning, and (5) possible contribution of each project/programme to the optimisation of growth of the economy. The choices are thus exercised in favour of only such options as are technologically feasible and economically viable, that is, only such projects are included in the plan as will satisfy all above criteria. (a) Besides, either the planner are themselves free to exercise choice between alternative goals or objectives, or alternatively, the goals and objectives of planning are chosen through political process. Then, these goals and objectives are given exogenously to the planners.

(ii) Evaluation of technological feasibility of projects or programmes involves a comprehensive and detailed analysis of their various engineering and technical aspects. For example, an irrigation project will have to be examined with a view to determine the fragility/strength of its structure and design on the one hand, and the impact on ecological balance of dam's location on the other. If the area of location of a mega irrigation dam is earthquake prone, being in the seismological zone, probability of its life being short shall be high, while in the event of its crumbling, damage to life and property may be immense. This has already happened twice in Maharashtra: once in Koyna (Pune) and once in Latur.

Then, plan programmes/projects have to be evaluated for their economic viability. For this, resource constraints, costs and all types of benefits expected to accrue from the execution and completion of the specific projects of development, have to be determined in advance. Not only this, the planning authority needs to know who bears the cost and how much of it is borne by different regions of the economy and different sections of the people, and how the benefits are likely to be distributed among the spatial units and different groups of people through time. In other words, equity and justice aspects of planned development require detailed analysis in advance over a sufficiently long period of planning, for which the likely changes in the distribution of incomes and wealth under the impact of planned development is required to be analysed. These aspects are important from the viewpoint of equity, welfare and growth. Consequently, the inclusion of any project or programme in the plan necessitates detailed techno-economic feasibility and viability studies. The evaluation of the technological feasibility and economic viability of projects, from which choices are made for inclusion or exclusion of particular projects from the plan, focuses on the *positive* as against *normative* aspect of planning.

(iii) Planning process should not, and in fact, does not stop with the selection of plan programmes/projects. Planning has to determine first the stepwise and stagewise strategic details of policies, designed to successfully implement the plan projects/programmes. In other words, the choice of instruments is as much an essential part of the planning as the choice of plan projects/programmes. From this viewpoint, planning is an agenda of action. If planning is not action-oriented, then it will be transformed into paper exercises, leading to the non-realisation of targets and non-fulfilment of preferred goals and objectives of planning.

(iv) Choice of strategies and their policy packages are guided and governed by the objectives and goals of planning. The goals and objectives of planning are, however, governed and guided by political and ideological considerations. Thus, the choice of strategies is determined by positive rather than normative considerations, though the objectives and goals, for the realisation of which the strategies have been formulated, are themselves an outcome of ideology and political context of planning. Choice of objectives thus represents the *normative* aspect of planning. But the choice of strategies focuses on *positive* rather than normative aspect of planning.

(v) Policies that constitute a given strategy have to be evaluated in terms of the outcomes that a particular course of action is likely to lead to. Likely outcomes of policy, and hence, plan implementation constitute the criteria of evaluation of plan projects and programmes. So the exercise of choice among alternative objectives, programmes, projects and policies imply that the evaluation exercises have already been completed.

(vi) Policies furnish instruments of planning, whereas expected outcomes of alternative policies are used as criteria of evaluation of effectiveness and appropriateness of chosen strategies. Policies have to be translated into agenda of action that has to be initiated during the planning horizon for the implementation of plan. Each action for implementation of policy has to be broken into hierarchical and sequential steps and stages in which implementation is proposed to be carried out. If planning is not action oriented, it will then be transformed into paper exercises, leading to non-implementation, and hence, non-realisation of targets, goals and objectives of planning.

(vii) Possible outcomes of implementation of plan projects will have to be compared with the targets and objectives of planning in general and each specific sectoral project in particular. It has to be noted that, though short and long run objectives may differ in certain respects from each other, yet short run goals and objectives are designed to converge ultimately towards long run objectives and goals of planning. Besides, long run objectives are often broken into short run goals and targets on the one hand, and short run objectives are mostly preparatory steps for the realisation of long run goals and objectives on the other. Therefore, shortfalls in achievements of short run targets and goals may lead to compromises even with the long term objectives of planned development. If the divergence between likely outcomes and targets and goals is markedly significant, plan strategy may need revision or even complete transformation. Alternatively, targets and goals may have to be revised to make them match the probable, if not actual achievements, otherwise frequent failure to achieve plan targets and shortfalls in realisation of goals and objectives plan after plan may elicit not only criticism but it may also infuse cynicism towards the setting of goals and targets of planning. Frequent shifting of target dates of realisation of the goal of universalisation of elementary education in India has made analysts and general masses quite sceptic about the pious declarations and proclamations of the policy makers in this regard from time to time. If planners find targets of the given plan to be too ambitious to be realistic relative to likely resource availability, then either targets should be lowered, or resources may be diverted from other sectors/projects, or alternative sources may be tapped for the mobilisation of additional resources during the planning horizon. Thus, chosen policies furnish the instruments of planning, whereas their likely outcomes provide criteria of evaluation of the effectiveness, efficacy and appropriateness of any given strategy and policy packages', that constitute the strategy. Criteria for evaluation is needed for assessing (a) feasibility, viability, and appropriateness of schemes and projects for realising both short and long term goals and objectives of planning, and (b) degree and direction of progress of plan implementation. If such monitoring and evaluation reveal some schemes or projects to have been wrongly included in the plan, or if their implementation is found to be tardy or faulty, corrective measures may be initiated during the pendency or operation of the plan itself. Evaluation criteria facilitates an assessment if actual development is converging towards the chosen short and long term objectives and perceived state of the economy and society.

(viii) Want of consistency in plan formulation, resulting in bottlenecks and constraints in plan implementation, has been a perennial problem of planning in India and elsewhere. Schools without teachers, buildings and even learning-teaching materials affected both the quantum and quality of learning in India. Similarly, shortages of wagons, resulting in the piling up of mountains of coal at the mining pits, while thermal power plants were forced to generate less than full capacity output of power due to shortages of coal. Power shortages, in turn, forced industries to produce less than full capacity output in India during 1966-69. Similarly, only one book per seven students could be made available in the Philippines. Such facets of planned development reflect the importance of consistent planning and the adverse effects of inconsistencies on plan performance. But consistency in planning requires balances between (a) consumption requirements of different goods and actual as well as planned sectoral output of these goods, (b) pattern of sector/ project-wise resource allocation and resource requirements, (c) intermediate inputs required for realising production targets of different sectors and commoditywise sectoral output targets, (d) requirements of manpower with different levels and types of education and level and typewise production of educated manpower by education sector, (e) demand for places and sanctioned intake capacities of educational institutions and their effective utilisation. Lange highlighted the importance of consistency in planning in the context of the problems of Polish planning performance 'First Five-Year Plan has been basically implemented with the development of heavy industry without expected rise in standard of living due mainly to the failure to develop agriculture, small industries, and handicrafts.' Consequently,'Distortions have developed between agriculture and industry, investment in fixed capital and availability of raw materials, owing to a shortage of the latter, fixed capital investments have not been fully utilised.There has also been a lack of balance between quality and quantity' (Lange, 1956). So planning has to be imbued with the property of consistency and material balances.

Planning refers to deliberate and conscious choices of (i) feasible and viable options, feasibility and viability being assessed by technical and economic criteria on the one hand, and criteria furnished by possible outcomes of plan implementation, and (ii) instruments selected for the realisation of goals, targets and objectives of development. Priorities and goals of planned development may be guided partly by political and ideological considerations, partly by resource constraints, partly by aspirations for future development, and partly by the stage of development of the economy at the time of plan formulation.

(ix) Choice-making exercises are designed to realise the multidimensional goals and objectives of planning in the minimum time period at the least resource cost. Besides, differential degree of importance of each goal and objective is assessed in advance. The goals and objectives of planning have to be ordered in advance according to their importance and the priorities of planning. *A prior ordering of objectives* will then govern the *priority ordering of plan projects and programmes* and resource allocation between sectors and between projects within sectors.

(x) Objectives and priorities of planning are generally determined by public agencies in whom the power and authority of planning have been vested by the political system of the country. Political ideology will, therefore, govern the nature of the objectives upon which will impinge the nature, extent and the type of planning on the one hand, and agents and actors to be involved and instruments to be used in planning on the other. Nature and degree of authority and power exercised by different layers of government and their agencies will, however, depend upon the political system, that is, dictatorial, theocratic, autocratic, democratic, or authoritarian structure of the polity. Institutional frame-work, layers of government, intergovernment transactions, and level and kind of authority wielded by each layer of government will then be determined by the nature of political system in operation in the country. However, maximum development during the given time-horizon, removal of regional and personal inequalities, removal of illiteracy and unemployment, provision of nutrition, sanitation, health care and education are kept among the important objectives of planning.

Improvement in the standards of living and ultimately quality of human life may be regarded as the long run fundamental goals and objectives of planning.

Socialistic or equity and welfare orientation of development planning may make it converge towards centralised planning, which will rely more on public and less on private sector for the realisation of plan objectives, while centralised planning will use more controls and regulation than inducements and incentives as instruments of planning. Market orientation of planning will, on the other hand, rely more on the efficacy of fiscal instruments, especially incentives and inducements of both punitive and promotive nature rather than to use controls and regulations. The emphasis on the role of public authority in the choice of objectives, programmes and priorities of planning should not imply exclusion of either the involvement or even the sole responsibility of planning being vested in non-governmental agencies. Even under centralised planning, individuals have to perform a variety of tasks and shoulder varied responsibilities in order to supplement state's developmental efforts. Nowadays NGOs are involved more and more in plan formulation and its implementation. Then, planning may not be confined to the state domain alone. Corporate planning, for example, is undertaken by the operators managing the planning departments of such enterprises. Therefore, the definition of planning has to be broad enough to include such facets of actual practices of planning as have been discussed above.

(xi) Objectives of planning tend to change with development. The very success of planned development ensures that the nature and number of problems and issues of development, techno-economic constraints and socio-institutional structures change through time, necessitating the transformation of goals and objectives of development on the one hand, and methods and approaches to planning on the other. As the society and economy move from lower to successive higher stages of development, several material and financial resource constraints, technological limitations, institutional bottlenecks are progressively loosened. As problems of preceding lower development levels are sorted out, entirely new ones emerge on the horizon. Inherited economic structure is diversified and several gaps of the economy are removed by planned development. Experiences gained from formulation and implementation of previous plans also provide useful guidelines for current and future planning. All these factors lead to improvements in knowledge about the theory and methodology of plan formulation and its implementation. Better plan formulation and its more efficient implementation result in accelerating development on the one hand, and above factors and impacts of their operations bring about qualitative transformation of planning on the other.

In early stages of development, it may be essential to expand such economic infrastructure as transport, power, communications, irrigation, marketing facilities, banking and insurance in order to remove constraints to development on the one hand, and facilitate spatial percolation of growth impulses widely to contain regional inequalities of development through creating new and expanding existing social overheads like health and education on the other. While development of basic and heavy goods industries will make development self-reliant and self-sustained in the long run, investment in economic infrastructure and social overheads mitigates spatial inequalities of development and it removes constraints to growth of remote and less developed regions of the country (Prakash, 1976, Prakash & Rajan, 1977). Technological constraints and shortages of investible resources may lead to the adoption of selectivity approach to industrialisation that accentuates existing and creates new regional inequalities of development. Considerations of technological feasibility, locational factors and resource constraints may also prompt planners to extend the principle of selectivity from industries to agriculture. Such mega multipurpose dams as Bhakra-Nangal, Rihand, Damodar Valley were not established everywhere due partly to resource constraints, partially to differential natural resource endowments of alternative possible locations and largely to technological considerations. Natural resource endowments, investment requirements and uncertainty of success prompted planners to adopt only 14 districts for initial propagation and diffusion of green revolution technology on an experimental basis in early sixties in India. Currently, World Bank sponsored *District Primary Education Project* was launched in 40 districts only, which has subsequently been extended to cover 60 districts. Selectivity approach to growth has now been extended from industry and agriculture to education. This has been prompted by the same considerations of resource constraints, socio-economic viability, administrative and technological feasibility to cover larger areas, and uncertainty of success of a programme of experimental nature (Prakash & Rajan, 1977; Prakash & Mohapatra, 1980). But most of the economic infrastructure and social overheads do not need such huge investment in fixed capital, do not involve such long gestation periods and specific natural resource endowments as are associated either with heavy industries, or mega multi-purpose irrigational projects. Besides, all socio-economic infrastructure constitutes prerequisites of development. Hence, investment in these activities has been conceived as the source of regional equalisation of growth in India (Prakash & Rajan, 1977; Prakash & Mohapatra, 1980).

In maturer stages of development, when resource constraints have been loosened quite a bit, considerable infrastructure and social overheads have already been created, and useful knowledge and experiences of planning have been gained, priorities and objectives of planning may shift to development of financial institutions, complex policy instruments, and R and D facilities on the one hand, and development of intermediate, small and consumer goods industries, handicrafts and agriculture on the other, in order to create balances between supplies of and demand for all varieties of goods and also to satisfy the growing and changing aspirations and expectations of improvements in living standards of the people with development. It is implicit that heavy and basic goods industries might have dominated earlier development of the economy. There are several models and varieties of development planning, which embody differential priority ordering of different sectors in the development design.

Feldman and Mahalanobis models of planned development assign pivotal role to basic and heavy goods industries, though Mahalanobis advocated allocation of only 33 per cent of total investment to heavy and basic industries and remaining 67 per cent of total investment to such other sectors as agriculture, irrigation, small industries and handicrafts, health and education, etc. to generate employment and confer purchasing power on the masses to meet their income needs on the one hand, and to create balances between supplies and demand for basic but essential consumer goods so as to avert inflation, which generally accompanies heavy industry dominated development, on the other (For Endogenisation of inventory effect on growth, See Prakash & Singh, S., 1996). As against this, Vakil-Brahmanada model of planned development considers development of sectors producing basic necessities to be of paramount importance in development design. Then, there is choice between export led or import substitution models of planned growth. Extent and direction of changes in objectives and goals of development, and hence, planning will, therefore, depend upon the nature of the model design of initial development and its priorities of planning and temporal changes therein since the base period. Determination of objectives and priorities of planning, therefore, depends partly upon (a) historical conditions, (b) stage of development of the economy, (c) aspirations for future development, and (d) political and ideological considerations at the time of planning.

Socialistically oriented planning has largely been centralised in nature. Under centralised planning regimes, plan formulation remains within the domain of Central Government and its functionaries, while plan implementation becomes, by and large, the responsibility of the lower layers of government and its functionaries, who have hardly any say in plan formulation. This leads to divergences between concepts and ideas informing plan formulation, and their understanding by the implementors, and hence, a wedge between precept and practice tends to emerge.

Besides, people for whose benefit planners undertake gigantic tasks of planning remain mere spectators of the planning and development processes that affect them vitally. But they have no say either in formulation or implementation of plans, and hence, in shaping the course of development and its nature. Public sector, controls and regulations rather than incentives and inducements, operating through market mechanism, will then play the dominant role in development and its planning. Excessive centralisation and reliance on controls and regulations under socialistic planning lead to inefficiency, time overruns, cost escalations and corruption.

Planned Development of Education

In the field of education, early phases of planned development have inevitably to focus on the quantitative expansion of facilities for wide spread networking of institutions, especially elementary schools to make at least elementary education accessible to the masses. But in maturer stages, concern with qualitative improvements and structural reforms of both economy and education on the one hand, and more rapid development of secondary, senior secondary education, provision of facilities for new disciplines, emerging as a result of knowledge explosion, expansion of R & D facilities in the existing and creation of facilities in new areas of research on the other, tend to emerge as priority areas of planned development of education. It is because of such shifts that medium term plans of IIEP and the UNESCO (1978-83) have emphasized the 'importance of qualitative changes in school system and, notably, the role of educational planning as an instrument in the service of educational reforms.' (IIEP, p. 8)

> *Objectives and priorities of planning change with development. Choices of objectives and priorities are guided both by positive and normative considerations. Planning proceeds on an explicit recognition of mutual interrelations between different sectors, including education-economy and economy-societal interrelations.*

The plan has propagated particular type of structural reforms and specific variety of educational planning. The plan emphasised that educational planning in the developed West should attempt to transform the educational systems to focus on the challenges of R & D for technological inventions and innovations for the post-industrial society on the one hand, and for development of technology of basic and heavy machines to produce machines, on the other; while educational planning in Third World should reorganise educational systems to cope with lower layers of industrialisation that focuses mainly on production of simple manufactures rather than basic and heavy industrial goods, designed to produce machines which is the educational and industrial specialisation suggested to be left for the developed West. The Developing countries should make their educational systems to focus on production of manpower for adapting and operating imported technology. The educational planning in Third World, according to this school of thought, should focus on the consolidation of gains of quantitative expansion of preceding educational development, qualitative improvements, more rapid development of elementary education, lower priority to higher, technical and professional education on the one hand, and promotion of imitative and adaptative R & D., on the other. This may perpetuate the dependence of the Third on the First World for a much longer period than what is warranted by the current development stage of such countries as India, Brazil, Mexico, Malaysia.

One may not, therefore, agree with this perception. The Third World under colonial rule missed opportunities of development through industrialisation during first industrial revolution, and their educational systems had been reduced to prepare manpower for white-collar jobs in administration, manpower for assembly line production and production of natural resource based manufactures for exports rather than to produce manpower for meeting personnel requirements of industrial revolution, technological transformation, and development of technology itself. Acceptance of such planning models will perpetuate the inherited maladies of the Third World's educational systems and their development.

Educational systems of the Third World had been designed basically to produce limited number of educated persons required for lower positions in colonial administration. Education itself was used as an instrument of linguistic and cultural hegemony rather than for the propagation of skills and capabilities designed for the development of science and technology. The post-industrial society, dominated by knowledge and information revolution, technology of information and communications, rapid technological developments, and consequently equally rapid technological obsolesence, requires educational planning entirely different from that advocated by international agencies for the Third World. If the Third World countries follow the advice of these international agencies, they will continue to import such technology, machines and equipment, embodying discarded technologies of the West, and/or produce goods and commodities under licence from the developed world. It implies perpetuation of third rate economic status for these countries and permanent dependence upon the developed West, and hence, perpetual exploitation of their resources for the benefit of others. It implicitly accepts the prevailing inequitous and exploitative international economic order and international division of labour among nations, associated with this order, as desirable and beneficial, though both the arrangements promote only national interests of the developed West at the cost of national interests of Third World. (Prakash, 1994; Prakash & Dutta, 1996; Prakash, Singh & Sharma, 1996)

If during this phase of third industrial revolution, educational systems continue to focus on the production of manpower for white-collar jobs in administration and assembly line production of simple manufactures, as India and other developing countries actually did during the British rule and in the first phase of planning during post-Independence era, or it remains confined to second or third lines of industrial production with obsolete technologies of the West, gaps of incomes and development between First and Third Worlds will be accentuated further. This type of educational planning and development have been the singular factor behind the differential roles that western education has played in Japan and India. Whereas the objective of planned development of the western education in Japan even during the Meiji restoration focused mainly on western science and technology, western education in India was designed and devised mainly to prepare petty clerks for the British administration. Even independent India has kept education geared to produce administrative manpower for white-collar jobs in government or public sector, though technical and professional education have been expanded on a limited scale to meet manpower requirements of assembly line production, based on imported technology, and/or even imports of goods in knocked down condition for assemblage. Courses designed for prestigious institutions like IITs and IIMs are poor imitation of the West and these are meant to cater to manpower needs of the developed West rather than those of India. Consequently, large proportion of graduates of such institutions migrate each year in search of greener pastures.

> *Objectives of planning are governed only partly by normative considerations. Historical conditions, developmental stage, and future perspectives of planned development affect the goals and objectives of planning considerably. In mature stages of development, focus shifts from quantitative expansion to qualitative improvements and structural reforms of both economy and education in order to move to a higher plane and into different directions to raise substantially the living standards, health and educational profiles of people.*

People's perception that education is the means for entry into white-collar jobs in government or in public sector enterprises, has naturally not been changed. Educational planning, that does not take into consideration R & D manpower requirements of production sectors on the one hand, and manpower needs of R & D sector itself on the other, will not be worth having in modern times. Determination of objectives of planning should, therefore, depend partly upon the historical conditions, partly upon the current stage of development of society and economy, and largely upon planners' vision and perspectives of future development at the time of planning.

Products, Actors and Processes of Planning

Planning comprises of theoretical paradigms. These paradigms furnish useful guidelines for plan formulation and intricate and sophisticated processes. Planning processes involve numerous stages and steps required to finalise the plan and sub-plans, products and by-products. Plans, projects and programmes result from the endeavours of planners and planning. Numerous actors and agents are involved in formulation and implementation of plans. Plans require information and data base for evaluating the current status, problems and future prospects of development. Analysis is based on specific methods and mechanisms of plan formulation. Organisational and institutional support base as required both for plan formulation and its implementation. Each element differs in nature, roles, functions and importance from other elements and components of planning.

Planning is, in fact, a multifaceted and multidimensional process, requiring:

(a) Involvement of numerous persons in plan formulation and even larger numbers in its implementation. All those who are involved either in plan formulation or its implementation may be designated as actors required for and involved in planning;

(b) Organisational and institutional support base both for plan formulation and its implementation. To start with, there may exist neither organisational structures, nor there may be institutions to undertake the task of plan formulation and its implementation. In such cases, first step will be to establish planning commission/board, or committee at apex level. Its lower feeder units will have to be created to make institutional support base percolate downwards to the lowest levels. All these hierarchical institutions and organisations will have to be organically linked together through elaborate and appropriate organisational structures with well-defined roles and functions. Their domains of power, authority, responsibility, and operations have to be delineated and their functioning has to be rationally coordinated in order to make their functions synchronise both in time and space and to subserve the goals and objectives of planning;

(c) Detailed, intricate and complex processes of plan formulation. The processes of formulating and finalising the plan is spread over considerably long time period. Formulation of a plan involves numerous steps and stages of translating goals, priorities and objectives of planning into concrete shape and form. These steps involve intricate and elaborate process of gathering detailed information, regarding current status of various activities and their outcomes, and future development scenario for each activity, envisaged to be undertaken at planned levels of each sector, subsector, department/division, etc. Then, this information has to be finalised into definite quantitative targets through detailed calculations and delimitation of qualitative contours of development. This involves long lead times and lags between initiation of plan formulation and its completion and finalisation;

(d) Elaborate and minute information and data base. Huge data, imbued with the properties of adequacy, timeliness, representativeness, and relevance have to be gathered and made available to planners and policy makers. (Prakash,1993)

Data have to be analysed to highlight current status, problems and prospects of future development of all sectors, social organisations and institutions. Without up-to-date, adequate and detailed information and data base, targets may either be inadequate in relation to people's needs, or these may be too ambitious to realise in view of shortage of resources mobilised and made available for achievement of goals and objectives of planned development. These unrealistically ambitious targets, goals and objectives will remain a utopia or mere aspirations, or at best, intelligent guesses and hunches;

(e) Sophisticated methodology. Planning methodology usually comprises of quantitative techniques–statistical and mathematical methods, that may deal both with quantitative and qualitative variables and parameters. These techniques and methods are required both for plan formulation and for testing its internal consistency. Methods and procedures for plan evaluation and monitoring during its implementation are also needed. In some cases, especially when one deals with planning for truly long periods, such heuristic techniques as Delphi and Cross Impact Matrix, Non-parametric Statistical Methods like Rank-Correlation, Signed Rank-Correlation, Sign Test, Random Walks, and such qualitative techniques as Binary Dummy Variables, and Logit Analysis may be quite useful.

Plan as Product or Outcome of Planning

All above elements are used jointly that lead to an outcome or product, which may be defined as plan, while different components/parts of the plan, that is, sub-plans may be defined as the by-products of endeavours of planners and planning processes. Subplans may pertain to sectors, subsectors, regions, programmes and projects. Each subcomponent will itself be decomposable into departmental and/or enterprise/ institutional level. The plan may be divided into distinct chapters, each devoted to particular projects and/or programmes, sectors, subsectors, for purposes of systematic organisation, neat presentation, coherent analysis and explanation.

The by-products of planning, like its main product, evaluate estimated costs of probable development targets of socio-cultural activities, development of health and education, and development projects of other sectors of the economy, regions of the country, and specified segments of special population groups such as the Tribal Component of main plan. Then, estimated costs are compared with resource allocation patterns, so as to judge adequacy or inadequacy of provisions made for implementation; costs are also compared with benefits envisaged to accrue from development.

Plan emerges as the end product and final outcome of endeavours of planners and as the consequence of processes of planning or plan formulation. The final outcome appears in concrete shape and tangible form only at the completion of plan formulation and plan finalisation processes. First product is the draft outlines of the proposed plan of development. Completion of draft plan itself involves numerous steps and stages through which numerous alternative proposals have to be developed, discussed, and even discarded altogether, if warranted, or modified and adopted for inclusion in the plan. It implies that plan appears first in the form of draft proposals from different sectors, agencies, departments, enterprises, establishments and such institutions as hospitals, schools, colleges, universities and institutes. But even before these draft proposals are invited and submitted for consideration, planning authority, the Planning Commmission in case of India, prepares 'An Approach Paper' to the given plan so as to furnish guidelines for evolving development proposals.

Alternative Modes of Plan Formulation

There are two alternative ways of approaching planning with a view to formulate a plan: one may identify and determine the most important but debilitating constraints to development in concrete quantitative terms. These constraints may pertain to physical and financial resources, that may be envisaged to be available or estimated to be made available for plan implementation, and/or these constraints may relate to availability of modern technology, food, and/or foreign exchange. In case of India, capital, foodgrains during the days of food shortages when the country lived from ship to mouth, foreign exchange, and modern technology have been the pivotal constraints as well as factors of growth. These factors have remained perenially in short supply. However, food shortages have now, by and large, been eliminated. In case of the USSR, availability of food constituted the most important constraining factor of planned development. Once this preliminary task of identifying and quantifying possible supplies, likely to be available during plan period for meeting both consumption and investment needs of development, has been completed, one may proceed to plan future development within the limitations of these constraining factors to growth. This school of thought in the USSR advocated the forecasting of likely size of future harvests first. Then, growth of output and employment in non-agricultural sectors was to be planned subject to the constraint of availability of food and other agricultural goods for industrialisation and for generation of non-agricultural employment during the planning horizon. Thus, plan size, and hence, investment for future development was to be determined decisively by the availability of food in the economy. Supplies of foodgrains have played similar constraining role in Indian development till the Green Revolution made the country self-sufficient. In India, likely supplies of (a) foreign exchange, (b) foodgrains, and (c) capital, from all sources for financing investment requirements of planned growth of output, are estimated first.

Planning is, however, the science and art of changing the currently obtaining system in a manner that all such debilitating constraints are removed at the earliest possible. Hence, another school of thought advocates the designing and devising of strategies to overcome at least partly, if not wholly, all constraints to growth through planning, howsoever severe these supply constraints may be. India has been successful in transforming its agriculture through Green Revolution not only to overcome food shortages of the past but also to become self-sufficient and exporter of foodgrains. It has also been accumulating sizeable stocks of foodgrains for the maintenance of price stability in the country. Similarly, White Revolution has removed the shortages of dairy and animal products such as milk, butter, eggs, chicken, etc. These achievements would have never materialised if possible outputs of all such sectors were taken to be autonomously determined and given exogenously for each plan. In practice, however, it is advisable to combine elements of both these approaches to planning. This happens to have been the practice in India.

Approach Paper to Plan

Preliminary output of planning in India is, however, defined as approach paper to plan. The plan approach paper delineates broad contours of future prospective changes in macro indicators of development, it highlights directions into which economy and its different sectors, regions of the country and different segments of population are envisaged to move from lower to higher plane of performance and achievements at the end of the plan period. However, anticipated results of planned development and its resource requirements are not identified in concrete quantitative terms, though broad dimensions of overall and sectoral growth may probably be highlighted in generic macro terms in approach to the plan. It will, however, broadly indicate the possible priorities of development strategies proposed to be adopted to find solution to the current and prospective problems to charter the planned growth path smoothly. It may also highlight the probable strategies of resource mobilisation and broad directions of resource allocation patterns.

Preparation of approach paper is the responsibility of the Perspective Planning Division of Planning Commission. Once it has finalised its approach to the forthcoming plan and it has been approved by competent authority, approach paper is released to the state governments, media and others for debate and analysis to elicit opinions, alternative options, and possible limitations and shortcomings of the approach to the plan. In the light of approach developed in approach paper to planned national development, state planning boards also prepare the approach papers to state plans of development.

Draft Plan

Draft Plan, prepared by the Planning Commission, emerges as the first finished product of planning. Draft plan is recommendatory rather than mandatory in nature. Draft plan is submitted for approval to the National Development Council. Proposals, and hence, draft plan approved by the NDC, is then taken up again by the Planning Commission for finalising the final plan. The NDC and the Government may or may not accept and approve the plan prepared by the commission.

Once the plan is finalised and approved subsequently by government, Planning Commission will proceed to prepare detailed and elaborate sectorwise draft proposals of the development. It is at this stage of planning that all sectors, departments, divisions, regions, enterprises and institutions are supposed to submit their broad proposal for the development. These proposals should be in conformity with the finalised approach paper, macro directions, and dimensions of proposed planned development that the Planning Commission itself prepares. The Planning Commission finalises the draft outlines of the proposed plan of development in the light of various proposals from its own constituent units as well as others, and the approach to macro dimensions of planned development.

The plan translates goals and objectives of planning into an agenda of action and production targets, as embodied in development projects and programmes, expressed in terms of coherent and consistent numerical figures. The production targets relate to the prediction/projection of development of the economy/society according to accepted approach, norms and priorities. But planning should not be confused with statistical and econometric predictions and forecasts of likely development. Planned development may only partially be approximated by predictions/forecasts of future on the basis of past and current trends. Planning being largely normative in nature. It is norms and objectives of planning that delineate the directions and magnitudes of changes in economy and society under the impact of planned development.

Different Planning Periods

'Duration of a Plan' may be defined as Plan Period, while the 'period for which planning is undertaken' may be defined as Planning Horizon. Depending upon the length of period for which plan is prepared and implemented, short and long-term plans may be distinguished. Short run may cover a period of one to three years, whereas medium run may generally range from five to seven years. Long period may be stretched over as many as 10 to 25 years, though long period may, at times, be spread over as long a period as 40-50 years to furnish long period perspectives of socio-economic development. Perspective plans pertain to long periods, while short and medium plans relate to relatively shorter durations of time.

Monitoring, Evaluation, and Appraisal of Plan

Even if plan is finally approved, and it becomes a legal document, it does not mean that actual action or policy will not diverge or deviate from proposed or planned programmes of action. Knowledge of new facts, developments in theory, methodology and practices of planning, emergence of unexpected problems and degree of success or failure of planning, revealed by mid-term appraisals or concurrent monitoring and evaluation of implementation of approved plan, may warrant changes in original, accepted and approved plan. Uncertain and unexpected changes in future course of development necessitate contingency planning. At one stage, concept of 'Rolling Plan' had been introduced in India for facing continuous but uncertain changes effectively during the course of development. Due to such facets and features as continuous but uncertain changes in future, short run planned development is more likely to approximate actual development than long run or perspective planned development. Such facets of planned development have warranted the institution of concurrent evaluation and monitoring of the progress of plan implementation and midterm appraisals of plan performance in order to detect possible short falls in achievements and probable deviations between actual and planned development paths during the plan implementation phase itself.

Main Features of Plans

Following are the chief features that characterise the finalised product (plan) and by-products (sub-plans) of planning for development (Cf. Tinbergen, pp. 7-8):

(i) Plan refers to future. It, therefore, looks ahead and beyond the known present into the unknown and uncertain realm of future possibilities. Naturally, future may not be an exact and precise replication of the past, notwithstanding the dictum that ***history repeats itself***. Plan furnishes the thrust of future changes in socio-economic forces, their operations and impacts on development processes. All the same, any plan, howsoever detailed and with whatever precision it might have been prepared, may not be an exact anticipation of the nature and directions of scaffolding of future configurations of various factors and forces in operation at the time of materialisation of outcomes of plan implementation and consequent developments. Many unforeseen changes may occur, while directions and magnitudes of impact of any given set of causative factors may turn out to be different from those observed in the past, or anticipated at the time of plan formulation;

(ii) Plan refers to an agenda of action, intended or proposed to be executed in future. But proposed goals and targets have to be specified in detailed quantitative terms in advance in order to leave no doubt about as to what is planned to be achieved. Correspondingly, proposed actions for plan implementation have to be explained unambiguously in the plan, so as to facilitate proper understanding of the conceptual framework, and hence, better operationalisation of planning by the implementers. Uncertainties of future may, however, warrant the institution of concurrent monitoring and evaluation as well as periodic appraisals of plan implementation in order to ascertain that implementation is on right lines and to ensure proper progress, and hence, achievement of goals and objectives of planning. But it is probable that actual course of development deviates and diverges from planned development path in one or more directions due either to (a) faulty implementation, or (b) limitations in plan formulation and development design itself, or (c) due to emergence of new but unforeseen factors and forces. There is, therefore, always a need for contingency planning in case actual course of development deviates from the warranted or planned development path;

(iii) Plan is an instrument of concretisation of well-defined goals and objectives into quantitative targets and specified qualitative improvements, howsoever hazy, ambitious or modest these goals and objectives may appear to be at first sight. The objectives are transformed into production or output targets, set for achievement by the end of the plan period. Qualitative improvements may also not remain as qualitative as these may sound to be. For example, minimum nutritional requirements or minimum levels of learning by all enrollees in elementary education are translatable into identifiable and measurable targets of planning, though measurements may at times be ordinal, or quantitatively imprecise;

(iv) Plan incorporates not only goals and targets but also means required for the realisation of these targets and goals. Resource requirements, both in financial and real terms, have to be estimated for each project, subplan, and overall plan separately, while adequate provisions have to be made in resource allocation exercises. Instruments or policies of resource mobilisation and allocation on the one hand, and instruments of plan implementation, on the other, have to be spelled out in full details much before the time of actual implementation. But all elements of these instruments may not be equally important. Strategic elements among these instruments have to be identified in advance and these may occupy higher priority in agenda of action. The planned interventions in social and economic processes in operation during the planning horizon will guide development processes, at least partially, if not wholly, towards the goals, targets and objectives. From this viewpoint, planning may be defined as the process of reducing uncertainty attached to the unforeseen and indefinite shape, structure and pattern of the society and economy in future at the end of the plan period in order to move both economy and society nearer to people's desires, dreams and aspirations on the one hand, and planners' vision and endeavours to translate this vision into reality of the state of self-sufficient, self-propelled and self-sustained development;

(v) Plan implementation requires coordination of the means and instruments on the one hand, and functioning of the actors/ agents, using the instruments on the other. This is the most difficult task in view of the fact that operators and actors involved are huge in number, scattered all over the country, and each group has a different (a) perception of plan and planning, (b) vested interests to safeguard, and (c) styles and modes of functioning.

Processes of Planning

Processes of planning have, however, to be distinguished both from the product and by-products of planning on the one hand, steps and stages involved in plan formulation, methods and techniques of planning on the other. Planning processes consist of several elements that relate to (a) end-product of planning, that is, plans and subplans, (b) steps and stages, (c) procedures, and (d) methods and techniques involved in plan formulation, its implementation, monitoring, and evaluation, (e) information and data base required for plan formulation, and (f) institutional and organisational base for development. It is possible as well as useful to distinguish between different elements of planning processes that are of different genre. The intricacies and elaborateness of steps and stages of plan formulation, complexities and subtleties of techniques and methods, involved in planning, depend upon the nature and degree of planning, and even more importantly, upon the number and nature of objectives and tasks to be accomplished through plans that are sought to be formulated through planning processes. But the elements that planning processes involve offer choices between alternative possibilities and numerous conceptual and operational options.

Planning involves various activities, which comprise of numerous steps and stages of work. All these elements constitute essential components of processes of plan formulation, its implementation and assessment of impacts of planning on development, and/or impacts of development on society and economy. These activities may be described as follows:

Forecasts as Building Blocks of Planning

As a first step, Central Planning Commission (CPC) or Central Board of Planning (CBP) obtains projections, predictions, and forecasts for building alternative scenarios of future for each step in the planning horizon. Purpose of these projections and forecasts is to foresee in advance probable patterns and possible structures of the systems and their constituent subsystems under alternative scenarios in order to (a) identify and choose the best scenario, either as it has unfolded, or with modifications, if warranted by the needs and objectives of planned development, from amongst those available to choose from, (b) compare outcomes of all scenarios, furnished by forecasting, with desired or planned outcomes of development in order to determine the best among all scenarios furnished by forecasts. Then, outcomes of the scenario, identified as the best, will have to be compared with the outcomes envisaged from planned development, and (c) identify the best instruments, means and mechanisms of their implementation and their possible impacts on development with reference to the targets, goals and objectives of planning.

Alternative scenarios are built on the basis of assumptions regarding (1) operating system and its constituent subsystems, endogenous variables and their functional relations with exogenous factors; (2) shapes, forms and nature of functional relations; (3) current as well as future exogenous factors or variables, called data, that are expected to operate and affect the system in future, and hence, likely to be involved effectively in functional relations; (4) parameters of functional relations between endogenous and current and/or future exogenous variables of the system: (i) best possible estimates of numerical parametric values of functional relations, and (ii) instruments, means and mechanisms of operationalisation of policies and their impacts on system and subsystems as well as their exogenous variables, and hence, expected changes in all facets and factors of development in future.

Projection techniques furnish the simplest method of scenario building. This simplest method of scenario building, based on projections, assumes that the system will continue to operate in future just as it has been operating in the past. It is also assumed that, if the system changes, it will undergo changes similar to those it had experienced in the past. Naturally, such expected changes as these will have impacts on the system that are similar in nature to those experienced in the past. If actual course of planned development traverses such forecasted path, then there shall never be any uncertainty about the future, and it will always be possible to make precise and exact predictions of the future changes in the economy and its development. Unfortunately, this seldom happens in reality. In effect, such projections assume current policies, variables and parameters of their functional relations to remain either the same, or to change in future in a manner which is similar to the manner of changes in the past. Operating factors are expected to have impacts on socio-economic systems in future similar to those as have been observed in the past without much changes and modifications in relations, rates and patterns of changes in numerical parametric values of functional relations. Changes will be either almost monotonic, or these may traverse the path embodied in the chosen forms and structures of functional relations of the system. These projections just attempt to foresee changes in future in accordance with the observed patterns of current and past changes.

Both prospective and observed changes are, however, bound to alter the future course of development. Since the essence of planning is introduction of such changes as are capable of radically transforming current structure of the system, development will seldom focus on either quantitative expansion alone, or on the continuation of patterns of changes in the past. Consequently, such projections may carry too large margins of projecting errors to capture likely future state of the system accurately. Then, since changes in new directions with a view to fill up the gaps in current structures and shortfalls in past performances are the basic motivating force of planning such projections will have only limited utility. This does not altogether negate the importance of such projections. Projections may be used to judge (i) magnitudes and directions of divergences between objectives of planning and the projected scenario; (ii) divergences among nature, degree and directions of impacts of current and past policies on development on the one hand, and impacts of development strategies on society and economy expected at the time of plan and policy formulation on the other. Such divergences between actual and perceived changes will highlight needs for policy changes, if any; and (iii) deviations between the expected impacts of proposed policies to be adopted during the plan and the projected scenario considered to be the best on a priori considerations.

Forecasting Errors

Projections, predictions and forecasts, howsoever precise, rational, detailed and scientific these may be, involve three types of projection/prediction, or forecasting errors: (a) such errors as remain confined to those variables, parameters of functional relations, and subsystems with which they are associated. But such errors are not carried forward from present into future and these errors do not also affect other variables or systems; (b) certain errors are in-built in method(s) used for projection or prediction of future values of the system. For example, linear trend cannot capture either possible non-linearities or breaks of system with the past trends. There is no way of controlling these errors, unless alternative method or technique is adopted, or assumptions regarding the behaviour of exogenous variable(s) are modified; (c) errors also creep into predictions, if assumptions used in projections diverge significantly from future reality; (d) percolation errors that flow subsequently from one step to another, one variable or parameter to another, and ultimately from one subsystem to another. At each step and stage of planning, percolation errors are compounded. Even small margins of such errors in any step/stage may ultimately assume large magnitudes, disproportionate to initial values of percolation errors through their cascading effects in the process of being carried forward from one step, stage or variable to another; (e) stipulated changes in policies and strategies from one to another plan are even more important sources of forecasting or prediction errors than the sources of errors discussed above. Then, likely consequences of either breaks in future from past trends, or drastic changes in future policies and strategies of development have to be foreseen and built into projected scenarios, otherwise negligence of such changes will lead to serious forecasting errors of percolation type. Such changes have to be foreseen and built into these forecasts. Therefore, it becomes essential for planners to develop alternative scenarios on the basis of (i) changing assumptions regarding expected turns in exogenous variables, (ii) likely directions and magnitudes of breaks from observed trends, and (iii) likely impacts of new policies and strategies of development. It implies that planners should have a complete command over methods or techniques of forecasting for scenario building on the one hand, and envisagement of likely outcomes of strategic interventions in socio-economic processes on the other.

Some degree of projection or prediction is always involved in planning, though planning neither begins nor ends with predictions. Planning, in fact, is neither prediction nor forecasting of future on the basis of statistical techniques nor is it just an attempt to foresee future as it is likely to be under the autonomous functioning of the system. Planning attempts to deliberately break from the past to move into directions that will propel the society and economy nearer to the scenario embodied in the vision and future perspectives of planned development. Therefore, it is essential for planners to have a command over policies and strategies and control over changes due to policy impacts in future on the system and its constituent components.

Consequently, forecasts are to be embodied in planning itself, and hence, planning forecasts are derived neither from projections of past trends into the future nor are these derived from workingout future outcomes of current policies and decisions, though both these types of forecasts may also be used in planning as preliminary steps. Forecasts required for planning are envisagement of consequences of implementation of proposed strategy of development and impacts of various projects and programmes of development, included in the plan, on the economy, education and society. It is, therefore, prior or ex-ante anticipation of outcomes of implementation of plans of development. Hence, forecasts involved in planning are normative in nature, encompassed as these are in the objectives and strategy of planning. The possible limitations of the means and mechanisms of policy implementation and delivery system of instruments have also to be determined in advance by the planners through such forecasts. If likely outcomes of plans and the associated strategies and policies diverge from desired targets and goals, then strategies and/or their instruments will be required to change. All these steps and stages of plan formulation constitute planning processes. Tinbergen highlights the usefulness of instruments of prediction to the 'planning agency' as follows: 'Planners have to 'investigate the probable effects of the use of various means of policy', and in all probability, results of such investigations will influence the policy makers' choices of instruments to a considerable extent'.

At the second stage of planning processes, outcomes embodied in alternative scenarios, built on the basis of forecasting on different assumptions and by different methods, under step one, may be compared with likely outcomes of the 'desired or planned state' of the system to be achieved through proposed agenda of action to be implemented during the plan on the one hand, and forecasted outcomes of impacts of proposed policies and strategies of planned development on the other. In other words, state of the system as it will obtain, if goals and objectives of planning were to be fully achieved, have to be compared with outcomes forecasted under different scenarios, that have been built-up on different assumptions and probably by different methods. If targets, goals and objectives of planning appear to be too ambitious, or these appear as less desirable, or even totally undesirable, unviable and infeasible in the light of results of such comparisons, goals and objectives may be lowered or raised to match likely outcomes and possible resources envisaged to be available for plan implementation. Alternatively, if targets, goals and objectives appear to be too limited in comparison to likely outcomes of present or proposed resource investment plans, policies and strategies, targets and goals may be revised and upgraded.

Thus, at times, targets and goals may be raised, if the original ones are found either below the planned levels, or these are lower than those warranted by resources earmarked for investment during plan period. In other cases, targets and goals may be lowered, if these are found to be too ambitious relative to grass roots realities and available resources. For example, universalisation of elementary education was decided to be achieved by 1961 in a period of only one decade. Once the target date was discovered to be impractical, it was shifted to 1965, though planners have failed consistently to adhere to any subsequent target dates for the realisation of the objective of UEE. Now UPE is stipulated to be realised by the year 2001, that too through the World Bank sponsored District Primary Education Project. It is both shocking and shameful that India had accepted not only financial but also technical aid from the World Bank for this project, which has, however, been consistently refused by the Government of India in the past.

Changes in means and mechanisms of implementation of instruments or policies, warranted by goals and objectives, have to be determined at the third step and stage of planning processes. Choice of means and mechanisms of implementation of instruments or policies and strategies of development is as pivotal to the success of planning as other elements of development processes.

These activities, various steps and stages, involved in undertaking these activities and performance of requisite tasks at each step and stage of planning processes, differ from one country to another and from one time to another within the same country.

Probable Errors of Choice of Development Design

Like two types of statistical errors involved in the rejection of a true hypothesis and acceptance of a false hypothesis, choice of development models, development design and strategies embodied therein, may also involve two types of possible errors of choice of development model and planning involved in its implementation: (a) a country may persist with a development model, its development design and strategies embodied in it, if it has succeeded at some given stage of development of its economy, even if the success of the model, its development, design and strategies have themselves transformed the nature of development problems it faces currently, and consequently such a successful model(s) may no more be relevant; (b) another error of choice is that, if a development model has succeeded in some other country at some point in time, other countries may imitate this successful model, even though it may not correspond to their development needs, stage of development of the economy/education, nature and degree of resource constraints, technological limitations, institutional and socio-cultural backgrounds. Hence, it may not be an appropriate model to follow and adopt for development planning in such cases. However, many countries do commit errors of either type in choosing development models, designs and strategies at some point in time or another.

Procedure of Planning

Procedure refers to the nature and time-patterns of contacts and coordination with the coproducers of plans, subplans, projects and programmes, or actors involved in plan formulation and its implementation. Ministries and departments under them, regional, local and sectoral planning agencies, trade and business organisations, public and private undertakings engaged in production of goods and services, professional associations, trade unions, employers' associations, research institutions, involved in planning processes, are called actors, who are invariably involved in planning procedures. Though it is possible to prepare plans without contacting all these agents/actors just on the basis of secondary data and information base, their involvement in planning is both desirable and useful. As these actors are directly involved in actual operations of the system and its constituent units at grass roots, interactions and exchanges of views and sharing of experiences with them will introduce (i) greater degree of realism because these functionaries at lower levels of administrative ladder have first hand knowledge and experience of actual problems at the grass roots, (ii) widespread participation, which will make large number of actors and operators of planning not only feel directly involved as partners, but it will also infuse enthusiasm in them for planning, and (iii) inputs of expertise, experience, knowledge and skills, possessed by such actors, will directly be used fruitfully in planning.

A general procedure is to prepare an approach paper, based on detailed technical analysis of macro constraints such as available foreign exchange, population growth, foreign loans and aid, centrally mobilised resources, considerations of economy wide impacts of macro policies and quantitative dimensions of these impacts on different regions and sectors of the economy, and well defined short and long run objectives of development, envisaged to be achieved during the period of a particular plan. The approach paper is widely circulated for (a) disseminating information to all other actors and agencies of planning, (b) eliciting suggestions for improvement, and (c) generating debate. Regional, local, sectoral, departmental and enterprise/ undertaking level plans will be prepared according to these guidelines. Representatives of state governments and other agencies are called by Planning Commission for direct discussion. In the light of such discussions, these agencies finalise their approaches and plan proposals. Subsequently, these subplans may be fused and coordinated into the national plan. Sectoral, regional and other subplans, revised and modified in the light of suggestions made by the Planning Commission for incorporation in original proposals, are submitted to the central planning agency(ies), which coordinate all components and parts into an integrated but organically synthesised plan-frame. In the light of preliminary exercises, mutual discussions, interactions, and exchanges among different actors, the proposed subplans of subordinate actors or co-producers, are finalised with appropriate amendments and modifications in the draft proposals. These may again be submitted for scrutiny to the Central or National Planning or Development Committee/ Council for final approval (Cf. UN, 1960).

Materials' Balances and Consistency Planning

When Russian planning started in the early twenties, there existed neither theory of planning, nor was there any institutional, organisational support, information and data base, nor was any methodology of planning available to guide the Russian planners. Gos Plan Authority, therefore, relied on *trial and error* procedure, adhoc mechanisms, and tentative methodology of planning. All these three elements of planning were transformed into Materials Balance Procedure of planning in due course. The procedure involved (a) supply of information and data directly from individual factories, farms, schools, colleges, universities, clinics, dispensaries, hospitals, banks, post offices, telephone and telegraphic offices, insurance, transport, and trade operators, (b) widespread participation of a number of functionaries in plan formulation, and (c) knowledge of current development status, both strengths and weaknesses of production structures at grass roots. All production units, enterprises, and operators were asked to inform Gos Plan Authority about (i) number, nature and quantities of goods and services produced by each respondent, (ii) quantities of such factors of production as occupation and educationwise labour, itemwise fixed and working capital, itemwise raw materials and intermediate goods used in production of given quantities of specific goods and services, (iii) layers and levels of technology employed in production, (iv) area and population covered by output of goods and services, (v) itemwise output proposed to be produced during the plan period on the one hand, and quantities of factors, intermediate inputs and raw materials that will be needed for implementing production plan, (vi) proposed improvement in designs, quality and technology, and (vii) production of new goods. This huge information and data were then tabulated, classified and aggregated in order to furnish estimate of (a) itemwise proposed output targets, and (b) itemwise input requirements. These data were further aggregated into sectoral inputs and output targets. Output targets were compared with input requirements in order to assess the adequacy of goods and services available for being used in production as intermediate inputs. This highlighted internal consistency or want of it in the plan design. If output targets and possible supplies of factor inputs, raw materials and intermediate goods were detected to be mutually inconsistent, proposals were sent back to farms, factories, operators of trade, transport, banks, insurance, health and education and other operators of production units of goods and services for revisions and modifications of their proposals in the light of available information. Several such rounds of consultations and calculations continued till a finally consistent plan-frame emerged. As all prices were administered and almost all means of production were state owned, there was hardly any role in planned development for market and financial instruments. All output targets and input requirements were, therefore, expressed in physical or real units only.

The material balances procedure of planning ultimately led to the emergence of Leontief's *Input Output Economics* on the one hand, and Sraffian system of *Production of Commodities by Means of Commodities* on the other, to furnish (a) theoretical paradigms of consistency planning, (b) mathematical methods of consistent plan formulation, and (c) identification of gaps between data available and data required for planning. In due course, other methods such as mathematical programming, quadratic programming, non-linear-programming, and linear programming were also evolved to endogenise various constraints directly into plan-frame. Numerous mathematical and econometric models of planned development have emerged since then as analytical tools and empirical devices for development planning.

India, having adopted the mixed economy and socialistic pattern of society, prepares its plans both in financial and real terms. Both output targets and their intermediate inputs and factor requirements are expressed in financial and real terms. It is imperative because some prices are (i) totally administered, (ii) some sectors operate under dual pricing policies, output being sold partly at administered and partly at market determined prices, (iii) consumption of some goods being subsidized and consumption of some goods being heavily taxed to depress demand for them, and (iv) prices of large number of goods and services are market determined. Unlike the Russian system, Indian system is not thus totally based on commands and executive fiats, or controls and regulations. Both financial instruments, and hence, market mechanisms, and physical controls and regulations operate in tandem in Indian economy. Naturally, planning is of both physical and financial varieties.

Procedural Choices

The procedure of planning thus offers a variety of choices between options and different alternatives. Following are some of the major features of these procedural choices:

(1) Planning may begin 'from above', as it actually operates under centralised planning. Alternatively,'planning may start from below', as it actually operates under decentralised planning. 'Top-down', or 'Bottom-up' procedures of planning are often conceived to be mutually exclusive, though it is possible to have a happy blend of these two together. Certain degree of decentralisation is not only compatible with centralised planning but it is also desirable to have it fused into centralised planning. Some elements of decentralisation may be operationalised with the chosen degree of centralisation. This is the case with 'joint planning' in mixed economies. It may also be noted that materials balance procedure of Russia did involve in planning all those actually engaged in production, though they might have not wielded as much power as the Gos Plan Authority. Russian planning has often been dubbed as centralised planning, notwithstanding the fact that planning through materials balance procedure involved all producers of goods and services in plan formulation.

Whereas 'Bottom-up Approach' involves some degree of duplication of work, 'Top-down Approach' involves sacrifice of realism and relevance on the one hand, and exclusion of large number of actual functionaries and actors and people on the other. Over the years, responsibility of planning tended to slip away from professionals and technocrats, who might have initially been entrusted with the task of planning, to bureaucrats. This happened in Russia earlier, and it has occurred in India also. The Indian Planning Commission has been taken over almost totally by bureaucrats, especially those belonging to IAS cadre. Bureaucrats are adept in forging political and administrative linkages for manipulating their movement into core positions and also to keep others under their thumbs. The crucial problem of procedure is to have right combination of elements of centralisation and decentralisation, since total decentralisation will pose serious problems of both material and manpower balances on the one hand, and closedness, consistency and coherence among local, regional and national goals and objectives of planned development on the other. Similarly, planning should involve both academicians and bureaucrats in order to reduce the gap and distance between plan formulators and plan implementors for ensuring scientifically correct formulation and proper plan implementation. These problems are seldom associated with centralised planning. Totally decentralised procedure of planning will have no means to ascertain macro constraints, macro impacts of micro decisions, or micro impacts of macro operations, while proper vision and perspectives of macro development will be totally missing. Parts cannot pull or drive the whole. The crucial and pivotal problem is the identification and determination of core constraints, strategic macro variables, and effective instruments and appropriate means and mechanisms of their delivery and operationalisation, irrespective whether centralised or decentralised procedure has been followed in plan formulation;

(2) Choice between different procedures should realistically relate to nature, number and frequency of contacts between different actors, operators, and planning agencies, while the nature of these contacts and consultations depends on the depth,

freedom, and frankness in expression of opinions and views in these consultations, number and nature of subjects taken up for discussion during such interactions in these contacts. Nature and degree of contacts among actors are directly affected by administrative hierarchy. Frequency of interactions and consultations and the nature of discussions in these contacts among actors in planning depends, to some extent, upon the methods of planning also. Method of trial and error involves more frequent consultations. Time frame is also an important factor of determination of the nature and degree of participation of subactors and coproducers of plans and planning processes on the one hand, and time lags involved between initiation of consultations and the finalisation of outcomes of consultations both for plan formulation and its implementation, and therefore, the timeliness of consultations is important, on the other. Fact is that the nature and extent of participation of different actors, professionals, and groups of people in formulating and implementing development plans will, to a great extent, determine the degree, representative character, nature and success of planning;

(3) Data and information for plan formulation are needed from different sources. Data requirements are huge in dimension, myriad in typology and complex in nature. Then, there are all varieties of available data that may or may not be relevant for plan formulation and evaluation of progress of its implementation. Untimely, inadequate, unrepresentative and unreliable data will compromise relevance, scientific nature and objectivity of planning. Nature and quantity of data and information, however, depend to a great extent upon (a) nature and degree of planning to be undertaken, (b) agencies and their spatial dispersions, which are involved in data collection, (c) time given to these agencies for data collection, (d) expertise, experience, skills and training possessed by generators of data, (e) modes, methods and designs, especially sample frame and sample design, used in data collection, and (f) scope and coverage of time, space and population size covered by data which are to be collected.

Time-Ordering and Phasing of Planning

Time-ordering and phasing of contacts and consultations among the actors and agencies on the one hand, and the phasing of plan formulation and its implementation on the other hand, are important elements of planning. Time-ordering should normally follow the order of data and information flows, and data needs for plan formulation. Whereas all relevant data should be made available to planners much before the commencement of plan formulation exercise, consultative meetings, seminar and conferences for the formulation of next plan may ideally be held periodically, when current plan itself is in operation in order to furnish timely inputs required for relevant and realistic plan formulation and its finalisation in time. Sequencing, phasing and time ordering are essential in the proper execution of plan projects and programmes also. If administrative hierarchy determines time-order, frequency and nature of these contacts, mutual interactions and consultations among various actors involved in planning, discussions in these meetings may be more ceremonial than real due to hesitancy on the part of juniors, or muzzling of juniors' views and opinions by the seniors. Then, society and economy are divided into sectoral, spatial and organisational units. The priority ordering for the plans and views of these different types of constituents of the economy and society, for and by whom planning is undertaken, may be determined according to their positions in the hierarchy on the one hand, and the importance attached to their roles and functions in the process of planned development on the other. Besides, the priority in time ordering for these sectoral, regional and organisational units may also be affected by the sectoral, regional and organisational dimensions of policy or instruments of planning. Hence, time ordering and nature of consultations with various agencies or their representatives may also be affected by such factors.

Publication of Planning Documents

Plans and plan related documents should be published both before and after the approval of plan by competent legislative and/or executive authority. Publication plays an important role both in dissemination of information about the plan and its effective execution. Approach paper, draft outlines of plan, sub-plans of sectoral, and regional components, including projects and programmes, have to be published for wider dissemination before the plan is finalised. Final plan can, however, be published only when its formulation is over and it has been approved by competent authority, say, by the National Development Council in India. But final plan should be published much before its commencement. Only then plan implementation can proceed smoothly under chosen policy and strategic guidelines, on which the plan is based and adherence to which determines, by and large, the full or partial realisation or non-realisation of plan targets, goals and objectives.

Time-Budgeting in Planning

Time budgeting of planning activities is as important as financial budgeting. The more intricate and complex the planning processes, the greater will be the importance of determining the sequencing and time-scheduling of planning activities to be undertaken right from the stage of plan formulation to the final stage of its completion. Success of planning depends a great deal upon the sophistication of time-budgeting and adherence to it in practice. There exists close relationship between (i) time and cost over-runs, (ii) time-slippages, and (c) shortfalls in realisation of plan goals and targets, caused either by want of time budgeting, or by non-adherence to time-schedule envisaged in the plan. Greater are the time over-runs, larger shall be the cost escalations. Both time and cost over-runs may be avoided by timely completion of plan, its projects and programmes. Timely implementation of plan and its projects depends upon (a) timely initiation of implementation process, (b) speedy and efficient execution of plan, (c) adequacy of both financial and physical resources on the one hand, and material and human capital on the other, and (d) proper designing of development and its adequate understanding and execution by implementors.

Time-scheduling is much more difficult in short than long run planning. Plan for each year, within the overall perspective plan-frame, should be available in advance to the finance ministry so as to facilitate its reflection in annual budgets. Budgets furnish most decisive financial instruments for (a) resource mobilisation, (b) determination of resource allocation patterns, and (c) guiding investment into socially desirable lines of production through incentives and limiting or totally preventing growth of output of low priority goods and services through taxes and physical controls and regulations. Both these types of instruments play pivotal role in the realisation of plan objectives. Annual budgets furnish effective instruments of implementation of plans and translation of policy designs into concrete actions.

Generally, statistical data, in socio-economic sense, pertain to socio-economic processes and the phenomena, that emanate from these operational forces and processes. Hence, these data reflect the socio-economic causes and their consequences, which must have materialised instantly and partially with lags, depending upon the functional relations between causative factors and their consequences. Therefore, requisite data must be available timely for the given plan year for which budget is to be prepared. This is not an easy task. Experience and historical antecedents suggest that strict adherence to time schedule is often difficult. Data that are available to planners and policy makers are neither timely, nor are these relevant and adequate for policy and plan formulation. For example, 'Economic Survey', presented each year to Parliament/Assemblies by the Finance Minister along with the annual budget papers, often does not contain up-to-date information and data for the year for which budget is formulated. Naturally, such data gaps lead to several distortions in policy thrusts. Many times even plans have been finalised after their actual commencement. Though its first year is over, the Ninth Five-Year Plan is still to be formulated. Thus, there is no question of its publication before implementation commences. Sometimes, duration of plan periods, and/or years of their commencement and completion have also been changed. For example, during plan holidays from 1966 to 1969, India did not formulate any five-year plan. Only annual plans were formulated and implemented. The plan periods have also been changed to match actual time of finalisation with the commencement of plans. Fourth, Eighth, and Ninth Plans of India and Dutch Plans of early' sixties furnish such instances.

Certain options and choices are, however, available in time-scheduling: (i) choice may be exercised between rigid and flexible time frames. Length of planning period and size of staff, involved in plan formulation, play decisive role in such choices. Liberal and relaxable time frames may overcome disadvantages of reliance on obsolete, incomplete and inadequate data and information base of long period planning. Temporal distribution of different elements and stages of planning may also offer some limited choices. Even temporal distribution of different stages and steps of the process of planning requires judicious choices.

However, subordinate actors should not be expected to adhere to rigid time-scheduling, when Central agencies flout their own time frames, though proper time-scheduling of auxiliary processes, emanating from subordinate actors will yield advantages. Most time consuming and difficult elements of planning warrant early starts in advance. Complicated preparatory work should also be started in advance.

Methods and Techniques of Planning

Methods of planning refer to scientific techniques and procedures used in plan formulation. Methods of planning may broadly be classified into two types: (1) trial and error methods, and (2) systematic methods of mathematical and statistical analysis of both quantitative and qualitative data and information. Trial and error method should not be confused with any arbitrary, irrational, unorganised or adhoc method of problem solving. Trial and error, in fact, is an established method of problem solving and mathematical analysis.

Conceptually, 'method' of planning refers to steps involved in procedure(s) of finding unknown values of endogenous variables in terms of known values of exogenous variables and their parameters. The values of endogenous variables of the system, found by the use of methods are such numerical figures as offer solution of the given set of equations and system that these equations constitute. Such values of endogenous variables are a solution in the sense that substitution of these values of unknowns in given equations will exactly match the known quantities or values on the other side of equations, that is, equations will be exactly and precisely satisfied. But the constraints and conditions attached to the equations will also have to be satisfied by the solution. For example, diet problem of linear programming seeks to determine such quantities of different foods, included in diet, as to meet minimum prescribed dietary requirements at the lowest cost. Consistent, feasible and optimum solution will not transgress predetermined constraints and conditions imposed upon the problem/system from outside. This implies that only such values of unknowns of the system may be considered to constitute the solution as (a) satisfy constraints limiting the system's current operations and restricting objectives of planned development, and (b) conforms to initial conditions imposed on equations. The solution has to satisfy conditions of consistency, its stipulated assumptions, definitions, constraints and conditions. In other words, solution should be characterised by the property of coherence. These constraints and initial conditions relate to (i) nature of relationships between different endogenous variables and their determinants in specified system. These relations describe the behaviour of variables, socio-economic constraints, assumptions, definitions or concepts used in the system and limitations within which variables and forces they represent operate, their time and spatial frame of operation for reference, and initial values of core variables and parameters. Unknown variables and parameters of functional relations are determined by the solution(s). Solution value(s) furnishes a type of 'forecast' of the likely state of the system. This should coincide or resemble the outcomes of successful implementation of the plan. One often searches for unique, optimum, and stable solution(s) through complex mathematical and/or statistical methods.

Trial and error method seeks to find such numbers as will satisfy conditions of coherence. Trials can, however, be repeated systematically. This is the case with 'successive approximations,' or 'decreasing degree of abstraction', which is associated with each successive step or stage of problem solving. Iterative procedure of trial and error may also be followed. Solution of each iteration is assessed to find if the solution happens to be that one is looking for. Simplex method, used in solving programming problems, is based on such iterations as gradually make iterative solution at each step move from less to greater degree of convergence towards the desired solution, till the desired optimum solution is finally found. Sometimes, there may exist multiple rather than a unique optimum solution. Unique optimum solution may be derived from the system of equations by the use of trial and error method, since some mathematical methods are also based on trial and error. Interestingly, solution of a large number of simultaneous polynomials, or equations, or inequalities may depend upon trial and error method of problem solving.

A given set of equations may constitute a planning model. These equations may relate to balances or equilibrium conditions of the system, definitional relations, relations that translate pivotal assumptions into mathematical expressions, while some equations will relate to technical, institutional and behavioural aspects and their interrelations, which underly structural and behavioural characteristics of the system. For example, assumption of perfect competition in the market relates to an institutional framework of analysis under which all prices converge towards cost of production. Identities, definitional equations, assumptional and functional or structural relations are also expressed as equations of the system/model. Equations involve endogenous and exogenous variables, parameters and structural/technical coefficients. Initial conditions in the base year are also specified. Exogenous variables and initial conditions constitute known data, which are required for solving the model. Statistical or mathematical methods are used for (a) estimating unknown values of endogenous variables, and/or (b) parameters attached to exogenous variables of the system from data furnished by exogenous variables and initial conditions.

Stages of Planning Methods

Phases or stages of planning, which offer choices of methods of analysis, may be distinguished. Initial phase refers to the macro-stage at which the processes of production in the economy, taken as a whole, are described by explicit specification of inputs to be used to produce the targeted output of goods and services. Interrelations between inputs and output may be specified by one or more production functions, chosen from alternative functions that are available in literature. One may conduct statistical or econometric experiments with alternative functions to choose the one that captures the given conditions best. It is also possible to choose different production functions for different sectors of the economy in the sectoral phase of analysis. Input-output analysis, linear/non-linear programming, or game theoretic approaches may be considered as analytical tools. Next comes the project phase of analysis. This phase will involve analysis for evaluating technical feasibility and economic viability on well-defined criteria. Appraisal of real resource costs, and expected benefits is of critical importance in the choice of projects/programmes to be included in the plan.

Organisational Base of Planning

Organisation refers to hierarchical structure(s) of authorities and their agencies of planning; (ii) demarcation of domains of operations, roles and functions of different authorities and agencies, entrusted with planning; (iii) delineation of rights and functions of personnel of different cadres of different agencies, involved either directly or indirectly in planning both within their own agencies as well as in dealings with personnel of other agencies; (iv) forms, structures and procedures of planning; and (iv) rules and regulations, governing the functions of all planning authorities.

As there is only one central but supreme authority and/or agency of planning in every country, it is possible to explain and describe their main organisational forms and structures. But regional, local, sectoral and institutional authorities and agencies of planning are far too many in number with too much diversified operational forms and structures to precisely explain and describe characteristics of their organisational forms and structures.

Organisational Features in India

These authorities and agencies of planning may either be internal or external to the economy, which has to be planned. For example, the Planning Commission, constituted by the Government of India by an Act of the Parliament, may be an external authority and agency of planning for the regional and local economies, while the State Planning Boards or Committees, constituted by State governments, may represent an external planning authority for sectoral or departmental authorities of planning. Externality or internality of planning authority is important insofar as the lower level agency or authority has to formulate its plan within the constraints, conditions and limitations suggested, recommended or prescribed by higher authority. Thus, externality or internality of authority or agency refers largely to relative hierarchical position. Within each planning authority or agency, hierarchical positioning of personnel also prevails to delineate and delimit powers and functions of each layer of operators. Internal organisation refers to the hierarchical division of labour between different departments, units, divisions, or cells within any given planning authority and agency. For example, the Planning Commission is divided into such divisions as perspective planning division, research division, etc. Roles and functions of each division and department/cell within each of them, are clearly demarcated. Then, there exists the hierarchy of functionaries. The Prime Minister is exofficio Chairman of the Planning Commission. Vice-chairman may either be the minister of planning, or a technocrat, or an economist, or a bureaucrat. Then, there is a secretary who may or may not be a professional or technocrat. There are full time members of the Planning Commission, who have the status and powers of ministers of state. Members are assisted by advisors, joint advisors, heads of divisions, and so on.

Data Generators

Central Statistical Organisation (CSO) is also attached to the commission to meet its data requirements. CSO's work is supplemented by such organisations as Office of Registrar General of India, who is responsible for decadal census operations. NSSO conducts regular as well as special sample surveys. This data base is further supplemented by the statistics generated by such ministries as health, education, labour, agriculture, etc. Five yearly census of industries and agriculture are also conducted regularly.

International Organisational Features

We may, however, describe major organisational features of planning authority in different countries. Most of these facets are common. Planning Ministry, Controlling Planning Commission or Committee, and Ministry of Finance are main external organisations for reference in planning. The controlling ministry is generally under the charge of the Prime Minister's or President's Office (PMO), depending upon the form of country's government. Both in India and Turkey, prime minister's office controls the Planning Commission. In some cases, CPC itself is a ministry; this is the case in Venezuela. CPC may be merely an office in other ministry as in Netherlands. Whatever its location. CPC will, however, have interministry and inter-departmental jurisdiction, having powers to contact and seek information from different ministries without permission of concerned minister. Successful operation of planning requires an access to all information available with the different organs of the government. Hence, CPC/CBP or its designated agencies will generally have mandatory powers to collect relevant information and data both from public and private sector industries, institutions and organisations. CSO, Directorate of Employment and Training, Statistics Division of Department of Education, Statistical Organisation of Ministry of Agriculture in India are examples of such organisations as regularly collect information and data. CPC should itself imbibe and display the trait of cooperation and flexibility of approach in its dealings with others.

In large and populous countries like India and China, and such other countries as practice centralised planning, based on extensive state interventions, pervasive controls and regulations, and exhaustive coverage of the society, economy and education, success of planning may require more than one authority and agency of planning. Decentralisation of planning necessitates wide networking of planning agencies, and directorates of statistics, each dealing with one region, or even one sector. Such agencies may function under one single agency or there may also be multiple controlling authorities and agencies. In case of multiplicity of authorities and agencies of planning, coordination assumes paramount importance.

Internal organisation of CPB/CPC will depend upon the nature and tasks of planning. There may be separate divisions to deal with short and long term planning independently. Perspective Planning Division (PPD) of Indian Planning Commission is an instance. Subdivisions deal with individual subjects and sectors such as industry, health, education, labour and employment, and agriculture. Functions of subdivisions may be demarcated to allow freedom of action, though independence in decision-making will often impinge upon the inter-dependencies among socio-economic phenomena, involving duplication, inconsistencies, and even conceptual and methodological incompatibilities. Coordination, integration and synthesisation of programmes, decisions and actions in time, space, dimension, and accepted plan frame in all such cases will be of prime importance.

Internal organisation of CPC/CPB thus offers vital choices: (i) well defined hierarchy, or cooperation among experts, usual actors and agencies on an ad hoc basis; (ii)separation of research from consultancy, advisory roles, routine administrative decisions, or mixture of two or more of above elements in different proportions is possible; (iii) same or different experts and sub-agencies may formulate short and long-term plans; (iv) formulation, organisation and presentation of short and long-term plans either according to sectors and regions, or according to the nature and principle of functionality of areas and subjects such as trade, consumption, investment, employment, industry, health, and education, etc., may be adopted; and (v) choices may be interpenetrating and mixed ones also.

International Comparison of Planning Processes

Department of Economic Affairs of the UN conducted a survey on the request of its General Assembly. A similar enquiry was also conducted by Netherlands Economic Institute in consultation with the UN. Out of 51 countries covered by the survey, 19 furnished detailed information. Various facets and features of planning in these countries have been inferred from their responses to schedules convassed among them. These have been summarised in details by Tinbergen in the Annexure of his book as follows:

1. Organisational structure, prestige and size of the planning agency depend upon (a) nature and degree of planning undertaken by the planning agency. Centralised planning needs services of large number of experts, administrators, and hence, large sized organisational and exhaustive data as support base for performing varied functions related to planning. This requires extensive powers and confers greater prestige. But in Norway and some socialist countries, personnel in different ministries discharge all functions relating to planning, reducing the size and prestige of planning agency.

2. Staff employed in planning agencies do not possess skills, training, knowledge, experience, and expertise in the methods, theory, policy and practices of planning before recruitment. This highlights scarcity of educational and training facilities in universities and institutes, resulting in clevage between manpower needs and manpower production by education sector for planning. Hence, learning by doing, on the job and in-service training have been main sources of manpower supplies for planning authorities. This highlights the role of training institutes like NIEPA and IAMR Italy, Poland, Netherlands, UAR, US, and Venezuela are among such few countries as have special courses, training schools and institutes of planning. Indian universities also offer specialised courses/papers in economic, manpower and educational planning. JNU, Calcutta, North-Eastern Hill, Jadavapur, Jamia Millia and Delhi University offer courses in planning as part of postgraduate programmes in economics and education. Now Ram Manohar Lohia University, Faizabad has also instituted courses in educational planning.

Economics of education and human resource development are taught as part of postgraduate courses of economics at Punjab University, Chandigarh, North Eastern Hill University, Shillong, and Guru Nanak Dev University, Amritsar.

3. There is considerable uniformity in tasks performed by planning agencies, highlighting similarities of planning procedures and processes.

4. Modes of formulation and execution of plans display considerable variations. In only few countries, CPB/CPC is responsible for implementation of plans it formulates. This shows hiatus between formulator and excecutor of plans. Hence, this clevage forms an important source of leaving wide scope for conceptual distortions, dilution, and divergence between precept and practice, on the one hand, and miscarriage of intents and purposes of planning in implementation, on the other. Administration and management of planned development require specialised skills, expertise and knowledge, which are generally not possessed by generalist administrators. Mismanagement of planning in India is due largely to its domination by bureaucracy, which was originally meant for collection of revenue and maintenance of law and order. This calls for plugging of seepages, leakages, and clevages through monitoring, midterm appraisals or even concurrent evaluation on the one hand, and institution of subjectwise all India services such as health, education, and engineering in order to take away technocratic, engineering, economic, and statistical services from being manned and/or headed by current IAS personnel.

5. Number of actors involved in planning is enormously large.

6. Considerable degree of uniformity seems to mark the objectives of planning and policy. Following appear as major goals and objectives of planning: (a) consistent rise in national and per capita incomes, (b) employment generation, (c) improvement in balance of payments, (d) maintenance of price stability, (e) reduction of inequalities in (i) income distribution, and (ii) regional development, (f) initiation and nurturing of self-reliant and self-sustained development in the long run. Now-a-days development of infrastructure and social

overheads, quality of life, environmental conservation, and hence, sustainable development figure among high priorities of planned development.

7. Policies and instruments, used for intervention in socio-economic phenomena differ in nature, number, and effectiveness. Systems of delivery of policies and instruments and plan implementation also diverge widely between countries and even within regions of the same countries.

8. Sectoral classification differs sharply among countries. Developing countries have much fewer divisions than the developed ones. The degree of details in planning also differs according to sectoral classification used in plans.

9. Employment does not figure much highly among target variables (Prakash, 1997).

10. Trial and error method is used extensively as a tool of planning. Mathematical methods and intricate planning models are used in only few countries such as the Netherlands, the USSR and India. Uniformity of approach in the planning of macro variables, especially those involved in macro stabilisation is, however, highly marked.

Above description is crude, rudimentary and tentative, since comparability is made difficult by such features as multiplicity of concepts, methodological diversity, varieties of analytical framework and approaches, and differences in nature and scope of planning in different countries. These are precisely the facets and features which have been revealed to be shared by survey responses of large number of diverse countries.

In conclusion, it may be reiterated that transition from the concept of ruling and an oppressive to welfare state, demonstrated success, effectiveness, and efficacy of interventionist policies of Keynesian type in macro stabilisation and their widespread acceptance in post Second World War period were pivots of state policy. Successes achieved by the USSR in telescoping that level of development in only a few decades which market economies of the developed West accomplished in several centuries, success of controls and rationing in mitigating wartime shortages and ensuring equitable distribution of available supplies established the efficacy of planning as an instrument of rapid development with equity and justice, specially the development of newly independent countries of the Third World. The accumulated experiences have amply highlighted the limitations and shortcomings of autonomously functioning market economies of the West. All these buttressed the case of planning and facilitated its adoption as state policy by numerous countries of the Third World during the post Second World War period. But now experiences have revealed shortcomings and limitations of planning.

References

Anderson and Bowman(1959), Theoretical considerations in educational planning, in Blaug, M. (Editor), *Economics of Education*, Penguin, p. 356.

Brahamananda, P.R. & Vakil, C.N. (1953), *Planning for an Expanding Economy*, Bombay.

Griffin, Keith B. and Enos, John L. (1970), *Planning Development*, Addison-Wesley Publishing Co., London.

Lange, Oskar (1938), *On the Economic Theory of Socialism*, University of Minnesota.

Lange, Oskar (1956), 'Prof. Oskar Lange's Interview', Published in *New York Times*.

Lange, Oskar (1967), *Essays in Economic Planning*, Statistical Publishing Co., Calcutta.

Learner, Abba, P. (1959), *The Economics of Control*.

Leontief, W.W.(1951), *The Structure of the American Economy*, Oxford University Press.

Mahalanobis, P.C. (1962), *Essays on Planning*, Statistical Publishing Co., Calcutta.

Myrdal, Gunnar (1954), *Economic Theory and Underdeveloped Regions*, Vora & Co., Bombay.

Myrdal, Gunnar (1970), *Asian Drama*, Abridged Students' Edition, Asia, New Delhi.

Prakash, S. (1960), Planning in India: Problems in an Underdeveloped Country', Published in *The Competition Master*, October, Ambala Cantt..

Prakash, S. (1976), 'Input Output Models of Education With Applications to Indian Data, Published in Mathur, P.N. (Editor), *Economic Analysis in Input Output Framework*, Vol. III, IORA, Bombay University.

Prakash, S. (1977), *Educational System of India: An Econometric Study*, Concept, New Delhi.

Prakash, S. (1977), 'Regional Inequalities of Infrastructural Development in India, Published in *The Indian Journal of Regional Science*, Kharagpur.

Prakash, S. and Rajan, P. (1977), Regional Inequalities of Rural Development in Madhya Pradesh, Published in *The Indian Journal of Regional Science*, IIT, Kharagpur.

Prakash, S. and Ghosh, S. (1978), Public Sector in Indian Economy : A Study of Its Role and Contribution, Published in Gupta, K.R. (Editor), *Organisation and Management of Public Enterprises*, Vol. I, Atlantic Publishers, New Delhi.

Prakash, S. and Mohapatra, A. (1980), Economic Development: A Study of Inter-Temporal and Intra-regional Variations in M.P. (India), Published in *Third World Planning Review*, Vol. II, Liverpool.

Prakash, S. (1982) Industrial Production and Its Determinants in India: 1951-76, Published in *The Economic Journal of Nepal*, Vol. 5, No. 4, Oct-Dec., Kathmandu, Nepal.

Prakash, S. (1993), *'Use of Sample Survey Techniques in Educational Statistics*, UNESCO, Paris.

Prakash, S. (1989), *Analytical and Historical Perspectives of Educational Planning in India*, Proceedings *Review Conference on Four Decades of Development*, organised jointly by NIEPA and Ministry of Human Resource Development, New Delhi, April 14-15.

Prakash, S. (1991), Financial and Real Development in India : Analysis of Growth of Income, Money and Prices, Published in *Indian Economic Journal*, Conference Vol., Bombay.

Prakash, S. (1994), Liberalisation of Indian Economy and Relevance of Nehru-Mahalanobis Strategy of Development, Published in Sinha, A.K. (Editor) *'New Economic Policy of India: Restructuring and Liberalising the Economy for 21st Century*, Deep & Deep, New Delhi.

Prakash, S., Singh, S. and Sharma, A. (1996), Effect of Liberalisation on Industry-Agriculture Interrelations and Terms of Trade, Published in *The Indian Journal of Economics*, Vol. LXXVII, Allahabad.

Prakash, S. (1996), New Economic Policy: Analysis of Actual and Perceived Impacts on Indian Economy, Published in Jauhri, B.M. (Editor), *New Economic Policy: A Critical Appraisal*, Commonwealth Publishers, Delhi.

Prakash, S. and Singh, Shalini (1996), Inventory Investment and Generalisation of Mahalanobis Model of Growth, Published in *MM'96:*

Macro Models on Integration and Development, University of Lodz, Poland.

Prakash, S. (1997a), Neo-Liberalism and Employment in India, Published in *Indian Journal of Labour Economics.*

Sraffa, Piero, *Production of Commodities by Means of Commodities*, Vora, Bombay.

Tinbergen, Jan (1967), *Development Planning*, Widenfeld & Nicholsan.

Tinbergen J. (1967), *Central Planning,*Yale University Press.

Parnes, H.S. (1964), Manpower Analysis in Educational Planning, in Parnes (Ed), *Planning Education for Economic and Social Development*, O.E.C.D, p. 73.

UNESCO & IIEP, *Educational Planning for the Future*, Paris.

United Nations (1963), *Planning for Economic Development*, New York.

4

Approaches and Strategies of Planning

Success or failure of planning depends a great deal upon the nature of plan formulation on the one hand, and the effectiveness of strategy of implementation on the other. Plan formulation depends upon the approach to planning and the strategy adopted for the realisation of goals and objectives of plans. But there is a wide range of options between different approaches and strategies of planning to choose from. Each approach to planning and strategy of development embodies specific goals and objectives of development. In other words, approaches to planning and its objectives are quite specific to each other.

Objectives and goals of planning are derived from (a) ideological considerations, (b) the gaps between current and planned stages of development of the system to be planned, (c) current problems and issues, requirements approach to educational planning warrants the production of manpower adoption of goal of producing requisite manpower, and (d) the approach to planning and strategy of development. For example, manpower with specified levels and types of education to meet the development needs of the economy; whereas demand approach may warrant development of education to be guided by its social demand. As against the approach(es) to planning, strategy may guides the instruments and mechanisms to be relied upon for the realisation of goals and objectives of plans. If the strategy is to rely upon private sector for development, state will rely upon private initiatives for development, on instruments that furnish incentives and reinforce efforts and enterprise of individuals and private organisations. If, however, public sector is to be relied upon for development, then state will have to initiate such measures, as are required for development and also mobilise resources for financing investment in educational development and arrange manpower and institutional support base for inspection, supervision, planning and management of education. Before discussing strategies and approaches to planning of education, it shall be appropriate if the concepts and meaning, nature and scope of the terms 'strategy', 'approach', and 'educational planning' are clearly delineated and differentiated from concepts of an allied nature. The foregoing attempts to propound operational definitions of all the three concepts that are under consideration.

Approaches, strategies and methodology of planning are conditioned and guided by the nature of economic regimes within the framework of which planning is undertaken. Besides, main objectives and strategies of planning themselves suggest the approaches to planning or vice versa.

Strategy

The concept of 'strategy' has been imported into economic and educational planning from military science. The concept of strategy has been developed in military science as an essential and inevitable part of the science and art of conducting wars. The term 'strategy' has itself been derived from the word 'stratagem'. Stratagem, in military parlance, refers to an 'artifice' or 'device' to deceive an enemy. This deceit is dictated by the ultimate goal of winning the war, or defeating the enemy by means of the superiority of (a) army in terms of capabilities of armed forces to accomplish the desired goals, and hence, to effectively perform assigned tasks and roles. Role of skills and capabilities of armed forces is crucial both in conceiving the 'strategy' by the army high command, consisting of senior generals and commanders, and its execution by cadres of different hierarchical order of the forces.

The concept of 'strategy' has been borrowed in economic and educational planning from military science. Strategy is concerned with the package of tactics and management of men and materials for conducting wars. The term 'strategy' has been derived from the concept of 'stratagem'. Stratagem, in military parlance, refers to an 'artifice' or 'device' to deceive an enemy.

The high command should formulate only such a strategy as the forces at its command are capable of executing to its last minutest detail both in letter and spirit. Importance of training and education, and hence, skills and capabilities is highlighted by the fact that in the evaluation of causes of defeat in the Second World War, German policy makers and planners concluded that the allied forces, led mainly by the British army, won the war as they proved superior to the German army. Their superiority was derived from their better education and training, and hence, better skills and higher capabilities than those possessed by the German army, i.e, materials, and even more important better tactics and more efficient management of men and materials than that of the enemy. It is the last element of above triplets that constitutes 'strategem', and hence, its derivative 'strategy'.

Strategy, in a broader sense, may be defined as the management of army and weaponry to (i) mobilise, and (ii) deploy men and materials so as to choose the time, place and conditions of one's preference, and hence, advantage for fighting the enemy on one's own terms. Obviously, superior strategy chooses that time, place, tactics and conditions of fighting which are disadvantageous to the enemy in the envisagement and perspective of the conceiving and executing strategies.

In the parlance of planning, strategy refers to (i) means, modes and methods of management of men and materials, (i) conceiving and executing tactics for optimum mobilisation and deployment of actual and potential resources, (iii) advance decisions and actions to find solution(s) of current and emerging problems and urgent issues, (iv) initiate and then sustain policies and actions to pull economic and educational system(s) from lower to higher levels and stages of development through time and space.

In military parlance, strategy refers to measures, programmes of action, and manoeuvres to turn the conditions of battles or wars against the enemy and in favour of the strategist and executioner of strategy. Strategy should, therefore, concentrate on exploitation of one's strengths and enemy's weaknesses on the one hand, and on overcoming, or at least, minimising and hiding one's weaknesses in terms of paucity of men and materials, or their logistic and other shortcomings from enemy's eyes through superior and tactical deployment for blunting enemy's strengths. Thus, superior methods, better modes and efficient mechanisms of mobilisation and deployment of available men and materials for optimal utilisation is the pivotal element in determining the effectiveness of the chosen strategy. This basic connotation of the concept of strategy has been imported into economic and educational planning from military science. This military concept of 'strategy' has, however, been suitably adapted and modified to sub serve the conceptual and policy purposes of economic and educational planning.

In the parlance of planning, conceptual contours and meaning of strategy refer to the means, modes and methods of management, optimum mobilisation and deployment of actual and potential resources, advance decisions and actions on the same to discover and impose solution(s) of current and emerging problems and urgent issues in order to move the economic and/ or educational system(s), its variables and parameters into better situations and conditions in time or space or both to make their converge towards the realisation of accepted and approved goal(s), objective(s) and outcome(s) of developmental planning. The main objective of planning is to pull the system from lower to higher levels and stages of development both through time and space.

Concept of strategic planning has been developed on the basis of the concept of strategy. Strategic planning takes care of formulation and effective execution of the plans both in vision and perspective to move the socio-economic and educational systems into right directions at correct time and proper space to accomplish specified goal(s) of development. Conceiving of strategy and its detailed formulation is only the preparatory phase. Execution phase of strategy requires timely decisions and their proper implementation through carefully prepared programme of action. Clarity of vision, concepts and ideas, that constitute the core elements of strategy in the envisagement of planners, is essential for facilitating its unambiguous and concrete expression in plans and programmes of action for plan implementation. It implies that pivotal organisational structures, materials and men are needed for conceptualisation, formulation and execution of strategy so as to translate it from drawing boards, papers and files into devices by means of which planning can be transformed into efficient actions that synchronise both in time and space. Aversion of seepages and leakages in the translation of concepts, ideas, methods, modes and tactics, evolved to tackle problems and to overcome hurdles and bottlenecks in development, are the pivots of success. Strategic planning is essential for aversion of shortfalls in the achievement of targets and in the avoidance of failures. This is an important aspect of planning, since the results often obtained in laboratory experiments, or through simulations, tend to be diluted in field conditions. Such leakages and seepages have to be neutralised for optimum achievements.

From strategic planners, conceptual framework of strategy of planning and its action programme percolate first to administrators and then to producers and operators working on farms and factories, production establishments, institutions, and organisations. Translation of ideas, precepts, concepts, and theories into action requires meticulously efficient operationalisation in accordance with the plan, needing efficient management of men and materials on the one hand, and synchronisation of decisions and actions thereof in time, space and among agencies and actors on the other.

Important ingredients of success of strategy are: (a) strategist's or planner's vision and perspective, concepts and ideas, which embody and encompass the chosen goal(s) and strategy of its realisation are completely understood by those entrusted with the task of executing it. First of all, it needs clarity of concepts and ideas in the minds of planners themselves and their clear explanation by the conceivers of strategy in the plan documents as well as through administrative decisions and orders to plan implementers. The job is decidedly intricate, subtle and complex. It involves enormous details of new and novel ideas, innovative actions and new methods and modes of operations. All of these need proper explanation by persons in responsible positions to an extremely large number of subordinates in the bureaucratic hierarchy; (b) temporal and spatial dimensions of decisions, modes and methods of implementation of programme of actions have to be meticulously explained, understood and operated; and (c) mobilisation and deployment of men and materials in requisite numbers and quantities have to be ensured just at right time and at correct places. The strategy involves the timing, forms, structures, methods and modes, tactics, mechanism and instruments.

Illustration

Suppose the objective is to eliminate illiteracy for which a strategy has been conceived and development plan has been finalised. Programme and mode of acting upon it will then involve identification of all potential and current illiterates, their spatial locations and socio-economic background. Strategy will require comprehensive knowledge about all members of target groups. Achievement of the goal warrants bridging of gaps between the current and desired state of development to be reached at the end of the planning horizon. Strategy translated the plan into steps and stages of actions to be undertaken. These should be explained and expressed in such terms and language, as are understood, assimilated and then smoothly executed by all would be operators of the plan. This simple task will itself need thousands of details of myriad actions under the plan of identification of illiterates. Then will commence the second step of meticulous execution of the minutest and the finest details of action programme, for example, name, gender, age, place of residence, occupational status, personal and family's socio-economic background of illiterate are to be prepared. Next step of enrolment of illiterates in adult literacy centres will require an appropriate strategy for each group of illiterates to be prepared in advance. Different groups may need different packages of incentives and instruments for arousing their dormant demand for literacy. Those, who habitually go to bars at such times as are in conflict with the literacy classes, will encounter resistance from liquor shop owners. An effective punitive action against those who dissuade or pressurise illiterates to keep away from literacy centres have to be placed in order. To cope with larger than usual number of enrollees and make them literate within given time profile will require an action programme for strengthening infrastructural and instructional facilities in literacy centres. Each centre will have to be enriched and prepared in advance to make the plan succeed. Such infrastructural facilities as classrooms and furniture, lighting arrangements, blackboards and reading-teaching materials adequate to meet the enhanced requirements, will have to be provided to each literacy centre in advance.

Essential Ingredients of Strategy

The essence of the concept of 'strategy' in the context of planning may be purveyed and conveyed lucidly with the operational design and policy objectives of reputed corporate houses. A reputed corporate house, for example, Tata, Godrej, Hindustan Lever or an MNC like IBM, says above all, we want a reputation for doing the little things better than others, and we want to do the tiniest things better now than in the past it implies that accomplishment of the smallest tasks better and more efficiently than others, distinguishes between good and bad performers, while improvement of past performance will convey the message that the particular producer cares more for its consumers than others operation in the market. But the differences in the efficiency of performance of one single task alone does not suffice to designate one corporate house as superior to another. An entire package, or set of all tasks, complementary and reinforcing to each other, has to be delivered more efficiently to yield greater satisfaction to those for whom the tasks have been undertaken. Performance of one task perfectly with the neglect of others may make the whole mission fail. A surgeon or an aeroplane pilot has hardly any scope for error in the performance of any one of the interconnected tasks. The job has to be done perfectly, accurately and precisely for the accomplishment of the mission. Compromise with perfection in precision and accuracy may prove fatal in both instances. In case of socio-economic and educational planning, fatality is not immediate but gradual, invisible and imperceptible in the immediate run. But it becomes perceptibly visible in the long run with almost fatal consequences as it slowly eats into the vitals of the system. Rather than performing only one task 10,000 times better, it is better to perform 10 interconnected but mutually reinforcing tasks two times better. This conveys the meaning, nature, scope and method of conceptualisation and implementation of strategy in the context of planning for improving the plan performance.

Basic Prerequisites

Strategy needs strategic organisational structure and institutional support base to achieve success in development. Only when the gaps in actual and potential performance levels of several known things are identified and the causes of failures, or the shortfalls in achievement of targets have been diagnosed, effective strategy for doing these numerous known things better, every time the given tasks are to be performed, can be evolved and implemented.

Quality of performance of one task by one group depends upon the quality of preparatory work of earlier stage or steps taken by other group(s). Therefore, conceptualisation and operationalisation of strategy happen to be the 'teamwork'. Both formulation and implementation of strategy, therefore, require a motivated and dedicated team of capable managers/ administrators and decision makers, who by their thoughts and deeds, can inspire other colleagues, subordinates and lower order operators to follow their leads, commands and guidance.

Following are other important factors involved in the formulation and implementation of any strategy: (a) conceptual clarity and firm ideological convictions occupy the centre-stage, (b) steady, rigid and sticky adherence to the cherished values and convictions makes all members of the team in charge of the mission, realise that certain things are non-negotiable, (c) orientation or bias towards action and implementation of ideas and concepts in reality ensure that plans and programmes do not remain confined to papers or files, (d) high motivation and urgent but constant rooting of implementers for achievement of cherished goal(s) prevent waivering and unsteadiness in resolve to work, (e) autonomy and enterprise in decision making and action ensure proper division of labour, sharing of responsibilities and devolution of powers and duties, (f) respect for others' views not only facilitates sharing of experiences and expertise but it also prevents antagonisation of functionaries by arrogance and egoistic behaviour of one or the others, (g) stickiness to ways and things one does the best as an insurance against faltering in midstream, or frittering of time, energy, and resources in doing the second best rather than the best things, or opting for means and ways other than the best, (h) simplicity of organisational structure and institutionalised forms of actions tend to make the system immune to the presence or absence of individuals. But it does not imply the adoption of steely frame of rules and procedures, leaving no space for individual's initiatives and well designed innovations, (i) looseness or tightness, rigidity or flexibility in thoughts and actions go a long way in successfully implementing the chosen strategy, (j) principles may be imbued with flexibility in according freedom and autonomy in action to real operators and implementers but rigidity in values and convictions on the one hand, and adherence to basic design and plan implementation within the given time frame, on the other, and (k) coordination and integration of decisions, action and work of different groups is of paramount importance in preventing haphazard and disjointed decisions and actions.

Leadership plays the most vital role in formulating the strategy and its implementation. The leadership should be capable of enthusing and inspiring subordinates by leading from the front through example rather than by precept and only pep talks about lofty ideas and goals. They should consider themselves as first among the equals. Besides, they should have vision and intuitive insights to diagnose the present and unravel the future to aim at the highest and the best that is possible to achieve under the given circumstances. Without a broad vision and realistic future perspective, it is difficult to comprehend and understand current problems, envisage the scaffolding of future scenarios. This inability will impinge upon the formulation of plans and evolving of strategy for planned development (Cf. Peters-Waterman).

Importance of following factors in conceptualising and executing strategy is self-evident; (Cf. Hickman and Silva): (i) vision and intuitive insights are needed not only for properly understanding the intricacies of problems and urgency of emerging issues but also for evolving the best mode and method of their solution. Vision and perspective planning enable not only arousal of future aspirations in general terms but it helps in their expression in concrete shapes and forms also. Vision is needed to move from the known present to unknown, uncertain and risky future. But movement presupposes the prior knowledge of goals or destination and the direction of movement. Intuitive insights are important in understanding and diagnosing the problem/situation. The correct diagnosis facilitates the evolving of corrective measures and devising of methods to undertake remedial actions; abilities between words of understanding, diagnosing, and devising of remedies and capabilities for getting the same implemented are required to be backed by focused and motivated actions for realising the goals; (ii) unrelenting focus and unflinching motivation for problem solving and goal achieving is an important ingredient of success; (iii) completion of assigned intricate tasks involves time and group work. The completion of such tasks require patience, tact and facility to interact with other members of the team; (iv) craving and penchant for having all details and the propensity to delve deep and understand their intricate interrelations make it possible to anticipate all implications and ramifications of decisions and actions. This determines whether one is overtaken by events, or events find one well prepared in advance to face them. These behavioural tendencies have to be inculcated as an essential part of work culture and operational environment; (v) action programmes for the achievement of big and complicated goals are time consuming and strenous in nature. These actions require forebearance and patience to wait for results to materialise. Haste and impatience, or untimely or premature initiation of action without adequate preparation and proper understanding of the problem and the mode, method and sequence of steps in which action is to be undertaken, may lead to unsatisfactory results and, at times, the mission may even fail altogether; (vi) correct timing, proper spacing and assessment of appropriateness of conditions under which action(s) is initiated determine the nature of outcomes; (vii) achievement of excellence is impossible without having proper environment and work culture. Successful completion of assigned tasks should evoke pride and elation, job satisfaction and confidence. But the efficient and timely performance should not only be to one's own satisfaction but it should also satisfy others, specially those for whom the tasks have been undertaken. This involves two groups of people; (a) superiors who assigned the tasks, and (b) final users of the end-product of the performance, that is, to whom the service is rendered, or for whom the goods are produced, or specific work is done. In other words, satisfaction of customers and clients is quite important.

Strategy leads to an extension of (a) inherent capabilities of workers, (b) reinforcement of organisational strengths, (c) subduing, dilution or mitigation of weaknesses, inexperience, inadequacy of expertise, resource constraints, and organisational limitations. Organisational structures, institutional support base and styles of functioning will set the limits to the degree of effectiveness of implementation of the strategy, and hence, its success or failure. More often than not, success is only partial. Hence, pragmatism warrants that efforts should be focused on raising the proportion of targets achieved by reducing gaps between actual achievements and plan targets.

Each package of tasks and the strategy associated with these tasks require specialised teamwork for its success both from behind and in front. Vibrant, vigilant and perceptive leadership, backed up by a competent, dedicated and motivated team of conceivers and implementers to support the strategy, leads to successful translation of strategy into action to achieve the desired goals fully rather than partially.

Need for Strategic Planning of Education

Strategic planning of educational system is needed to tackle problems of (i) demand mobilisation among weaker sections of population, whose demand is currently dormant, so as to realise the elusive goal of UEE, (ii) eradication of mass illiteracy, (iii) controlling of massive number of dropouts, (iv) bringing the enormously large number of non-enrollees into school system of education, (v) improvement in the low quality of learning-teaching, and (vi) mitigation of mismatches between skills needed by the economy and those produced by the educational system on the one hand, and prevention of deployment of people on jobs for which they neither have the aptitude, nor they have education and training, or possess the expertise required for such jobs on the other.

Alternative Strategies of Planning

If we consider the Soviet theory and practice of development planning, we may distinguish among three distinct strategies: (i) Teleologist's Strategy; (b) Genetitists' Strategy; and (iii) Materials' Balance Strategy of Consistency Planning for Development.

Teleologists' Strategy

Protagonists of the teleologists; strategy may be considered to partially follow the deterministic philosophy of social systems. They subscribe to the view that infusion of pragmatism and realism in planning, on which its success depends, needs the recognition of autonomously determined, and hence, exogenously given factor(s) that exercise the greatest stumbling and hampering influence on development. Such factor(s) may relate to social structures, institutional support base, organisational forms and their limitations, and/or resource constraints and bottlenecks to planned development. Once such constraints and bottlenecks have been identified and reckoned explicitly in plan formulation, planning will become not only realistic but its chance of successful completion and full rather than partial achievement of targets will be enhanced. The explicit recognition and accounting of constraints, bottlenecks in plan formulation will lead to the setting up of achievable goals and targets. If such constraints, bottlenecks, and limitations are overlooked in plan formulation, planning will become too ambitious to be realistic, leading to its failure. There will be shortfalls in achievement of targets and realisation of goals. Repeated failures and shortfalls in the achievement of targets at the end of each plan of development may lead to dis-illusionment, disappointment, and even cynicism about planning among the masses as well as administrators and policy makers. This will also afford an opportunity to bureaucrats to shift the blame on planners and their planning design for their own administrative bunglings. Bureaucratic inefficiencies may lead to shortfalls in the realisation of plan targets and goals. Failure of planning may be mainly due to faulty implementation rather than defective design of the plan, though inconsistencies and imperfections in plan formulation are not ruled out. But even perfectly conceived and formulated plans may result in constraints and bottlenecks, if execution of one or some projects involves time slippages and cost over-runs.

Repeated failures may evoke and elicit carping criticisms from analysts, media and opponents of planning. Some core bottlenecks and constraints may be too severe to overcome during the short run. But it may be possible to remove such constraints and bottlenecks gradually as the economy proceeds along its development path from lower to higher stages of growth. The constraints and bottlenecks will be loosened under the impact of growth.

The Constitution makers of India stipulated achievement of universalisation of elementary education within a short span of only one decade in total disregard of the fact that (a) education has had an elitist bias in colonial era with the result that the masses found both the direct and indirect costs of education beyond their means, (b) only a microscopic proportion of population was covered by educational facilities, leaving enormously large number of children, both in relative and absolute terms, out of school system. The goal of UEE by the target date of 1961 was too ambitious to be realised in view of (i) availability of extremely limited number of qualified teachers to meet manpower requirements of phenomenal expansion in intake capacities of existing and those of additional schools opened in widely scattered spatial locations for UEE, (ii) extremely limited schooling facilities which were confined, by and large, to urban areas, (iii) shortages of financial and real resources to meet infrastructural and instructional requirements. Teleologists' strategy warranted that the constraining influence of (a) qualified persons available for teaching jobs, (b) financial and real resources available for development of elementary education should have been kept in view in determining the target date for the realisation of the goal of UEE. Indian planners very soon realised the mistake and shifted the target date to 1965, which also proved to be unrealistically ambitious. Unfortunately, the shifting of target dates of UEE has become a perennial but routine exercise since then, generating cynicism and doubt both among the analysts and masses about the sincerity of planners and policy makers. Another instance of such disregard of constraints is furnished by reckless expansion of facilities for medical and engineering education in the early sixties, resulting in as high a shortage of teachers as about one-third of total requirements (Prakash, 1977).

Constraints to Growth in the former USSR and India

Teleologists in the former USSR pleaded that supply of food was the most pivotal constraint to planned development in general and industrialisation in particular. Therefore, the forecasting of future harvests at each step of planning horizon was suggested to be the first step of planning. Probable non-farm employment and development of non-farm sectors could have been determined once expected supplies of food were known. Development of the economy was, therefore, to be planned within the constraints imposed by the autonomous growth of farm sector to be given exogenously from outside the system.

As against the USSR, following factors have continuously been constraining planned development of Indian economy: (i) inadequacy of supplies of foodgrains has been a problem even in colonial India. India emerged as a food deficit country after separation of Burma. 'Grow More Food' campaign had been launched in British India. But the Green Revolution, triggered in the mid-sixties, has almost totally eliminated shortages of foodgrains. This constraint is no more operative. A large amount of foreign exchange was used in financing imports of (a) foodgrains to meet shortages of domestic supplies, and/or to stabilise prices, (b) such agroraw materials as raw-jute and longstaple cotton to cover the gaps in inadequate domestic supplies and intermediate input requirements of jute and cotton textile industries. These industries were and still continue to be large foreign exchange earners for the Indian economy, (c) oilseeds and edible oils, shortages of which necessitated imports not only to meet shortfalls in domestic output relative to demand but also to contain the cascading effect of rise in their prices on general inflationary pressures in the economy. These shortages of oilseeds and edible oils necessitated large scale imports to overcome excess demand, which absorbed large quantum of foreign exchange. These shortages of oilseeds and edible oils also accentuated inflationary pressure in the economy. Foreign exchange, which used to be absorbed by imports of above goods, is now available for financing investments in imports of capital and intermediate goods needed for development; (ii) inadequacy of capital formation mainly due to low savings rate has been an important constraint to growth. Savings rate has also now been raised from as low level as 3-3.5 per cent in 1951 to approximately 22-24 per cent of the GDP, though India still faces shortages of capital relative to its growth requirements; (iii) dependency for technology imports on the developed West mainly due to low technology base of the economy and inadequacies of indigenous R & D efforts. India shares this facet with all countries of the Third World. Technology imports not only absorb precious foreign exchange, but these imports also make the country dependent upon others and discourage indigenous R & D by obviating its need on the one hand, and make the country remain satisfied only with such old and obsolete technology as the exporters are willing to part with; (iv) inadequacy of foreign exchange to finance consumption and capital imports obstructed growth by limiting supplies of capital goods and intermediate inputs on the one hand, and compromised consumption levels, while excess demand for consumer goods released inflationary pressures in the economy. Shortages of imported raw materials and intermediate inputs even triggered recession in the mid-sixties for the first time. This difficulty is accounted mainly by low level of export earnings. Balance of trade, in fact, still continues to be adverse, whereas balance of payments assumes alarming crisis proportions periodically.

Geneticists Strategy

But the geneticists opposed the teleologists' strategy of planning. They argued that planning is the art and science of mitigating the constraints, bottlenecks and limitations to growth through planned state interventions in the autonomously functioning parts of the system. For this, appropriate instruments have to be forged and used to accelerate the growth of constraining resources. Hence, the implications for Indian and Russian planners were to focus on accelerated development of agriculture to bring it in line with the growth requirements of other sectors of the economy rather than to accept current food shortages as constraints to growth and bottlenecks of development and, therefore, allow limited food supplies to be determined autonomously and to be given exogenously from outside on the one hand, and recognise food shortages to limit growth and impinge on development planning on the other. Geneticists' view ultimately prevailed to guide plan formulation. But the strategy resulted in bottlenecks and constraints, resulting from inconsistent planning. The strategy warranted the higher priority of agricultural development than what it actually received in the Soviet planning. Consequently, Russia still continues to face food shortages and remains dependent on its imports. Similarly the implication of geneticists' strategy for Indian planning was that, if higher priority had been accorded to accelerated the development of education in general and elementary educations in particular, (a) adequate supplies of teachers should have been ensured through higher priority to teacher education and in-service training, and (b) much greater amount of resources, both financial and real, must have been mobilised and allocated for educational development to ensure adequate supplies of infrastructural facilities and instructional materials to avoid compromises with quality that quantitative expansion, disproportionate to resources allocated to education, forced upon it. It has been observed that, whereas flow inputs were inadequately provided for, stock inputs were diluted both in quantity and quality. This holds true particularly about teachers' qualifications, infrastructural facilities and instructional materials (Prakash, 1977).

Materials' Balance Strategy

Materials' Balance Strategy (MBS) to planning had been evolved through incessant experiments with the method of trials and errors in initial stages of evolution of planning in the former USSR. Ever since its development, the 'technique of balancing' has played the most 'distinctive role' as pivotal strategy of 'modern planning'. (Kindleberger, Chapter 9). The materials' balance strategy has been evolved to avoid (i) institutional and organisational limitations, (ii) transgression of resource constraints, and (iii) maintenance of consistency between sectoral output targets and their factor and input requirements through an exhaustive accounting of intra and inter sectoral linkages of both backward and forward nature.

The materials' balances refer to equality between (a) sector and itemwise output targets of goods and services and the factor and intermediate input requirements for their production, (b) requirements of physical and human capital for production of planned/targeted output to yield surpluses for meeting rising demand for investment and consumption. Just as output targets have to be determined itemwise, sector and plant/farmwise resource requirements have also to be determined correspondingly, plant farm, and sectorwise so as to facilitate synchronisation of supplies of each goods/service, primary and other resources with the requirements for each user, enterprise/

producer, or consumer both in time and space. It implies balance both in technological and economic senses. In economic sense, demand has to be matched by supply, while in technical sense, requirements have to be matched by availabilities. Whereas output targets of high priority goods, services and resources are derived primarily from the basic objectives and goals of planned development, requirements of resources, factors and intermediate inputs, that is, output targets of sectors producing intermediate and other investment goods, are determined by technical coefficients of production per unit of output. These coefficients tend to change with changes in technology of production. Till the techniques of production remain invariant, production of larger or smaller output and allocation of more or less resources do not affect input requirements per unit of output. If, however, the quality of resources improves or techniques of production change, per unit input requirements also tend to change.

Resources comprise of (a) labour, the primary factor of production, which is accumulated through population growth; (b) human capital, partly innate and partly acquired capabilities of men, which are accumulated through investment in health and education; (c) physical capital, which is accumulated through the generation of surpluses to be diverted from consumption to production by raising savings, and hence, investment rate. Besides, natural resources, raw materials, and intermediate goods such as power, packing materials, metallic, non-metallic and chemical goods are also needed from the growth of sectoral output.

Important materials to be balanced or sector/commoditywise balances refer mainly to the equality between: (i) commoditywise targets of output and their itemwise input requirements, (ii) requirements of manpower of the economy with different levels and types of education, training and skills, and level and typewise manpower produced by education. Occupation, skills and educationwise manpower requirements may be derived from techniques of production used in various plants, establishments and their output targets. If the technology is to be imported, manpower coefficients may be borrowed from the country of origin of the imported technology. If the technology has been indigenously developed, norms of manpower requirements have to be discovered through its actual use in production, though some norms may emerge from R & D efforts at laboratory stage itself. If manpower requirements exceed supplies, general or specific manpower shortages will either constrain growth, or skill, training and educational levels will have to be lowered to overcome shortages. Alternatively, manpower may either be imported, or less qualified persons may be trained both within and outside the country. Otherwise manpower shortages will lead to 'jammed growth'. If manpower requirements fall short of supplies, policy makers may often be forced to balance demand for employment with supplies of job opportunities through 'relief employment'.

Avoidance of such remedies may warrant either the raising of output targets of commodity production sectors generally or specifically, or opting for more labour intensive techniques by transferring production and resources from more to less capital and from less to more labour absorbing sectors, or plants or techniques. Mahalanobis model, which guided second and the third plans, incorporated growth of traditional handicrafts, small and cottage industries in the plan frame as not only generators of employment but also as suppliers of consumer goods to satisfy consumption demand of the masses. This was an excellent matching of growth of output, consumption, and employment requirements of the economy. Raising of output targets may, however, transgress resource constraints. Another alternative may be to control population growth on the one hand, and slow down the growth of education to contain the demand for employment on the other.

Following are the major aspects of materials' balances need special attention:

(1) generation of skills, education, and sector-wise employment opportunities should match level and type-wise output of educated manpower. Ultimate objective of planned development is to raise living standards of the masses. This objective can be realised only when (a) currently unemployed and new additions to labour force get employment at wages,

adequate to meet the income needs of the households, (b) wage levels are raised continuously to neutralise inflation so as to prevent erosion of real wages by price rise, on the one hand, and to confer benefits of improvements in productivity of workers to raise their real wages, on the other, (c) human capital formation keeps pace with manpower requirements, and (d) available human resources are optimally deployed and utilised. Relief employment, partial employment, employment mismatched with skills, training, education, and unemployment manifest sub-optimal deployment and utilisation of available human resources. This lowers the growth performance of the economy, though it contains social unrest and discontent. Generation of 'relief employment' is generally easier than the mobilisation of more resources, or reallocation of available resources, downward revision of output targets, or change in production techniques. The First Five-Year Plans of China and India had to generated relief employment for absorbing excess labour supplies. This represented patching-up of planned growth, since relief employment was not a part of core plan. Relief employment is normally warranted to cope up with such unforeseen natural disasters as famines, floods and earthquakes. Relief employment may, therefore, be considered as a device of only disaster management. This should not be a regular feature of planning. Relief employment, for covering gaps between planned generation of productive employment and excess supplies of labour-force, highlights the weakness of planning, resulting in growth of employment at rates lower than those warranted by actual manpower supplies. This might reflect either unplanned growth of population, or lower than planned growth of the economy, and hence, employment, or more than planned growth of education, or unbalanced growth of different sectors of the economy. The imbalances between the planned and actual employment growth had been deftly covered by provision of 'relief employment' in simple capital projects, village industries and traditional handicrafts in China and India (Malenbaum, 1956).

Materials' balance strategy of planning has been evolved through trials and errors. USSR stumbled upon the materials' balance strategy and theory and method of planning associated with it through experimentation. Transgression of balances between (i) sectoral output targets and available factors, raw materials and intermediate inputs to meet production requirements, (ii) manpower with different levels and types of skills produced by education and employment opportunities offered by economy, and (iii) savings or investible surpluses and investment requirements of growth necessitate balances. Manpower shortages necessitate either the jamming of growth, or human capital imports, while manpower surpluses force the generation of relief employment.

As contrary to this, overambitious production targets may require generation of employment opportunities in excess of available manpower, leading to the transgression of human capital constraints. Short-term imports on limited scale from outside world may relieve the shortages. Hence, shortages may be overcome by 'hyperemployment' as was done by the Nazi Germany during war years by the revision of age structure of workforce, reduction of holidays, compulsory overtime and synthetic substitutes for basic production. Lowering of educational qualifications, on the job and in-service training and short term crash courses may also raise supplies of human capital to cover quantitative shortfalls and qualitative deficiencies of available human resources. Reversal of these processes may relieve and mitigate the incidence of unemployment to some extent. The first three plans of India, China's second and Japan's first five-year plans attempted to establish consonance between employment opportunities and available manpower through such measures. But India has had extremely limited success. Indian plans have invariably carried forward rising backlogs of unemployment from each preceding to successive five-year plan. Thus, while importance of physical balances and consistency have been recognised and even over emphasised need for balances between manpower supplies and demand has either been totally overlooked or grossly underestimated (Cf. Kindleberger, 1956, p. 147).

(2) Second facet of materials' balance relate to the determination of an optimal pattern of location of production facilities, on the one hand, and population and employment growth on the other. Production units may be so located as (a) minimises transport costs, (b) transport network should synchronise with current and potential requirements to the maximum extent, minimising needs for new facilities and avoidance of possible bottlenecks. If these balances are transgressed, transport bottlenecks will be converted into resource constraints to growth. For example, in the case of coal accumulated at coal-pits, while power plants and factories operate below capacity due to shortage of coal since piling mountains of coal could not be moved from coal-pits to production centres due to want of railway wagons. This highlights the importance of synchronisation of demand for and supply of commodities, human and physical capital, and intermediate inputs, both in time and space.

Relief employment deftly covered imbalances between manpower supplies and employment opportunities in India and China during first plan.China and Japan took adequate care of this balance in their second plans. Manpower imbalances reflect not only mismatches between education and economy, but it also highlights imbalance between demographic growth and economic development.

Location balances are as important as temporal and physical balances between demand and supplies of commodities and manpower. Locational balances have initially been overlooked both in India and China. Migration reflects spatial imbalances between location specific demand for manpower and its supply for employment due mainly to regional inequalities of population growth and economic and educational development.

The temporal and locational patterns of production should ensure full utilisation of local resources, including human capital on the one hand, and adequate supplies of non-local materials to match local demand on the other. Only then dovetailing of commodity and human resource supplies into spatial and time patterns of resource requirements could be effected. Locational balances have not always characterised planning in India or elsewhere, especially during early stages of planned development, though subsequently greater care has been exercised. In the field of education, locational balances have often been transgressed, leading to excessive pressure of numbers in urban and underutilisation of intake capacities in rural areas (Prakash, 1977). China's first plan has also displayed locational imbalances. Locational balance received better attention in the second and subsequent plans of China 'as to the geographical distribution of industries, the policy is to combat the tendency towards over concentration and that towards neglect of correlation (China's Second Five Year Plan, Quoted from Malenbaum).

(3) Physical targets of production of goods and services are required to be balanced by the provision of matching financial resources. If financial allocations to different sectors and segments of the monetised economy fall short of requirements, physical resources may also remain under or unutilised. Alternatively, prices of commodities and factor rewards will have to fall below equilibrium levels, unleashing recessionary phase. An excess supply of finances will release inflationary pressures in the economy. In the first five-year plan of India, financial allocations fell short of physical targets of production. But the second plan attempted to 'modify money income flows so as to maintain a balance between the supply of consumer goods and the purchasing power available for being spent on them' and a 'balance between savings and investment' and between 'receipts and payments abroad' was to be maintained. (The Second Five Year Plan)

Draining of financial resources, reflected by more than unit deposit-credit ratios for rural areas and developing regions, also manifest spatial imbalances. Spatial imbalances have percolated to educational development, leading to underutilisation of facilities in rural and pressure of numbers in urban areas.

Balancing of financial and physical resources as an essential as the matching of sectoral output targets with demand. Obviously, centralised planning and materials' balances strategy of planning were developed in USSR.

Thus, the plan focused attention both on internal and external balances between physical and financial resources, on the one hand, and the equilibrium between demand and supply of resources, on the other. But unprecedented inflation and foreign exchange crisis during the second plan belied expectations. Periodic foreign exchage crunch and perpetual inflation and deficit financing in all subsequent plans reflect the transgression of this balance in the Indian planning. It is distressing to observe that the financial and physical resources allocated to education in different five-year plans in India have invariably fallen short of output (enrolments) targets, resulting in the dilution of quality of stock inputs, though the flow requirements have been adequately met, by and large. Consequently, quantitative expansion resulted in compromise with quality, especially of infrastructure (Prakash, 1977). Besides construction of campuses of educational institutions were invariably delayed because the supplies of such materials as cement and steel seldom matched their requirements, though financial allocations, were made both in macro and micro budgets. This highlights the importance of balancing the matching of financial and physical resource allocations.

These trends of development continued up to the third five-year plan. Attempts have been made to reverse the trend. During the seventies and the eighties, focus shifted to (a) consolidation of quantitative gains rather than to further accelerate quantitative growth, and (b) for plugging the gaps in infrastructural and instructional facilities for education. Qualitative improvements have emerged as the major goal of educational planning. Besides, education has grown ahead of population and economy, resulting in mismatches between economic growth and output of educated manpower.

(4) Requirements of all intermediate goods are needed to be matched with the sectoral production targets. This determines

sectoral consistency of planning. Mismatching of requirements of such goods as railway wagons, metallic and chemical intermediate goods with their production and import targets pushed the Indian economy into recession towards the close of the sixties. Even in the former USSR, materials' balances strategy could be transformed into a comprehensive and efficient instrument of planning only after the experience gained from the first two plans guided the planners thereafter to avoid earlier mistakes. It is but natural that the countries like India, China, and Poland have taken time to acquire proficiency in materials' balances strategy of planning. Input-output and programming techniques are highly useful tools for consistency planning that does not transgress resource constraints and conforms to materials' balances in terms of physical, financial and human resources.

Centralised planning and materials' balances strategy of planning originated in Russia after the Bolshevik Revolution of 1917. It subsequently percolated from there the East European countries such as Hungary, Poland, Romania, Czechoslovakia, and Yugoslavia. China, among the socialist countries, and India, among the developing economies, attempted to (a) avoid the mistakes of pioneering Russian planners, on the one hand, and (b) incorporate indigenous institutional structures and experiences into their respective planning models rather than totally imitating the Russian model blindly.

Approaches to Planning

Two approaches to educational planning may broadly be distinguished; (a) Business Economics Approach and (b) Welfare Economics Approaches. Conventional distinctions between different approaches are encompassed within these two broad groups of approaches to planning. Specificity of planning to temporal stages of development and its spatial dimensions compel planners to opt for specific approach and strategy of planning. Modernisation of social structure, institutional set-up, organisational forms, and rapid economic development embody all activities and sectors of the economy, including education. But planning itself is affected by the pattern of social organisation and economic structure in operation.

Either business economics or welfare economics, approach may guide to development planning. (Tinbergen, p. 4). Business economics approach to development planning seeks to maximise growth of income from given investment. Alternatively, planners seek to minimise investment required for given output and its growth. In the first case, given investment in plan projects and programmes is made to go to the farthest in yielding income/ benefits. Levels of living of the masses may or may not improve perceptibly, even though income may grow phenomenally primarily because maximum surpluses may be mobilised for investment rather than for raising living standards in the short run. Social welfare, defined as total satisfaction from consumption, may not be maximal in the immediate run. But the short run maximal growth will facilitate maximisation of consumption, and hence, maximisation of social welfare in the long run. In the second case, level of income and its growth is given a *priori,* while investment required for it is sought to be minimised. Standards of living may or may not rise in the immediate run. These are alternative routes of solving the same problem. Naturally, both solutions have identical values.

Impact of growth on the standards of living depends upon pattern of growth, and the proportion of surpluses utilised for investment. If the pattern of development is dominated by the growth of capital and intermediate goods industries, their entire output emerges as investible surplus. This limits the growth of living standards, despite the growth of incomes. If development is dominated by the growth of agriculture and consumer goods industries, surpluses will be available, by and large, for consumption. This will lower the pace of development, though levels of living will rise relatively faster. Obviously, approach and strategy of planning determine the nature of short and long run objectives of the development or vice versa.

Approach of welfare economics views development as the means to maximise social welfare. Overall social welfare is sought to be maximised. The approach does not directly focus either on maximisation of (a) income or its growth, and (b) growth gains of plan projects/programmes, or (c) minimisation of investment for reaching the given income level and its growth. But for the analysis of temporal and spatial patterns of welfare maximisation is important. Conceptualisation of welfare, its measurement, and distribution over time, among spatial units, groups of people and even individuals within groups are important aspects. Maximisation of welfare in the immediate run may ultimately lower long run welfare or vice versa. All regional components of the economy and groups of individuals may not gain equally, while possible conflicts in group interests may pull welfare in opposite directions. Therefore, temporal and spatial pattern and sharing of costs and benefits of development among different regions and groups of people have a direct bearing upon planning and planned development through this approach. The choice between two approaches is neither easy nor unambiguous, nor it is clear.

Both approaches are normative insofar as the choice between maximisation of either growth or welfare as the goal of development planning is based on ideology. Optimisation may, however, reflect rationality as optimisation of the objective function, is guided by methods that objectively reckon the given conditions and constraints rationally. Hence, differences between both the ends and means distinguish these approaches.

Operating Economic Regime

Policy, approach and strategy of planned development are derived largely from the nature of economic system in operation. In the narrow sense, economic system is considered to be exogenous. In the broader sense, choice of economic system may be guided by objective conditions and constraints and relative merits and demerits of alternative systems. Only such system may be chosen as is characterised by instruments, means, and mechanisms, the essential components of systems, as is capable of yielding optimum outcomes. Consideration of impacts on development of alternative systems may thus be the decisive determinant of optimality of the system. Choice of approach and strategy of development planning depends on institutional set-up, organisational structure, patterns and stages of development of the economy. An optimum economic system may require private interests to be coterminous with social interests and individual decisions to coincide with the optimum social well-being (Cf. Tinbergen, pp. 80-82).

Underdevelopment of almost all sectors of the economy, all segments of society, and backwardness of socio-cultural and politico-institutional structures of the countries of the Third World necessitate comprehensive approach to planned development. Planning imparts an impetus to the selection of only the optimum from all available options and choices. As impulses of modernisation spread, changes in almost all spheres of life and human activities, going beyond 'economy' or 'purely economic spheres' become 'desirable goals of the development'. Whereas interventions become 'apt for policy', whenever these are warranted by backwardness and underdevelopment (Cf. Myrdal, p. 170). Improvement in nutrition, hygiene, housing , sanitation, health, education, banking, insurance, transport, communications administration, cultural and psychological barriers to change, and rigidities of social stratification directly contribute to development. Scarcity of resources and technical viability force selectivity in development approach regarding location of such mega projects as multipurpose dams, basic and heavy goods industries, requiring heavy capital investment and highly specialised resource endowments. Impulses of growth are then conveyed from centre to periphery only through the spatial dispersion of economic infrastructure and social overheads; while education mitigates socio-cultural barriers to change and it removes blocks to growth. (Prakash and Rajan, 1977; Prakash and Mohapatra, 1980). It is, therefore, natural to infer that state policies focused on the improvement of non-economic conditions have an instrumental value for development. Unwanted socio-cultural conditions act as barriers to modernisation, perpetuate inefficient administration, while inadequacy of economic infrastructure and social overheads constitute constraints and bottlenecks to development (Cf. Myrdal, p. 170). 'Planning', therefore, 'becomes the development intellectual matrix of the entire modernization ideology' (Myrdal, p. 711).

Limitations and imperfections of the market mechanism, purporting to promote welfare, and success of controls and regulations as instruments of management of wartime shortages and equitable distribution of available supplies, persuaded policy makers to tilt towards centralised planning. As against this, experiences with centralised planning through extensive controls and regulations, purporting to promote both growth and welfare, have resulted in serious failures and suboptimal outcomes. This has not only disenchanted the masses with the growth performance but it has also disillusioned analysts and supporters of this approach, resulting in a move towards market oriented decentralised planning. Planning may, therefore, be approached either through price mechanism, or through widespread network of state controls, regulations and licensing. This does not preclude the existence of private, cooperative, and joint sectors to operate along with public sector. Within the price mechanism, dual system of pricing may also be used as an instrument of inducing private investment into planned directions and effecting more equitable distribution of goods and services. Foodgrains, sugar, cement and steel industries of India used the instrument of dual pricing. Thus, planning has either to accept the institutional and organisational structure to be exogenously fixed, within the framework of which the approach, strategy, and methods of planning will then be determined optimally. Alternatively, inherited social and organisational structures and institutional set-up will be discarded in favour of those warranted by preferred approach to planning. Whereas Western economies and some developing countries favoured the first option, the former USSR, China, India, and numerous other developing economies opted for the second alternative. Countries like India chose the middle path of using existing structures as best as possible, while new structures were instituted wherever needed. But its mixed economic structure has to put up with the limitations and shortcomings of both the systems.

Macro Planning Approach

While the former USSR developed central planning, macro economic planning was developed by the capitalist countries of the West. Capitalist macro planning focused on periodic cyclical fluctuations, necessitating state interventions through short run policies of stabilisation of either Keynesian or Friedmanian variety on the one hand, and sustenance of the long-term growth, on the other. Like central planning, macro planning refers to the planning of the national economy as a whole. But unlike centralised planning, macro planning deals only with macro aggregates and average, and it uses selective fiscal and monetary instruments rather than direct controls and regulations. The fiscal and monetary instruments focus both on incentives and disincentives to private initiatives. Whereas centralised planning deals both with the short and long-term management and development of the economy. Capitalist macro planning deals mainly with the short-term management with a view to put the economy on its development path and normal functioning. 'Statistical concept and method of social accounting, Keynesian or Neo-Supply Side Economic Policy Prescriptions, and reliance on market mechanism to respond to monetary and fiscal instruments led to the emergence of macro planning. This ultimately culminated in economywise macro econometric models, whose capability to explain and forecast economic phenomena comprehensively furnish guidelines for development planning. Continuous expansion of the range and scope of such models have facilitated the formulation of Computable General Equilibrium (CGE) models. Computable General Equilibrium models converge rapidly towards comprehensive planning models. CGE resembles centralised rather than macro planning in detail.

Supply side economic policy prescriptions have staged a resurgence to challenge Keynasianism. But emphasis on monetary and fiscal tools is common both to Keynasianism and Neo-Classicism. Whereas Keynesians emphasis rise in money supply and increase in public expenditure for removing deficiency of demand. Neo-monetarists emphasis reductions in fiscal deficits and public expenditure, and hence, shrinkage in government activities, irrespective of whether the economy is in recessionary or inflationary phase, or whether the economy is growing slowly or rapidly. Wartime experience with controls, rationing and regulations gave necessary confidence to the governments of Western countries to evolve interventionist policies to cope with economic fluctuations and problems of growth and stabilisation by guiding the market into socially useful and desirable channels through regulations and controls. These countries, however, continue to repose faith in the efficacy of the market mechanism to arrive at rational and optimum decisions in a decentralised fashion. Their policy interventions are designed to release appropriate signals to the markets for their guidance. Mostly fiscal and monetary instruments are relied upon to perform this function of guiding the market forces. It is implicitely believed that abnormalities and aberrations of market operations need corrections through market interventions. Alternatively, state is supposed to supplement rather than substitute, stimulate, and reinforce rather than control and regulate the market.

These two approaches have recently tended to converge towards each other. Western countries have also used such detailed methods of research and analysis for policy formulation as input-output, programming and general equilibrium analysis. Development of such techniques and their use in practical application have been facilitated by new developments in mathematics, statistics, and econometrics, emergence of powerful computers for complex numerical analysis, and availability of extensive data. These methods and tools of analysis are extensively used to test internal consistency of comprehensive plans, evaluate policy impacts and examine repercussions of changes due to interrelatedness of modern economic structures. Then, the developed world as a whole has been keenly interested in the development of the developing countries, on the one hand, and learning and benefiting from each others' experiences, facilitating convergence of different models, methods, strategies, and approaches to planning, on the other. Market oriented macro planning uses selective fiscal and monetary instruments to guide the market. Computable

General Equilibrium models resemble central planning rather than macro planning in detail. Macro and centralised planning have, however, been converging towards each other recently.

Russian priority to the development of heavy and basic goods industries, mechanisation and collectivisation of agriculture and low priority to consumption goods sectors have facilitated rapid industrialisation and accelerated development of the economy. The long run growth of consumer goods industries was assumed to depend on the short run growth of heavy and basic goods industries. Backward linkages of consumer goods sectors and forward linkages of heavy and basic goods sectors furnish the basis of this assumption. But the time lags between income generation, and hence, demand creation, and production of investible, and consumable surpluses to match the anticipated demand for different varieties of goods, need careful analysis. Mismatches between the demand for and supply of consumer and producer goods will otherwise lead to the constraining of growth on the one hand, and inflation/deflation on the other. The strategy of development of basic goods industries ahead of other sectors of the economy and its rationale may be inferred from the opinion of Strumilin, Chief of Gosplan, (former Soviet Planning Commission) that the heavy and basic goods industries would have to grow at a rate of 18 per cent, if consumer goods sectors were to expand by 10 per cent per annum. This strategy resulted in low supply of foodgrains and other consumer goods, and hence, lower levels of living, accentuating popular discontent. Heavy goods development strategy has, however, facilitated rapid growth of (i) Production capacity, (ii) R & D, and (iii) scientific and technical manpower. All these factors accelerated development of the economy. This was achieved by mass base of elementary education and rapid growth of science and technology education in the former USSR. High priority to education in the Soviet planning facilitated both accelerated development and industrialisation. Education and electricity have, in fact, been accorded as high a priority as heavy and basic goods industries in its planning.

The former USSR as well as other countries have drawn appropriate lessons subsequently from such experiences.

Monetary rewards to enthuse the people, especially the peasantry, and to some extent decentralisation of decision making have been introduced into the Soviet planning. China has attempted to achieve second agricultural revolution through cooperative farming under planning to sustain industrialisation and also to close the gap between the rich and the poor peasantry, first revolution having been achieved before the dawn of planning era. Then, household industries and handicrafts have been accorded great importance in the first and the second plans for generating employment and augmenting supplies consumer goods. Lifu-Chun, Chairman, the Chinese Planning Commission, on the eve of the launching the second plan, declared 'local industries and handicrafts in the country, to play an important part in supplying the needs of both the urban and rural population'. India also relied upon small and cottage industries and traditional handicrafts for generating employment and supply of basic necessities.

Educational Planning

Concepts, theories, and policies of educational planning were developed before the development of the corresponding concepts, theories, and practice of economic planning in some cases, while educational planning has generally been led by conceptual and methodological developments in economic planning.

Planning for the development of the economy is usually comprehensive in nature and scope. This somehow has been the case in socialist and mixed developing economies. Economic planning has, therefore, to focus on the planning of the development of all sectors of the economy, regions of the country and segment of the population. Special attention has, however, to be paid to the intricate and complex web of interrelations based on interdependence among different sectors, especially those sectors of the economy which are assigned a pivotal role in development. Education is one such sector. Educational planning, therefore, constitutes an essential and inseparable part of economic planning. Educational planning belongs to the core of economic planning. The post Second World War perspectives have made education the focal point of socio-economic development. However, development of the concepts, theories, and policies of educational planning preceded the development of the concepts, theories, and practice of the economic planning in some cases, while educational planning has generally been led by conceptual and methodological developments in economic planning.

General concept of educational planning is modelled easily on the pattern of the concept of economic planning. Educational planning may, therefore, be defined as the process of deliberate choice of the projects, programmes, and policies designed to attain well defined and predetermined objectives of educational development. The objectives of educational development are directly related to the socio-economic development of a country/region. This definition of educational planning will have all the essential features that have been discussed in relation to the conceptualisation of economic planning. This definition will, however, be relevant for macro educational planning. Besides, some further discussion and elaboration may be needed for the proper conceptualisation of the objectives of educational development as these may partly be internalised and endogenous to the particular stage of development of education, and these may partly be derived from and/or embodied in the wider socio-economic objectives of development: Maximisation of the internal efficiency of educational system, both at micro and macro levels, has always been and will continue to be among the primary objectives of educational planning. The drop-out rates at the elementary stage of education, pass ratios of the various levels and types of education, degree of departure of actual from optimum unit real resource costs, etc., are important indicators of internal efficiency of an educational system/institution at any given point of time, whereas the temporal movements in these indices highlight the degree and direction of change in the internal efficiency. As there is always some scope for improvement, educational planners normally include improvement in internal efficiency among important objectives of educational planning.

External efficiency of education is as important as the internal efficiency. Internal and external efficiencies are highly related.

Spatial location of schools, levels and patterns of creation of intake capacities and their levels and patterns of utilization, extent of coverage of 6 to 14-year old children by the school system, levels and patterns of unemployment, nature of employment of manpower with each level and type of education, degree and direction of utilization of available educational facilities by different strata of population and patterns of spatial and personnel distribution of educational services associated with given patterns of development of education of different levels and types are some of the important indicators of external efficiency of education. The objectives of equity and welfare may capture numerous socio-economic objectives, including prevention of transmission of present into future generational inequalities of income through equalisation of educaticnal opportunities. However, one has to be fully conscious of the possible outcomes of planned development and each policy package. Mutual trade offs between policy packages and specific outcomes that are expected to flow from their respective implementation have to be worked out by planners in advance.

The objectives and concept of educational planning may, however, depend upon the approach adopted for planning. Following major approaches to educational planning have been distinguished in literature; (a) rates of returns to educational investment, (b) manpower requirements, (c) social demand, correlation/regression, (d) international comparison, and (e) development indicators.

Rates of Returns Approach

Educational planners are usually interested in determining the optimum levels and patterns of resource allocation between (i) educational and non-educational sectors of the economy, and (ii) various subsectors of education. Resource allocation to education has been determined by the socio-political and economic processes. The chief objective of educational planners is to allocate educational budget among different levels and different types of education. Then, resources allocated to each level and type of education optimally distributed among various institutions so as to maximise returns to overall investment in education. Alternatively, the guiding principle of the educational planner is to minimise the cost of producing the given amount of education of each level and type, which is considered to be preferable (Prakash, 1977, 1997; Prakash and Chowdhury, 1995). This is the prime objective planning of educational development, if the planning approach is based on rates of returns to investment in education. In such cases, educational planning may be defined as the deliberate choice of the best pattern of resource allocation from alternative resource allocation patterns. That pattern of resource allocation adopted will lead to (i) equalisation of the returns to investment in educational and non-educational sectors of the economy, (ii) equalisation of returns to investment in different levels and types of education, and (iii) equalisation of returns to investment in institutions of different levels and types of education. Thus, the above objective and concept of educational planning have been derived from the specific approach of rates of returns on educational investment on which educational planning is based.

Manpower Requirements Approach

Manpower requirements furnish an alternative approach to educational planning. If this approach is adopted, the chief function of education will be to supply such quantities of manpower with specific level and type of education at each point of time and spatial location which approximately match manpower requirements with the given levels and types of education of current as well as future development of commodity production. Educational planning may, therefore, refer to the process of scheduling the inputs of students' labour and time into the production processes of education of various levels and types so as to bring them out into the economy as finished products, that is, qualified manpower with different levels and types of educations to meet the manpower need. Supplies of qualified manpower are thus to be dovetailed appropriately into the spatial and temporal patterns of investment and output so as to match these with requirements of manpower, having each level and type of education, of different sectors of the economy at different points of time, locations and organisations. This definition of educational planning is obviously different from the preceding one. Outcomes of the policy packages that may correspond to each of these approaches may also differ significantly.

Manpower Planning

Manpower planning should not be confused with the concept of manpower requirements. The conventional concept and the theory of manpower planning have been based on the direct relationship between the production sectors of an economy and its educational system. But the most important and the strongest link between the economy and education in a society is generally forged through the interrelations between the demand for human capital generated by production sectors of the economy and supplies of manpower that emanate from the educational sector. According to one view, the single most important function of educational system is to furnish and equip the students with skills and abilities that will be required for the operation of commodity production processes. Therefore, the educational system must be geared to meet the manpower needs of the economy. The manpower requirements or needs will have to be derived from the levels and patterns of output various goods and services from the technological interrelations between output of goods and services and their manpower requirements. The levels and patterns of output of various goods and services will, however, depend upon the levels and patterns of allocation of physical capital and other inputs among different production sectors of the economy. The conventional approach, therefore, focuses upon the enabling and constraining influences of physical capital on output, whereas the growth promoting role of human capital remains dormant. This is in-built, at least partially, in the concept and design of conventional manpower planning, which has almost exclusively concentrated on the determination of manpower requirements on the basis of planned growth of sectoral output of goods and services. This has appropriately been called the forecasting, or the projecting of manpower requirements as are enclosed in the planned production targets. However, the projection of the unknown values of any variable(s) is generally based on the past trends, whereas the planning postulates deliberate and conscious policy interventions in the autonomous working of the market mechanism and the foreseeing and/or predicting the likely outcomes of these decisions so that the actual results do not diverge from the desired outcomes and objectives of planning. Therefore, alteration of the observed course for moving the economy on to its desired developmental path is the essence of planning, include the planning of employment and education. Therefore, concepts and theories of manpower planning should be much broader and more exhaustive in nature and scope than the much too narrow and technical concept of projections of manpower requirements.

Manpower planning may refer to the deliberate and conscious choices of such programmes of human resource development from the feasible alternatives as are consistent with socio-economic needs of development planning on the one hand, and the needs and objectives of planned educational development, on the other. Manpower planning should seek to ensure those temporal and spatial patterns of development and accumulation of human capital of each level and type, which will match the levels and patterns of demand for manpower to meet the socio-economic needs so that neither the supply bottlenecks will constrain growth nor education will produce manpower of any level and type that will exceed demand. It implies that the development of commodity production and education sectors of the economy should be balanced. Besides, actual levels and patterns of utilisation of human resources, that are available at any given point of time, should correspond to the optimum levels and patterns. It requires that the manpower planner should be able to determine the expected levels and patterns of (i) demand, and (ii) supply of each level and type of manpower. Then, those levels and patterns of economic growth and educational development can be worked out which will equalise demand and supply of (i) places in educational institutions, and (b) output of manpower and job opportunities at each point of the planning horizon. This will necessitate equilibrium between (i) supply and demand for goods and services, (ii) demand for capital and other material inputs for the planned growth of production of goods and services and their allocation between different sectors, (iii) supply of manpower and its demand, and (iv) demand for places and intake capacities of educational institutions (Prakash, 1977; Prakash & Chowdhury, 1996). But the optimum levels and patterns of human resource development will flow only from those levels and patterns of resource allocation between sectors producing goods and services and human capital which strike balances between all above variables. It envisages a simultaneous change in (a) development strategy; (b) effective planning and proper utilisation of available manpower as well as physical resources; and (c) balancing the process of growth.

The following are the objectives and the major thrusts area of manpower planning: (i) monitoring and evaluating the employment conditions in various segments of labour market, (ii) furnishing estimates of additional employment by levels and types of education for the elimination of current unemployment or underemployment on the one hand, and for the absorption of additions to current job-seekers expected to flow from current operational levels of educational processes; (iii) in case of general or specific shortages, estimates of additional manpower by levels and types of education should be furnished along with the detailed information about the occupations and sectors, bearing the impact of shortages and methods adopted by employers to overcome these shortages along with the temporal patterns of shortages, output levels, and changes in production techniques, production designs, and production mixes, if any, (iv) full and timely information about these should be transmitted both to economic and educational planners so as to facilitate the designing and implementation of appropriate policy responses to the emerging scenario, (v) determination of the impact of structural changes upon labour absorption capacity of the economy as a whole, its constituent sectors and their occupational patterns in the course of movements of the economy from lower to higher stages of development, and from less to more efficient techniques of production. At each stage, structural changes and determination of their employment implications will furnish the base for the determination of manpower development programmes in the short, medium and long runs with reference to the behavioural propensities of labour and education markets; (vi) appropriate policy packages for moving the actual towards the designed behavioural paths of labour and educational markets have to be evolved and tested, (vii) overall demand for manpower has to be decomposed into sectoral, skill, trainings and educational components so as to facilitate the transmission of appropriate signals from the production to education sectors of the economy for necessary and timely initiation of requisite responses, (viii) similarly, signals emanating from educational sectors regarding the number of graduates with their levels and types of education likely to be released at each point of planning horizon should be transmitted to commodity production sectors, policy makers and labour market of the economy, while emerging changes in demographic and commodity production sectors should be available to economic, employment and educational planners (Cf. Prakash, 1977; Cf. Parnes, 1964).

Social Demand Approach

Social demand offers another alternative to the above approaches to educational planning. Under this approach, the chief objective of educational planners will be to arrange the supply of places in educational institutions of various levels and types so as to ensure that the social demand for these places is satisfied at all the temporal points of planning horizon and spatial locations of demand. Therefore, educational planning may refer to deliberate choice of such policy packages, projects and programmes of educational development as will ensure the supply of places in the institutions of various levels and types that correspond to the temporal and spatial patterns of social demand for these places. It is imperative that the action required for capacity generation synchronises with the emergence of demand both and in its temporal and spatial dimensions. But social demand for education need not necessarily coincide with the aggregate of private demand for education. Demand for education may be defined as desire backed up by willingness and ability to pay for education on the one hand, and possession of eligibility for admission into an educational institution, on the other (Prakash, 1977; Prakash and Chowdhury, 1992). We find that those who appear in tests for admission into IITs, IIMs, Regional Engineering Colleges, and Medical Colleges far outnumber those who are finally selected for admission. Thus, the aggregate of private demand exceeds aggregate supply determined by planners and policy makers. As against this, policy makers have been striving hard to realise the goal of UEE. Numerous parents do not send their children to attend schools, though schools are accessible and intake capacities remain underutilised. In this case, aggregate of private demand is deficient. Social demand may, therefore, be defined as the number of places that public authorities deem desirable to supply. Supply of places by public authorities will manifest major objectives of educational development.

Correlation/Regression Approach

Education and economy are bidirectionally related. Capacity of an economy to invest in education depends upon national and per capita incomes. National and per capita incomes, in turn, depend upon the stage of development. Higher the development stage, greater shall be the national and per capita incomes. This will enable the country to accelerate its development further by relatively more investment in production of goods and education. If, however, the development stage of the economy is low, its national and per capita incomes will be low. Consequently, capacity to invest in education will be limited which will also limit the growth of the economy. As against this, the current stage of development, and hence, national and per capita incomes of a country, are determined by investment in the physical and human capital in the preceding periods. Human capital formation depends largely upon investment in education. In view of both visible and invisible interrelations between economy and education, some analysts advocated that right amount of educational investment at any given point in time may be inferred from the coefficient of correlation between national or per capita income and the level of educational development.

The correlation coefficient may be estimated either from cross section or time series data. Time series data will obviously pertain only to one particular country or region, while cross section data may relate to different countries or different regions of the same country. The exercise on the basis of which this approach was advocated used intercountry data. But the proponent(s) of this approach overlooked the following facts: (i) current investment in education prepares manpower for future development, hence, current students, where education investment is made, do not contribute either to national or per capita income, though they will decided be an asset for future when (a) they join the labour force, and (b) they are deployed for productive work; and (ii) coefficient of correlation does not indicate causal relation between variables. In any case, it cannot be decided on the basis of statistics as to which variable is the determinant and which is the determined variable. We have already discussed above the nature of bidirectional interrelations between economy and education. The type of the inference which had been drawn by the proponents of this approach from their estimates of correlations would have been justified if current income was regressed on past educational investment (Prakash, 1977).

International Comparison

This is a simple approach. It suggests that an economically and educationally less developed economy may examine the nature and quantum of educational investment made by a currently developed country, or a group of countries, when their level of development is comparable to that of the country under consideration. The approach assumes that the development path is uniform irrespective of significant differences between socio-cultural structures and patterns of the economies of different countries when they happen to be at comparable stages of development.

Composite Index of Development

Harbison and Myers compiled a composite index of development for countries at differential levels of development. They used data pertaining to a large number of variables that reflected the nature of relationship between educational and general development. Such indices suggested the broad directions of educational development, though exact magnitudes of educational investment and other educational variables are difficult to infer from such coefficients.

The above discussion establishes the pivotal role of basic objectives in the conceptualisation of educational planning. One may suspect that different approaches, and hence, the concepts based on them, are independent of each other. This is neither the case in theory nor in practice. Private decisions to invest in education of a particular level and type are governed largely by differences in the probabilities of employment or unemployment and expected earnings after the completion of specific level and type of education. But probability of future employment is generally reckoned by individuals on the basis of current state of labour market. If current supplies exceed demand, it will reflect both low employment probability in future and even lower expected earnings. It may induce the shrinking in current private demand for that level and type of education. As against this, if current demand for any given level and type of education is too high relative to future job openings, it will eventually lead to a fall both in employment probability and earnings associated with that of education. The Indian empirical evidence lend a very strong support to this hypothesis. Therefore, the theoretical 'either' and 'or' categorisation of social demand, rate of returns and manpower requirements approaches to educational planning may be inappropriate. There is an urgent need for both theoretical and empirical explorations to workout the complex web of mutual relations of these approaches and their implications for educational planning (Prakash and Chowdhury, 1996).

The structured discussion of the concepts of economic, educational, and manpower planning has also highlighted the linkages and interrelations among different approaches to educational planning.

References

Anderson and Bowman (1959), Theoretical Considerations in Educational Planning. In Blaug, Mark (Editor) *Economics of Education.* Vol. I, Penguin.

Govt. of China, *Second Five Year Plan.*

Harbison, F. and Myers, C.A. (1964), *Education, Manpower, and Economic Growth: Strategies of Human Resource Development,* McGraw Hill.

Kindelberger, Charles, P. (1956), *Economic Development.* McGraw Hill.

Mahalanobis, P.C. (1962), *Essays on Economic Planning,* Statistical Publishing Society, Calcutta.

Malenbaum, W. (1956), India and China: Development Contrasts. In *Journal of Political Economy.*

Myrdal, Gunnar (1953), *Economic Theory and Underdeveloped Regions,* Vora, Bombay.

Myrdal, Gunnar (1970), *Asian Drama—An Enquiry into Poverty of Nations,* Vol. I, II, III, Pantheon, New York.

Parnes, H. S. (1964), Manpower Analysis in Educational Planning. In Parnes, H.S. (Ed.) *Planning Education for Economic and Social Development,* O.E.C.D., Paris.

Prakash, S. (1976), Input Output Models of Education with Applications to Indian Data. In Mathur, P.N. (Editor) *Economic Analysis in Input Output Framework,* Vol. III, Input Output Research Association.

Prakash, S. (1977), *Educational System of India: An Econometric Study,* Concept, New Delhi.

Prakash, S. & Rajan P. (1978), Regional Inequalities of Rural Development in Madhya Pradesh. In *The Indian Journal of Regional Science.*

Prakash, S. & Mohapatra, A.C. (1980), Economic Development: A Study of Inter-Temporal and Intra-Regional Variations in Madhya Pradesh (India). In *Third World Planning Review.*

Prakash, S. (1989), *Analytical and Historical Perspectives of Educational Planning.* Review Conference on Four Decades of Development, Ministry of Human Resource Development, Government of India, and NIEPA, New Delhi, April 14-15.

Prakash, S. and Buragohain, T.J. (1989), *An Inter-Industry Model of Economic Effect of Education.* In Proceedings of National Workshop on Economics of Education, July 21-22, NIEPA, New Delhi.

Prakash, S. and Buragohain, T.J. (1992), *Theoretical and Methodological Base of Education-Economy Nexus and Economic Value of Education.* In Proceeding of Plenary Sessions of XI International Conference on Input Output Techniques, Seville, Spain.

Prakash, S. & Chowdhury, S. (1992), A Probabilistic Approach to Private Demand for Education. In *Manpower Journal.*

Prakash, S. & Chowdhury, S. (1996), *Expenditure on Education: Theory, Growth, and Models,* NIEPA, New Delhi.

Prakash, S. (1997), *Cost of Education: Theoretical Explorations and Empirical Prognostication,* Anamika, New Delhi.

Strumilin (1930), *Second Seven Year Plan of USSR.*

Tinbergen, Jan (1969), *Centralised Planning*, North Holland.

5

Types of Educational Planning

Development and Educational Planning

Economies of pre-industrial societies are primitive in nature and primarily agricultural in structure. Such economies do not have much demand to put pressure on their educational systems. Education in such societies has moral trappings, philosophical moorings, and religious orientation. Consequently, education has no direct relationship with the economy. It is generally left to individual initiatives, requiring no planning by the state. Industrialisation, however, endows education explicitly with an economic value through the forging of both direct and indirect backward and forward links between education and economy. It has been empirically established that as the economy moves from lower to higher stages of development and from simpler to complex forms of industrialisation and tertiarisation, not only the range of goods and services produced in the economy is enhanced and diversified but the technological base of production is also upgraded. This leads to changes in occupational structure and enhancement of skill and knowledge requirements for employment. Education also undergoes structural transformation along with the economy. Besides, educational technology changes radically which not only raises unit costs but also diversifies the patterns and structures of educational expenditure (Prakash and Chowdhury, 1996). Consequently, backward linkages of education with the economy are deepened and diversified, whereas the backward linkages of the economy with education are also transformed. Naturally, education-economy nexus becomes stronger in this process. Education-economy linkages may be both visible and invisible, and direct and indirect. These education-economy linkages bestow on education economic roles and functions in general and development in particular. The degree and nature of linkages makes the role of education in development pivotal. But education-economy inter-relations are bidirectional rather than unidirectional (Prakash and Buragohain, 1992).

Reign of *laissez-faire* during the first industrial revolution, however, warranted that education, like other socio-economic sectors and activities, remained within the individual rather than social domain. The non-interventionist policy made education almost an exclusive concern of individuals or households. Individuals or their families could buy as much education from private tutors/teachers and institutions as they wished and/or could afford. As against this, the centralised large scale production of goods and services, based on factory/farm rather than guild/manor system, required production of education also to be organised on a mass scale for matching the manpower requirements of the economy with the production of manpower. The new factory system of commodity production, based on modern technology, comprising of mechanical processes, required educational institutions also to be locationally concentrated to produce manpower not only on large scale but the synchronisation of manpower supplies with demand both in time and space was also needed. Manpower production has to be commensurate with the manpower requirements of large scale commodity production. Education has, therefore, to be organised on a factory like centralised system of large scale production, necessitating concentration of large educational institutions at few places/regions, especially in urban areas, experiencing rapid economic growth and industrialisation. The establishment, management, and operation of such educational institutions required supervision and planning by the state. As the concept of welfare state had not emerged as yet, education, like other goods and services, could be purchased and sold in the market according to the needs of the individuals, state planning for its provision and supervision notwithstanding.

> *Unawareness of direct and indirect and short and long run benefits of education among the poor parents made their educational demand dormant, while their low incomes made costs/prices of education unaffordable. These twin facets limited educational demand to the affluent persons of the society. This limited the growth of education as private demand for education did not grow as much as it should have.*

Low incomes of the poor parents made educational costs/ prices of education unaffordable to them, while their ignorance and illiteracy made them oblivious of the direct and indirect and short and long run benefits of education. The second factor made educational demand of the poor dormant, while the first factor put it beyond their reach. These twin factors limited educational demand only to the affluent of the society. This directly impinged upon the growth of education. Demand for education, and hence, educational system did not grow as much as it was warranted by the growth of the economy and structural transformation of society. Utilisation of places in educational institutions, supplied by public authorities, naturally followed private demand for education. It implies that educational development was demand driven rather than supply driven. But educational demand, at least partly if not wholly, is the derived demand. Demand induced educational development needed hardly any planning for removing deficiency of demand for education by public authorities. As private demand for education was concentrated among the rich of largely big industrialised urban centres or affluent land owners, supply was largely confined to urban regions. Planning of education by public authorities was constrained by the policy of *laissez-faire* and the prevalence of ruling rather than welfare state both in precept and practice during the early stages of the first industrial revolution.

> *Planning of education by public authorities was constrained by the policy of laissez-faire and the prevalence of the ruling rather than welfare state.*

Education was treated neither as an industry nor was it sufficiently profitable to attract private investment on commercial scales. Provision of supply and its utilisation was mainly in the individual rather than social domain during the early stages of first industrial revolution.

As education did not yield profits comparable to those fetched by investment in industrial or commercial sectors, and education had not emerged as an industry or business till then it did not enthuse and attract private investors, pursuing profit motive to invest in education to supply places in institutions to common users. Public authorities also do not evince keen interest in educational development as it had not emerged till then as a public or merit good. Therefore, it did not become the public concern till then (Prakash,1977). This may be called pre-compulsory non-free education phase insofar as introduction of an element of compulsion was considered neither necessary nor was it regarded desirable to transform it from education for classes to education for masses. Like other social and economic activities, education was also guided by autonomously operating forces of the market, which required no planning by the state.

Planning of education focused mainly on bringing all children to schools with a view to promote mass literacy in this phase of educational development. Dominance of consumption over investment component of education resulted in relatively low priority to public investment in education, limiting investment in education to the residual investible public funds which were left after meeting priority needs of other sectors.

Transition from the concept of ruling to welfare state and recognition of contribution of education to (i) economic growth, (ii) promotion of social welfare, (iii) psychological factors of behavioural motivation, (iv) social changes, and (v) reduction in intra and intergenerational inequalities of incomes and wealth transferred education from private to public and from autonomous to planning domain (Prakash,1977; Prakash and Buragohain,1992). In early phases of transition, education continued to be received and provided as a consumer service.

Rich and perceptive parents could envisage far-reaching consequences or impacts of educational investment on future careers of children. Entry into high income and prestigious occupations/professions depended upon the training, skills and knowledge. The envisagement of future impacts on careers, and hence, earnings required foresight, perceptivity, enterprise and innovativeness. The poor conspicuously lacked these qualities. Then, the multifarious roles of education were not recognised and conceptualised even by policy makers and analysts. This directly affected the objectives and approaches to educational planning (Cf. Marshall,1961; Prakash,1997).

Planning of education in the second phase of development focused mainly on bringing all children to school with a view to promote mass literacy and social welfare. Dominance of consumption over investment component of education resulted in relatively low priority being accorded to public investment in education. Consumption benefits of education were well recognised. It is, however, empirically impossible to identify and separate consumption from investment component of education (Prakash, 1977) though it may easily be distinguished conceptually. But educational investment for consumption benefits could be afforded only by the rich. Even though employers started recognising positive but imperceptible effect of literacy and education on workers' productivity, yet they did not invest in education. Investment in education was limited to the residual investible public funds that were left after meeting investment needs of other sectors, enjoying higher priority in the scale of public preferences. Subsequent recognition of investment component of education as the source of accumulation of human capital changed the concept, approach and scope of educational planning and led to massive public investment in education. Public investment rose continuously in agricultural extension education, higher, technical, and scientific education, and R & D. Capital component of educational expenditure in such areas is directly visible (See Historical review in Prakash,1997).

Recognition of human capital as an agent of growth transformed not only development economics but it also led to the resurgence of educational economics. The productivity enhancing effect of education and its differential impacts on income in accordance with differential educational endowments of workers attracted attention of policy makers and analysts. Naturally, educational investment emerged as the main concern of economic and educational planning. The emphasis shifted subsequently from quantitative expansion to efficiency, improvement in quality and reforms in educational system. Recognition of education as the main source of R & D also led to the perceptible shifts in intraeducational priorities of planning and investment. R & D comprises of two distinct phases and three different stages of education: (i) generation, (ii) dissemination, and (iii) utilisation of new knowledge on commercial scales for development. First phase is research stage, when new theories are formulated through observation, experiments, analysis and deduction of laws. This is also experimentation, deductive/inductive testing and evaluation phase of logical structure of new hypotheses. This is a laboratory and library phase of research. The developing countries undertake research in adapting and modifying imported technology to suit their requirements. The developed countries generally deny latest technology to the Third World. Developing countries, therefore, undertake imitative research and development, on the one hand, and resort to research based on reverse engineering, on the other.

The second phase of research may lead to the application of new principles and theories to technical problems with a view to test and verify the validity of new knowledge, laws and principles embodying it. In these twin phases of initial stage, knowledge is confined to laboratories, libraries, and experimental fields/stations. Books and journals, carriers and preservers of knowledge, serve the purpose of dissemination of new knowledge on a wider scale.

Economic growth or development depends not only upon the generation, dissemination and utilisation of new knowledge, pertaining to natural and physical sciences and technology. Knowledge about man, his interpersonal relations and psychological motivations of behaviour on the one hand, and natural and economic environment, institutional set-up and organisational structure on the other, are equally important for economic growth and social transformation. Social engineering plays as important roles in economic development and social transformation as science and technology.

In the second stage, new knowledge is conveyed from laboratories and/or libraries to fields/farms/factories on an experimental basis. The purpose is the verification of the validity and potential use of new knowledge on commercial scale. Once the prospect of potential practical use of new knowledge, innovations and inventions is successfully assessed, commercial exploitation of R & D starts. None of these phases and stages of R and D is the concern of people, seeking new knowledge at leisure, or those who routinely engage in teaching and training. Both these stages need originality, perseverence and discipline in the pursuit of knowledge and enterprise for its commercial exploitation. Both these stages have now been completely professionalised and institutionalised. Besides, economic growth and development depend not only upon the generation, dissemination and utilisation of new knowledge pertaining to natural and physical sciences and technology. Knowledge about man, his interpersonal relations, psychological forces underlying his behavioural motivations on the one hand, and natural and socio-economic environment, institutional set-up and organisational structure on the other, are equally important factors of economic growth and agents of social transformation.

Social engineering plays as important role in the economic growth and the social transformation as science and technology. Machines, the carriers of technology, management techniques and organisational methods are invented by man. Besides, the degree of utilisation and its efficacy depends upon man. But new technology, innovative management techniques and strategic organisational methods have to be matched by the capabilities of the men on the job. For the development of such human capabilities, education and training are needed. Hence, educational planning focuses on (i) mass base of elementary education, without which output of secondary and college graduates cannot be raised substantially, and (ii) promotion and nurturing of R & D. Modern R & D is highly costly. It needs expertise of super specialists in different disciplines and extremely expensive equipment and infrastructure. Multi-disciplinary research is team based. These facets of R & D compel even advanced countries to jointly undertake research in frontier areas of knowledge, while it becomes essential for the states to initiate, nurture and finance R & D in all countries of the world, political and ideological differences notwithstanding. Private endeavours at best supplement public efforts and investment in R & D nowadays.

Planning was first evolved for conducting wars and for efficient implementation of chosen strategy of war. Hence, paradigms of planning are as old as the science and art of conducting wars. Concept/ theory of planning gradually percolated from the science and art of conducting warfare to the economy, from where it seeped into social sectors and other areas of human endeavours. The forms and nature of planning have, however, been changing with development of new paradigms, emerging from accumulated knowledge and experiences. Consequently, concepts, nature and scope of planning have not been settled finally even as yet.

Modern R & D is highly expensive, it needs expertise of super specialists in many disciplines, extremely costly equipment and infrastructural facilities, compeling even advanced nations to pool both physical and human resources to jointly undertake research in frontier areas of knowledge. Private entrepreneurs cannot undertake research without government support. This forces governments to initiate, nurture and finance research in all countries of the world, political and ideological differences notwithstanding. Paradigms of planning have first been derived from challenges to solve problems of development. Structural differences between planning practices of different countries manifest their ideological predilections, different socio-economic structures and techniques used in plan formulation.

Paradigms of planning have been influenced by actual practices evolved to solve practical problems and challenges of development. But both the problems and practices change from one stage to another stage of social transformation and economic development. Besides, problems of development and their solutions differ from country to country and time to time. Different methods, policies and practices of development planning have naturally been evolved in different countries. Intertemporal and interspatial differences in planning arose partly from ideological differences, partly from socio-political systems and partly from logical needs of development. Consequently, concepts, approaches, scope, nature, theory, and degree of planning have differed both in time and space. This led to the emergence of different typologies of planning.

Rationale and Basis of Planning Typologies

Planning, both economic and educational, is of numerous types and varieties. Broad typologies and categories of planning in general and educational planning in particular are discussed in this chapter. Planning is, however, not classified randomly. Various criteria may be used to delineate and delimit various typologies and varieties of planning. Differences in the precepts and practices of planning are mainly accounted for by the differences in social and economic orientation either towards market or socialism or mixed economy. The structural differences in planning manifest ideological predelictions of different countries. Differences in the socio-economic and political systems lead to highly marked differences in instruments used for plan formulation and its implementation, objectives, nature and degree of planning.

Different typologies of planning are, therefore, distinguished both conceptually and empirically. Various criteria are used to delineate planning typologies. The main factors and criteria used to delineate planning typologies are as follows: (i) instruments used for formulating and implementing plans, (ii) actors involved in plan formulation and its implementation, (iii) kind of resources involved in plan formulation, (iv) products of planning, (v) methods, techniques and processes of planning, (vi) spatial spread of units planned and scope of planning, and (vii) duration of the planning horizon.

Typologies of Planning

The following planning typologies are generally distinguished in literature on the basis of above criteria: (1) planning by incentives and executive fiats and legislative measures; (2) fiscal/financial and physical planning; (3) comprehensive and indicative planning; (4) micro and macro planning; (5) centralised and decentralised planning; (6) spatial/sectoral and institutional planning; (7) perspective, long and short-term planning; and (8) contingency planning to cope with unforeseen emergencies.

However, certain facets of planning of different types may be overlapping, and hence, planning typologies may not be exclusive. Above typologies and varieties of planning will be discussed both with reference to education and economy.

Planning by Incentives and Administrative Orders

The distinction between planning by incentives and planning by executive fiats and administrative orders is based on differences between instruments of plan formulation and implementation. These typologies of planning furnish examples of classification of planning on the basis of the nature of instruments of plan formulation and implementation. The instruments depend on the economic framework and policy thrusts within which the economy operates. Economic environment is determined by the structure and role of the market in the economy. Three important forms of planning by inducements and incentives may be distinguished: (a) planning by incentives and inducements in a purely market economy, (b) planning by incentives and inducements in a mixed economy, (c) incentives and inducements used in planning in a socialist economy for the realisation of plan objectives through private initiatives to supplement state endeavours. Indicative planning and strategic planning may also be discussed under these rubric categories. Planning by executive fiats and administrative orders is an exclusive type, as it were. It can be practised in a nationalised socialist economy. The former USSR, East European countries and China practised planning by executive fiats and administrative orders till the eighties. Drastic changes have now been introduced in the nature, coverage and methodology of planning in Russia, China and East European countries, erstwhile members of the former Soviet Bloc, since the introduction of structural reforms under the triple processes of globalisation, liberalisation and privatisation. UK and France may be cited as the proponents of planning by incentives and inducements on the one hand, and indicative planning on the other.

Arthur Lewis (1963) was probably the first economist to distinguish planning into different typologies on the basis of instruments used for plan formulation and implementation. He differentiated between planning by inducements and incentives from planning by administrative orders under given operational or policy regimes. Differences between these typologies of planning are also derived from the reliance on market, prices and fiscal tools on the one hand, and state interventions, controls and regulations on the other, in the formulation of plans and realisation of objectives of planning.

Planning by incentives and inducements can be practiced in a purely market or partially or fully mixed economy. Incentives and inducements can also be used in nationalised socialist economies. But incentives and inducements need not necessarily be financial alone; these can be both monetary and non-pecuniary.

Planning exclusively by 'executive fiats' and 'administrative orders' can be practised in a nationalised socialist economy, where either autonomously functioning market does not exist at all, or its role is marginalised by the state. Illustrations of these planning typologies are furnished by the planning in the former USSR, China, and Eastern Europe, on the one hand, and planning in France, US and UK on the other. The first group of countries relied more on administrative and legislative measures for the realisation of objectives of planning, while the second group of countries based the formulation of plans and policies on signals released by the market and left the plan and policy implementation to the autonomous market with a view to attain the goals of planned development. Signals released by the market are used for plan formulation in an effective manner. If prices of certain goods are high, it signals shortages or existence of excess demand, warranting more investment in such sectors to raise productive capacities, and hence, output. If, however, market signals general rather than specific rise in prices, it is a manifestation of inflation, which may require the use of fiscal and monetary policies to contain money supply, fiscal deficits, and public expenditure. In case of demand recession, fiscal and monetary measures to remove the deficiency of demand may be used. Similarly, if parents do not enrol their children in primary or middle schools, scholarships, free midday meals, dress, books, etc., may be provided to encourage such children to enrol. Rajasthan has made education of all levels and types free for girls, while each girl child is provided a stipend of Rs.10 per month on enrolment in schools in Haryana.

Three forms of planning by inducements and incentives in Western countries may also be distinguished. Almost all countries of the West use policy and planning for stabilisation of the economy during the downward or upward phases of cycles. Fiscal measures, monetary policies and public expenditure furnish effective tools of stabilisation. United Kingdom had, however, relied upon nationalisation of certain core industries, infrastructural facilities and social overheads, though it used to leave enough space for private enterprise and its market operations. France had developed indicative planning. Public authorities indicate the directions of changes that private entrepreneurs are expected to initiate. Magnitudes of targets are also specified. These are backed by the state through positive inducements and incentives, while undesirable private initiatives may evoke penalties or punitive measures and taxes.

Under planning by executive fiats, physical controls, regulations, public ownership of means of production and almost complete substitution of private by public sector will be needed. Bureaucracy replaces the market. Market plays hardly any role. Naturally, fiscal and monetary policies or prices do not play their natural roles in such economies. Physical quantities of goods and resources will naturally enter into planning as units of measurement and allocation. Consequently, this type of planning tends to converge towards physical rather than fiscal planning. Besides, planning has to be quite extensive and exhaustive in coverage. In other words, physical planning tends towards comprehensiveness and centralisation. As against this, planning by incentives and inducements ultimately converges to fiscal planning on decentralised basis.

Legislation and policy interventions become essential due to imperfections and failures of the market, making incentives and inducements ineffectual. Since poor parents are unaware of potential benefits of education in future careers of their children, or they do not respond to incentives and display disinterest in investment in children's education, legislative and/or executive measures are invoked even in market economies.

An exclusive reliance either on market and private initiatives, or an exclusive dependence on legislative and administrative measures is neither sufficient, nor is it practicable, or even desirable for achieving social and economic goals of planned development. In the fifties, the UK had to make it obligatory and legally mandatory for parents to admit their children in schools, failing which they faced prosecution. Autonomy and independence given to parents to decide whether to educate or not to educate their children frustrated the public objective of universalisation of elementary education. Incentives and inducements proved inadequate motivators for parents, particular the poor, to enrol children in schools under the debilitating impact of inadequacy of family incomes. The US had also adopted such legislation. Legislative and executive measures become essential if incentives fail to pursuade parents to invest in the education of children, or if they are unaware of potential benefits of education in future careers of their children.

But inducements are not used in market economies alone, while executive fiats are not the sole privilege of the socialist economies. Just as capitalist countries had to use executive fiats and legislative measures to realise the objectives of educational development, similarly, the former USSR and China had to introduce incentives for peasants to enhance production on their small private farms after collectivisation and communisation of farming. It should not be inferred that only socialist countries use executive fiats and administrative orders for realising objectives of planned growth of agriculture or any other sector of the economy. The US as well as the EEC countries practised policies of subsidization and minimum support prices for accelerating agricultural development. Bumper crops used to be burnt standing in fields, or dumped into the sea after harvesting, or used as foreign aid to developing countries under PL 480 by the US in order to ensure that agricultural prices did not fall below the prescribed minimum levels. India uses not only the policy of subsidisation of agricultural inputs but it also lends support to agricultural prices through direct purchases from farmers at minimum procurement prices, announced before harvesting for accumulation of stocks to be used for public distribution. The policy is triple edged as it induces farmers to invest in yield raising inputs for maintaining the momentum of agricultural growth, it safeguards the interest of consumers by distributing foodgrains through PDS at subsidised prices and maintains price stability through market operations by containing inter and intra seasonal price fluctuations within reasonable limits. These policy measures and interventions in the market impart stability to prices. Education of the masses has been promoted through the mixture of elements of both incentives and compulsion. Schools provide free meals and study materials to children in the United Kingdom, while most of the advanced countries of the West provide maintenance grants to students at university level. India has also introduced schemes of free meals and stipends to girls and children of Scheduled Castes and Scheduled Tribes in several states.

Financial and Physical Planning

Nature of resources involved in policies of allocation and investment may also be used to categorise planning into different types. Involvement of monetary or real resources distinguishes financial from physical planning. Under financial planning, money is an accounting, measuring and resource allocation unit. The underlying philosophy is that money is both a medium of exchange and measure of value. As money embodies purchasing power, allocation of financial resources among different sectors manifests the pattern of distribution of real resources. Real resources can be mobilised through fiscal resources. Financial planning relies heavily on fiscal and monetary instruments, which may be used as tools of inducements, incentives and disincentives. Monetary resources, allocated to various sectors, therefore, empower beneficiary sectors to mobilise required physical resources in requisite quantities. It is implicitly assumed that fiscal resources will facilitate acquisition of physical resources commensurate with financial resources. An appropriate matching of financial with real resources is, therefore, envisaged to be achieved, if planning relies exclusively or even largely on financial and monetary instruments.

Financial planning envisages balances between financial and physical resources involved in planning. Balances between financial and real resources depend upon (i) level and structure of current prices and changes in future, and (ii) balances between demand and supplies of goods, services and factors. If prices are stable and physical or real resources are neither surplus nor are these short in supply, financial resources may easily be matched by the mobilisation of real resources of requisite types on adequate scales.

Matching of financial with physical resources of requisite types in adequate quantities at right times and places often poses serious problems. Levels and prices, used for financial resource allocation, differ in time and space. Technological improvements, changes in product designs, incessant inflationary pressures accompanying development, lead to almost continuous changes in the levels and structure of prices. Then, trade, transport and tax margins make prices vary both overtime and space. At times, transport bottlenecks also block movement of goods to desired destinations. Besides, actual output, and hence, supplies of physical quantities may be more or less than the planned supplies. Time over runs in the completion of projects result in cost escalations, necessitating supplementary financial allocations. Thus, the balance between financial and real resources depends upon (i) level and structure of current prices and likely changes in future, and (ii) balances between demand and supplies of goods, services and factors both in time and over space. If prices are stable and physical or real resources are neither surplus nor are these short in supply, financial resources may easily be matched by the mobilisation of real resources of requisite types on adequate scales. Neither prices remain stable through time and over space, nor supply and demand balances obtain in reality. Levels and structures of prices do change in the process of development, and general or specific shortages or surpluses of physical resources do emerge periodically due to the transgression of balances and constraints in plan design itself, or due to inefficient plan implementation, resulting in shortfalls in the achievement of plan targets and goals. All such factors tend to create clevages between fiscal and physical resource requirements. Financial planning has, however, been practised widely in practically all countries of the world both through annual budgets and medium and long run plans.

Mismatching of time-scheduling of supplies and resource requirements, on the one hand, and imbalances between physical and financial resources involved in plan formulation and its implementation, on the other are, decisively exposed by experiences of bottlenecks, constraints, and under or non-utilisation of available resources.

Mismatching of time-scheduling of supplies and resource requirements on the one hand, and imbalances between physical and financial resources involved in plan formulation and its implementation are decisively exposed by experiences of bottlenecks, constraints and under or non-utilisation of available resources. Numerous experiences highlight such deficiencies. Textbooks are often made available to students after prolonged delays. At times, books may arrive in the market/institutions just before the completion of an academic year. Inadequacy of financial resources or limitations of financial planning may not be responsible for this. Timely preparation of textbooks is not sufficient by itself to ensure their availability to students in time.

The distribution of books among students should synchronise both in time and space with their demand. During phenomenal quantitative expansion of education in sixties, large number of school buildings, and equally large number of college and university campuses have to be constructed. Simultaneously, multipurpose dams, irrigation wells, canals, factory buildings, industrial townships, roads, rails, passenger coaches and wagons, power plants, coal mines, bridges, office, and houses have also to be constructed. All such development programmes and projects generated excess demand for such construction materials as cement and steel, resulting in their acute shortages. Even priority allocation of construction materials to education and development projects could not avert the mismatching of financial with physical resources. Materials' imbalance was in-built in inconsistent planning and inefficient plan implementation. This diluted the efficacy of planning.

From fifties to seventies a large number of schools, numerous universities and colleges were established in various parts of India. Whereas Central and State governments and the University Grants Commission had allocated financial funds for the construction of school buildings, and college, and university campuses to these institutions as development grants under the five-year plans. These institutions invariably found it difficult to complete their construction programmes during stipulated time, since monetary grants were not matched by physical resources. Consequently, the construction of new campuses progressed haltingly. The construction had to be stopped for a while, when steel and cement allocated to new institutions was finished. Next round of construction could start only when permits were granted by local supply offices. Such problems lead to bottlenecks and physical resource constraints and inflationary pressures in the economy during the course of development raised costs. Monetary grants are sanctioned on the basis of current prices, shortages of materials inflicts both time and cost overruns, making such projects and programmes unfeasible without supplementary grants. Testing of consistency of output targets and their resource requirements can obviate such problems.

Mismatches between financial and physical resources are not a problem in physical planning. Resources are accounted and allocated in physical units of measurements. Consequently, absence of financial accounting eliminates possible mismatches between physical and financial resources. Prices have not much role to play in physical planning, though use of inducements and incentives as well as disincentives and punishments is not ruled out. This is also compatible with planning by executive fiats and administrative orders. Materials' balances between resource requirements and planned outputs furnish the criterion of consistency. As already discussed earlier, materials' balance strategy had been practised extensively in the former USSR, which is a concrete example of physical planning. As against this, one criticism against the Indian planning is that it has been nothing more than annual budgeting, the five-year plans notwithstanding (Prakash, 1977, 1996, 1997). This is not to deny the fact that the Indian five-year plans express planned targets of output in physical terms.

Indicative and Comprehensive Planning

Public programmes under indicative planning and their guidelines are made known to private agents and operators, who formulate and implement their programmes and policies at the level of production units, according to their own objectives and resource constraints, without violating the guidelines furnished by public authority. The market machanism is instrumental in operationalising both public and private programmes. The plans are continuously modified and adjusted according to the emerging needs of the market at each point of planning horizon. The shortfalls or surpluses in the achievement of targets and goals of both private and public plans furnish criteria for judging the efficacy of planning.

Nature, form, and extent of involvement of public authorities in plan formulation and execution may also be used as a criterion for distinguishing indicative from comprehensive planning. Under indicative planning, public authorities are fully involved in plan formulation, while their involvement in execution is minimal, if not almost nil. They determine only broad objectives and directions of changes in the economy. The public programmes under indicative planning are in the nature of guidelines. These are made known to the private agents and operators to help them in formulating and then implementing their own development programmes and policies at the level of production units. Their projects and programmes have naturally to conform to public objectives on the one hand, and they seek to fulfil their own objectives within their resource constraints on the other. But they are not to violate the guidelines furnished by public authority even if they are motivated by profit maximisation, growth and diversification of their production structure. The market is used for the operationalisation of both public and individual programmes. These programmes are continuously modified and adjusted according to the emerging needs of the market at each point of planning horizon. Shortfalls or surpluses in achieving plan targets and goals of both private and public plans may be used as critieria for evaluating the efficacy of planning. Planning is almost continuously monitored and evaluated.

France developed indicative planning, which it has been practising quite successfully. India has practised indicative planning in the field of school and collegiate education to some extent. Numerous private schools and colleges were established in the expectation of ultimate takeover by the government, failing which grants-in-aid for the payment of teachers' salaries and capital grants for buildings and equipment would have been available. In fact, the policy had been to provide 80-85 per cent of total expenditure incurred by private managements or deficits, whichever was less. Such signals were periodically released by public policy. This encouraged establishment of a large number of private schools, colleges, and research institutes, though universities remained in public domain for long. Recently, legislation had been passed by the Parliament for the establishment of private universities also. Then, towards the close of the seventies, policy underwent a radical transformation. Policy shifts have indicated that private institutions will get public recognition for affiliation and examination without any obligation on government for grants-in-aid, prompting managements to charge full or more than full cost fees from students for school, higher, technical and professional education. Even admissions depend upon capitation fees and/or donations. Meanwhile, shortage of places in public institutions for professional and technical education and ever rising demand from students for such education prompted private enterprises to enter into the field with capitation fee institutions, which function not only in an autocratic manner but they are also motivated by profits.

Under comprehensive planning, public authorities not only formulate detailed and extensive and exhaustive plans but they also shoulder the responsibility of implementing the plans, though private sector may be allowed to supplement public enterprise under the government controls and regulations. The market mechanism will, therefore, play only a subsidiary role, if any, under comprehensive planning. It supplements rather than supplants public sector.

Macro and Micro Theory

Classification of planning into macro and micro typologies is patterned on a similar classification of theory into micro and macro economic theories. For understanding the basic differences between micro and macro planning, it will be useful to discuss the differences between micro and macro economic theories. The size of analytical and planning units are used to distinguish macro from micro planning.

Macro economic theory deals with big entities, while micro theory treats small units. Macro theory, in fact, analyses the system as a whole, as it were, and its micro counterpart treats only parts of the system (Mehta, 1958). Thus, macro economic theory deals with broad entities, having such large magnitudes, aggregates and averages as national income, per capita income, national expenditure on consumption and investment, public revenue and expenditure, total money supply, levels and patterns of resource allocation, exports and imports, foreign exchange reserves, balance of trade and payments, national population and its age and gender structure, total enrolments and enrolment ratios, etc.

As against macro theory, micro economic theory analyses consumption and investment of households, prices of particular goods, output, sales and purchase decisions of individual firms and industries. Micro economic theory, therefore, deals with smaller units and smaller magnitudes of decision variables. Difference between small and big is of one degree; the difference is relative rather than absolute. Firms are smaller than industries they belong to, industries are smaller than the economy in which they operate, the national economies are smaller than the world economy. Therefore, the difference between micro and macro is that of viewpoint (Mehta, 1958). If firms are analysed from the viewpoint of industry, analysis shall fall within the purview of micro theory. If, however, the focus of analysis of firms is relative to consumers, then the analysis may be macro in orientation. As against this, analysis of industry from the viewpoint of the economy will be micro. Analysis of Indian educational system as a whole will be macro in character. If, however, we focus on the analysis of problems and processes of either professional and technical education, or higher education, or secondary education, it may be considered to be micro. Again, households demand for education may be considered micro, whereas social demand for elementary education is macro. Analysis of problems of particular educational institutions shall also be micro.

The tiniest element of micro analysis is the behaviour of an individual or household. But behavioural propensities of individual agents reflect their psycho-mental processes. The micro analysis thus focuses on essential facets of human mind and individual behavioural responses to internal and external stimuli. Micro economic theory, therefore, involves an analysis of human mind in an essential manner (Mehta, 1958). But aggregates and averages, which macro theory analyses, exclude any direct involvement of human mind and individual behaviour. Individual behavioural traits and attributes of mental responses to internal and external stimuli of individuals or households are eliminated in the process of aggregating and averaging of variate values or attributes. Hence, there is no reference to individual behavioural traits, effects of psychological motivations and mental responses to stimuli in macro analysis. However, foundation of macro economic theory are laid essentially on micro postulates.

> *Micro economic theory deals with behavioural propensities of individual agents, reflecting their psycho-mental responses to endogenous and external stimuli. It involves analysis of human mind and behaviour in an essential way. Aggregating and averaging eliminates direct involvement of human mind and behaviour in macro analysis. But the foundations of macro economic theory are based essentially on micro theory.*

Macro and Micro Planning

Like economic theory, economic and educational planning may also be approached either at macro or micro levels. Above differences between macro and micro theories also distinguish macro from micro planning. Macro planning, like macro theory, deals with planning of the system as a whole rather than its constituent parts. Whereas macro economic planning deals with the planning of national economy, macro planning of education is concerned with the planning of educational system as a whole. As against this, micro planning deals with smaller constituent units of national economy or national system of education. National economy and national system of education constitute the accounting units and analytical entities of macro planning. Whereas firms and industries, on production side, and individuals or households, on consumption side, are the smaller units of economy, schools, colleges, and universities, on production side, and individuals receiving education, on users side, may constitute the accounting and analytical units of micro educational planning.

Macro educational planning deals with large aggregates and averages like total enrolments, total number of institutions in the country, total number of teachers and other staff employed therein, enrolment rates/probabilities for the population of reference age groups, transition ratios, stationary/dynamic 'Markov Chain' process of students' movements or flows among educational processes and institutions, repetition, drop-out, pass and failure rates/probabilities (Prakash and Singh, 1996).

Micro economic and educational planning, unlike micro economic theory, may refer to spatial rather than behavioural units. Micro entities or units of micro economic and educational planning are defined with reference to spatial size, location and spread. State, district, block, and village may constitute the basic accounting and analytical units of micro economic and educational planning. Micro economic and educational planning, unlike micro economic theory, will naturally deal with aggregates and averages like gross and per capita incomes, investment, consumption of these smaller spatial units. Within spatial boundaries of each layer and level of planning, defining and accounting units, there will be still smaller spatial and other units. Thus, differences between the entities and magnitudes of micro and macro planning may be one of degree or quantitative rather than qualitative.

Shift from the behavioural to spatial units of observation, accounting, analysis and planning in moving from micro to macro planning may probably be accounted by the fact that the theory and policy, right from their very inception, have been evolved to focus mainly on decision making processes by public authorities to determine, (i) levels and patterns of allocation of public resources, (ii) location patterns of publicly owned production units, (iii) levels and types of goods and services planned to be produced, (iv) norms and standards of distribution patterns of goods and services produced for realising predetermined objectives of planned development. These objectives are arranged according to a *priori* priorities. As against this, private decisions regarding consumption and investment at the level of individuals or households and private firms directly involve neither public resources nor public authorities. Naturally, such behavioural units do not fall within the purview of micro economic or educational planning.

This may, however, hold true fully neither for economic nor for educational planning. When planning focused on agricultural development to make India self-sufficient in foodgrains, government not only directly sponsored research in new farm technology, but it also invested heavily in extension education to ensure the diffusion of new technology among all regions of the country and the largest possible number of farmers. Minimum support prices and subsidisation of modern farm inputs constitute the pillars of public policy and planning of agriculture which directly influence private decisions at farm level. Similarly, when non-realisation of the objective of universalisation of elementary education has been found to be the deficiency of private demand, government came forward with a variety of packages of incentives and inducements to remove the deficiency in educational demand of the poor or unenlightened parents. All the same, conceptualisation of micro economic and educational planning necessitates substitution of spatial for human behavioural agents of accounting of micro economic theory. It implies that one of the factors accounting for differences between micro economic and educational planning may be the size of the spatial units of planning.

Centralised and Decentralised Planning

Differentiation between micro and macro economic and educational planning on the basis of differences between the size of population, geographical area, or administrative entity as spatial units of accounting and planning may, however, overlap with the classification of planning into centralised and decentralised categories. Under centralised planning, the authority to plan is vested generally in central authority like the Planning Commission in India, or Gos Plan Authority of USSR. The Central authority undertakes comprehensive planning for the entire country, whole economy and society, though it may involve authorities at lower levels and layers in planning in such ways as have been discussed under materials' balances strategy of planning. Under decentralised planning, power to plan is delegated to authorities working at lower levels and layers of spatial units. Planning at the level of state, region, division, district and local area may be distinguished on this basis. Planning can never be comprehensive and all encompassing without it being undertaken at national, regional, state, district, block, village, and town, sectoral, production units and institutional levels.

Perspective, Long and Short Run Planning

Planning may be distinguished according to the duration of period for which plans are prepared, that is, planning horizon may be adopted as the criterion of defining planning temporarily. But distinction between short and long periods is quite nebulous. It is one of degrees. Economic analysis distinguishes short from long period on the basis of the method of raising output that is possible to be adopted within the given timeframe. Level of output of an industry depends upon (i) number of firms, (ii) size of individual firms, and (iii) rate of output per unit of time. New firms can be established and productive capacities of existing firms can be raised only in the long period. Both for the establishment of new firms and expansion of capacities of production of existing firms, supply of both fixed and variable factors of production has to be enhanced. This is possible only in the long period. But the rate of output can be raised by enhancing the supply of variable factors to utilise fixed factors of production more intensively. Fixed factors of production include, besides human and fixed capital, technology of production, managerial techniques, organisational forms and institutional structures also. No such clear distinction between different time durations is attached to long and short-run planning. Short-term planning may cover from one to three years, five seven-year plans may be defined as medium term plans. Long period plans may range from eight to fifteen years. As against this, perspective plan is a very long-term plan. Its duration may cover as long a period as 20 to 30 years. During such long periods, current resource constraints may be expected to be removed, socio-economic transformation may be completed, current methods of production, managerial techniques, organisational forms and institutional structures may be totally changed. Hence, the exact shape and structure of society and economy will be quite hazy. Only broad directions of movements may be indicated and ultimate objectives of development and growth may be spelled out. But the perspective plans furnish the overall framework within which short and medium-term plans have to be viewed.

Contingency Planning

There is many a slip between cup and lip. This applies to planning also. More often than not, there occur seepages and leakages between achievements and goals and targets of plans either due to improper plan implementation and the emergence of unforeseen situations and emergencies for which provision might have not been made by planners. Under such circumstances, contingency planning has to be undertaken. Experience has taught that planners try to introduce flexibility in plan frame and make provisions for contingency planning in the eventuality of an emergency. Such planning may be defined as contingency planning.

We have discussed all the major typologies and categories of planning. Important points to be noted are that planning of different types are distinguished on the basis of differences among (i) nature of instruments, (ii) extent of coverage and scope of planning, (iii) type of authority empowered to plan, (iv) spatial/behavioural units of planning, and (v) viewpoint from which the system or its part(s) is planned.

References

Lewis, Arthur (1963), *Principle of Planning,* Allen and Unwin.

Prakash, Shri (1977), *Educational System of India: An Econometric Study,* Concept, New Delhi.

Prakash, S. & Chowdhury, S. (1996), *Expenditure on Education: Theory Models and Growth,* NIEPA, New Delhi.

Prakash, S. (1997), *Cost of Education: Theoretical Explorations and Empirical Prognostication,* Anamika.

Prakash, S. & Singh, Shalini (1997), 'Markov Chain Processes of Students' Flows and Universalisation of Elementary Education. Published in *Multivariate Statistical Analysis,* Vol. 23, University of Lodz.

Mehta, J.K. (1958), *Studies in Advanced Economic Theory,* S. Chand & Co., Delhi.

6

Institutional Planning

Need for Institutional Planning

The preceding chapters have made it clear that planning, as it originated in the former USSR, was comprehensive in coverage, centralised in nature and macro in typology. The power of plan formulation was vested in the Gos Plan Authority of the former USSR. Hence, planning was centralised, though processes of collection of information and plan formulation for individual production establishments involved all production units, big and small. The farms and factories, producing goods and units producing services were spread over all the regions of the country and sectors of the economy. Each production unit supplied information to the Gos Plan Authority regarding its current development status, output of goods and services produced and itemwise inputs used in production process to produce these given output levels. Each production unit also formulated draft proposals for its future development and submitted the same to the Gos Plan Authority for including these proposals in the final national plan of development. Thus, categorisation of the Soviet planning as centralised and macro is at variance with the materials' balances strategy of planning adopted by the Gos Plan Authority for formulating Seven Year Plans of development. The final plan was centrally formulated. But the final plan document comprised of plan proposals developed at the grass roots on decentralised basis. Actual plan formulation was operationally centralised but it was decentralised in structure. It was macro in conception but it had micro production units as its pivotal base. Operations for implementing the plan were also decentralised, though the operational guidelines were finalised centrally and these were furnished to implementing authorities and operators at the grass roots. Both plan formulation and implementation guidelines were based on centralised processes, while the contents were really developed at decentralised levels. Thus, the plan was macro in conception, centralised in form, decentralised in structure and micro in nature and contents, which reflected largely the concerns and programmes of micro production units on the one hand, and national objectives and priorities of planned development on the other.

All the same, analysts fondly classify Soviet planning as centralised and macro. This description is derived from the classification of planning into centralised and decentralised, and micro and macro categories. Distinction between micro and macro planning is based on the size of spatial units of planning. In the market oriented economies, micro planning may refer to firm or industry level planning. This has reference to corporate planning. Corporate planning plays a crucial role in indicative planning.

> *Micro educational planning may refer to planning of education at the level of individual educational institutions by the institutional authorities within the given policy frame of the government and the specific goals and objectives of individual institutions. Institutional objectives are not expected to be at variance with those guiding and governing the basic thrusts of public policies. Institutional planning is the planning at the level of individual educational institutions.*

When the move from centralised to decentralised planning started, basic idea was to move down to lower spatial units for planning. First step in this direction was to move from the centre to states/provinces as the agents and units of planning. As the movement towards decentralisation gathered momentum, it was realised that the problems at grass roots could be addressed better only if planning is further shifted from top down to the lowest spatial and/or administrative units in the geographical and bureaucratic hierarchy. Spatial units like village, town/city, block/subdivision, district and division are the spatial units below the state just as states lie below the nation. Micro planning may thus be taken up at any of these spatial units which constitute the basic units of planning, including educational planning. Micro planning of education may forge a step ahead of economic planning, since real micro units of educational planning are individuals or households on the one hand, and educational institutions on the other, which are not spatial in character. Main process of education, that is, learning and teaching takes place at the level of individual students, teachers and institutions. Students and teachers are the real transactors in this process, though administrators enter the scene as interventionists and facilitators, as agents, policy formulators and implementers of policy. Thus, students, teachers, academic administrators, educational administrators and policy makers are the transactions involved in education.

Parents also partake in these educational processes as facilitators and auxiliary transacters. These are smaller *behavioural entities,* and naturally they differ from the micro spatial units of planning discussed above. Individual educational institutions, which are behavioural and decision making units, are the real micro constituents of an educational system. This shift away from spatial to behavioural units in micro educational planning is facilitated by the fact that an educational system all over the world is owned, at least partly if not wholly, by public authorities. Even privately owned and operated segments of the educational system are funded/aided, controlled/guided and or regulated by the public policies of education. Public authorities, dealing with education, wield considerable control over the decisions of individual institutions. Micro educational planning may, therefore, refer to planning of education at the level of individual educational institutions by the institutional authorities within the given policy frame of the government and the specific goals and objectives of individual institutions.

Institutional objectives are not expected to be at variance with those guiding and governing the basic thrusts of public policies. Institutional planning refers to planning at the level of individual educational institutions. An educational institution, as the basic unit of institutional planning, is much smaller than the spatial units of micro planning. Besides, institutions are behavioural in nature as these are the decision makers and implementers of policy. Institutional planning may, therefore, pursue the objectives which are similar to the objectives pursued by firms of an industry in its production planning. Basic question which a firm considers are (i) what to produce, (ii) how to produce, (iii) how much to produce, (iv) where, when, and whom to sell its output, and (v) what prices to charge. All these aspects of production planning are relevant for institutional planning also. An institution has to determine (i) what level and type of education to impart, (ii) what intake capacities to instal, (iii) how many teachers to appoint, (iv) whom to admit and whom to refuse admission, (v) what fees to impose as user charges, (vi) what course contents to adopt, and (vii) what pedagogical methodology to use.

Materials' Balances and Institutional Planning

Under materials' balances strategy of planning, each plant, factory, farm, hospital and dispensary, and educational institution was required to submit detailed information about (a) its current operational status, (b) future programmes for expansion, diversification and development into new directions, (c) itemwise output targets during the planning horizon, (d) current itemwise amounts of inputs used up in current production, and (e) future requirements of itemwise inputs, including manpower along with their skills and occupational structure and educational profiles, anticipated to be needed for producing output planned to be produced by each institution. Each institution was supposed to evaluate its current performance and development status in relation to (i) targets fixed for achievements, and (ii) national objectives, goals and priorities. Current status was to be evaluated with a view to identify strengths and weaknesses, achievements and failures, shortages of both instructional and infrastructural facilities or their underutilisation, as the case may be, with a view to remove these operational deficiencies in the next plan. Targets were supposed to be fixed with reference to (i) resources available, (ii) target population of the students in the command area expected to be covered by education during the planning horizon, and (iii) programmes for the removal of current operational deficiencies. These institutional proposals were submitted to the central authority of planning. The Gos Plan Authority tested internal consistency in order to dovetail these detailed plans proposals and programmes of micro production units into national plan after several rounds of mutual discussions so as to make these decentralised proposals, projects and programmes consistent and in consonance with (i) national goals, priorities, targets and objectives of planned development, (ii) resources available/allocated for sector/space specific planned output levels, and (iii) input requirements of planned output.

Just as farms and factories are the basic micro production units of agricultural and industrial goods, schools, colleges, and universities are the basic micro production units of education. Under the Soviet system of planning, each educational institution was naturally required to undertake planning for future development of the institution concerned, giving rise to the need of institutional planning. Institutional planning may, therefore, be considered to be a special case of micro planning. Institutional planning is comparable to corporate planning by industrial sectors of the economy both in nature and scope, though the methods and objectives of these two layers of planning may be quite different.

Materials' balances strategy made the Soviet planning macro and centralised in form but micro and decentralised in structure and contents. Projects, programmes and proposals of development of individual farms, factories, hospitals and dispensaries, educational institutions and establishment of trade, transport, communications, and other production units constituted the core of centralised planning in a consistency framework. The need for consistency became essential (i) to provide national thrust and direction to development, (ii) integrate local, sectoral and regional development into national development plans in such a manner as to make regional, local and sectoral plans and programmes consistent with the objectives of national development on the one hand, and make these components conform to national priorities and resource constraints, and (iii) maintain balance between resource requirements and material input needs of production programmes included in the plan. Whereas national goals and objectives encompassed national concerns for (a) rapid transformation of a backward agrarian economy into a highly developed, industrialised and modern economy, (b) conversion of feudalistic and fragmented social structure into a unified and integrated, advanced and forward looking society, full of vigour, willingness, ability and enthusiasm for socio-economic growth and enhancement of human capabilities, and (c) making the monarchic and highly differentiated into an egalitarian and socialistic economy and polity through the elimination of economic inequalities. All the same, analysts fondly dub the Soviet planning as centralised. In order to differentiate, contrast and distinguish the theory and practice of planning in the former USSR with the theory and practice of planning in other countries, planning itself is classified into such categories as centralised and decentralised, and macro and micro planning. But from our analysis of materials' balances strategy of planning, developed and practiced in the former USSR and the procedure of planning associated with it, obviously that Soviet planning was neither purely centralised nor was it purely decentralised. Soviet planning was neither purely macro nor was it purely micro in nature, scope, and methodology. Planning, in the true sense of the term, may probably never be decentralised in the sense in which the term 'decentralisation' has popularly come to be used in literature.

Distinction between micro and macro in economic planning has basically been derived from the classification of economic theory into micro and macro economics. However, the basis of classification of planning into micro and macro may be slightly different from that of economic theory. Micro and macro planning may be distinguished mainly on the basis of the size of spatial or production units to be planned. Spatial or production units may be the basic entities of the decision making, policy and planning. Each spatial unit of planning may be characterised by homogeneity, while different units may be heterogeneous. Spatial units may be formed for the purpose of administration, geographical contiguity or similarities in agroclimatic conditions, or these may coincide with economic regions. The easiest basis of forming spatial units is administration.If production establishment is the planning unit, it may coincide with factories, farms, health and educational institutions, etc. In market economies, micro planning may refer to planning at the firm, farm, or an industry level. Corporate planning has firm as its planning unit. Theory and practice of corporate planning plays pivotal role in indicative planning. The Strategic Corporate Planning has come into the centre-stage with the initiation of the triple processes of globalisation, liberalisation, and privatisation almost in all the countries of the world, including erstwhile socialist economies of the Second World and countries of the Third World. Countries of the First World have been practising corporate planning knowingly or unknowingly for long.

Institutional Planning: A Special Case of Micro Planning

Economic and educational planning in the former USSR were the mixture of macro and micro, decentralised and centralised planning in conception, contents, scope and methodology. Interestingly, institutional planning was developed in the former USSR along with economic planning on the basis of materials' balances strategy. Soviet planning furnishes concrete concept and method of institutional planning.

Micro planning, in the modern sense, was developed in response to the explicit recognition of the need for supplementing macro or centralised planning to make planning focus on problem solving at the grass roots. Problems of real life at the grass roots often tended either to be blurred or totally lost in macro planning due to its concern with macro or national aggregates and averages. The processes of averaging and aggregating values of variables and parameters of micro units eliminated individual facets and diversities of the problems of production units. National/regional level macro aggregates and averages entered as essential elements of analysis, decisions and policies under macro and centralised planning. These averages and aggregates furnish the basis of macro programmes and projects for plan formulation at macro level. This is true for macro educational planning also. Consequently, problems and issues of development of individual farms and farmers, factories, and industries, educational institutions, students, and their educators got submerged in aggregates and averages.

Spatial units like village, block, district and state, as against a nation or a region as a whole, constitute the basic units of micro economic and educational planning. Macro planning of economy and education move mostly together or parallelly. But micro planning of education in real sense has forged one step ahead of economic planning in one respect. Micro educational planning deals essentially with such small *behavioural or decision making* entities as either schools, colleges and universities or households. These planning entities are much smaller than such micro production units as farms and factories, or such spatial units as states, districts, blocks or villages. Such educational institutions as schools, colleges and universities, which are decision making and behavioural units or planning agents, are the micro constituents of an educational system. This shift from the spatial to behavioural units, as one moves from economic to micro educational planning, is facilitated by the fact that the educational systems all over the world are owned, at least partly if not wholly, by the public authorities; while privately owned and operated segments of education are largely funded, aided, controlled, guided, and/or regulated by public policies of education. Public authorities, dealing with education, wield considerable control over the decisions of individual institutions.

Planning at the level of an individual institution is called Institutional Planning, and micro educational planning may, therefore, refer to planning of education at institutional level by institutional authorities within the given public policy parameters and overall framework of national objectives of educational development on the one hand, and goals and objectives that individual institutions choose for themselves on the other. Institutional objectives are not expected to diverge from national objectives of development as institutional policies and planning have to conform to public policies and thrusts guiding and governing national development. An institution as the basic unit of micro educational planning is much smaller than the spatial units of economic planning and an educational institution is also a behavioural entity in nature.

Planning at the level of an individual institution is called institutional planning. Objectives of institutional planning are expected to conform and to be in consonance with the national objectives of educational development and not to diverge from public policies guiding and governing the basic thrusts of national development.

However, an educational institution may consider under institutional planning almost the same questions as a firm has to consider in its production planning. A firm has to take decisions regarding the following basic questions: (i) what to produce, (ii) how to produce, (iii) how much to produce, (iv) what prices to charge from consumers, and (v) where, when and whom to sell its output. All above questions are highly important for educational planning at institutional level also.

Level and type of education to be imparted, intake capacities to be installed, qualifications of teachers, infrastructural and instructional facilities to be provided, fees to be charged, location of the institution, board or university of its affiliation are important questions for the deliberations of educational planners, when decisions to establish a new institution, or to expand, or to upgrade and/or diversify an existing institution are taken and plan to implement these decision is formulated. Nature, direction and scope of planning by institutions already in operation have naturally to be different from those of newly established institutions.

Types of Institutional Activities

Institutional planners, unlike macro planners, have limited space and scope for free and independent operations. Guidelines and parameters of macro public policies are exogenously given to institutional planners, which they can neither influence nor alter. But they have ample scope and opportunities for operational space within the constraints imposed by public policy, thrusts and directions of national objectives of educational development.

Activities of an educational institution may broadly and conveniently be divided into following two categories from the viewpoint of institutional planning: (i) those activities which an institution undertakes each year in a routine manner. Preparation of timetable for each subject/class/teacher, admission schedules, schedule of extracurricular activities, fixation of minimum achievement levels for admissions into an institution for pursuing a particular level, and type of education, etc. fall in this category. (ii) Certain parameters and time schedules are determined externally and the institution has to dovetail its programmes into this time frame and externally determined parameters. Just as micro consumption and savings decisions are planned and executed at the household level, whether to enrol or not to enrol, or whether to pursue general or professional education of a particular type after passing senior secondary examination are the decisions made by students and their parents. Individual institutions may not be in a position to alter the pattern of individual preferences and choices much. Thus, private demand for education, and hence, investment in the development of human resources, like private expenditure on other goods and services, is planned and activated at the level of households. Schedules of external examinations, duration, dates of commencement and end of the academic year, contents of the courses or curricula to be pursued at the given level and type of education, time schedules and the number and nature of inter-institutional literary, cultural, games and sports meets, etc., are determined externally. Curriculum, and hence, course contents, are determined by the Boards of Secondary Education and the Universities. Schools and colleges have hardly any say in these decisions. Apart from the universities and the Directorates of Education or their District level units, which themselves plan the time schedules of such activities for their colleges and teaching departments and schools, all other institutions have to take these time schedules as given and fixed. Institutional planning, however, does not encompass the planning of such activities, even though the internal organisation of such activities also involves planning of one type or another; (iii) Those activities which relate to development programmes of future expansion and/or diversification of the academic programmes, programmes of qualitative improvements in learning and teaching processes, and/or other curricular activities which will have a direct bearing upon the academic development of the given institution fall in the second category. Expansion of infrastructure like buildings, laboratory and other equipment, library, etc., also fall in the group of development programmes. However, the affiliating boards of education and universities prescribe certain minimum standards for these facilities before recognition and affiliation are granted to the individual institutions. The institution of new posts of teachers and administrators, introduction of new academic disciplines or subjects and additional courses/papers, that might have been developed recently in a subject or those might have been left out by the institution in its earlier programmes, upgradation of the level of education currently imparted in the institution, etc. constitute the developmental programmes.

But developmental activities may be classified into two groups: such activities as focus on overcoming current deficiencies and shortcomings of either instructional or infrastructural facilities or on effecting improvements in the current profiles of the institution; and such activities as attempt to further develop on the basis of current achievements by diversification, expansion and development.

Some of the chosen objectives of institutional planning may preferably be expressed concretely in quantitative terms, while several objectives may be qualitative in nature and may probably be difficult to measure quantitatively. Such objectives may be specified as concretely as may be feasible in the given state of knowledge. But all objectives have to be translated into clear and unambiguous goals and targets.

Institutional activities may also be classified from the functional viewpoint into the following typologies: (a) academic, (b) para or semi academic, (c) administrative, (d) auxiliary or supportive, (e) community service or extension activities. These various types of activities are associated with the provision of (a) students' services, both instructional and infrastructural. Appointment of teachers and assignment of work and duties to them, and provision of laboratory and library facilities may be designated as academic activities of an institution, whereas provision of buildings, equipment, furniture and furnishings, playgrounds, etc., may be called infrastructural activities, (b) recruitment, promotion, placement and provision of opportunities for professional development to the teachers is one of the most important activities of the institution, (c) administration deals with the routine assignment of work and duties to teaching and non-teaching staff, coordination of the activities of various transacters involved in education, enforcement of rules and procedures and liaison with outside agencies are important administrative functions.

Organisation of cocurricular and extracurricular activities fall in the category of auxiliary and supportive activities, (d) then financial provisions are among the important functions of educational management, (e) community services may encompass the involvement of both students and teachers in such activities as literacy campaign, environmental education, traffic regulation, etc. Howsoever intricate, comprehensive and elaborate the institutional planning may be, it is not an easy task to forge linkages between above institutional activities and the core objectives of institutional planning and development. At times, coordination of activities of different parts and components of institutions, specially the large ones, may rather be difficult.

Various activities may be grouped under the institutional plan according to the nature of programmes, projects and subplans to be undertaken during the planning horizon. But different activities may need different types of planning. For example, planning for improvements in teaching and learning processes will require planning of a type which will be entirely different from planning warranted for improvement in cocurricular and extracurricular activities of the institution.

Stages in Institutional Planning

Four distinct stages may be differentiated in institutional planning: (i) Normative stage, (ii) Strategic stage, (iii) Operational stage, and (iv) Stage of monitoring and evaluation of the progress of plan implementation.

In the normative stage, planners decide what ought to be done. In this preliminary stage of planning, planners have to choose from several alternative objectives that may be feasible within the resource constraints, number and nature of problems that the institution faces, and aspirations, expectations, and possibilities of development in future.

In the strategic stage of institutional planning, planners have to identify the technically feasible and economically viable projects and programmes and the best possible ways of implementation of schemes in order to realise the chosen objectives. The strategy has to break down the major objectives into subcomponents, tasks and various steps needed for their accomplishment in the course of plan implementation. This is the crucial stage for narrowing the gaps between promise and performance.

Operational stage refers to the stage when actual plan has to be implemented by activating the programmes. It is the stage of translation of intentions into deeds. In this stage, the programme of action has to be implemented. Hence, various operational steps have to be identified and undertaken with utmost care.

Next comes the monitoring and evaluation stage. Some analysts think that the monitoring and evaluation can be undertaken only when the given task(s) has already been accomplished. This view may have a certain grain of realism. For example, some project proposals for evaluating the impact of Navodaya Vidyalayas just one or two years after the introduction of the project/programmes were rejected on the ground that one/two years were too short a period for assessing the impact of this project on the quality of education. Similarly, the introduction of career orientation of education and vocationalisation of first degree is monitored and evaluated only after the lapse of couple of years of its introduction. But such prudence may be valid only for the evaluation and monitoring of some particular aspects of planning. So far as the assessment of the progress of plan implementation is concerned, monitoring and evaluation have to be concurrent. Concurrent monitoring and evaluation will facilitate the initiation of corrective measures if the implementation of the plan programmes is faulty, tardy or misdirected, otherwise the exercise will result only in crying foul after the milk has already been spilt. Above discussion should not lead to the inference that these stages are the loose ends of the chain or end-points of the joints or these are sequential in nature. These are in fact the points of a continuum.

Steps and Procedure of Institutional Planning

Institutional planning may follow a definite procedure, involving certain sequential steps in planning at the institutional level. The procedure and its steps are described below:

Choice of Objectives and Goals and Target Setting

Like all other types and varieties of planning, the first step of institutional planning is to choose the objectives of planned institutional development. As has already been discussed, this is the normative phase of deciding what ought to be done. This may however be guided by the problems and needs of the institution under consideration. But objectives chosen with a view to focus on problem solving will be specific in nature. Choice of such objectives will have to be preceded by an exercise to identify the problem areas, their resource requirements and resources available to the institution. Available assets and resources of the institution will have to be linked to specific projects and programmes designed to find solutions to institutional problems. Specific objectives of institutional planning will, however, be short-term objectives, since the number and nature of problems of each institution tend to change from one to another level of development. General objectives will be designed to have an overall view of not only short term but also medium and long-term development of the given institution.

Distinctive Objectives of Institutional Planning

It may be noted that individual institutions may, by and large, pursue almost the same objectives as inform national and regional planning, though special objectives of institutional development may also be pursued. In fact, the pursuance of specific objectives of institutional development imparts a distinct flair to institutional planning. But the choice of objectives of planned institutional development may pose serious problems to planners. It may be quite instructive if we have an idea about the nature of objectives that educational institutions proclaim to pursue. Most of the institutions find it useful to enlist their purposes and objectives in their prospectus in order to make themselves stand out as different and distinct from other institutions. Unfortunately, a perusal of prospectuses of numerous institutions will reveal that most institutions prefer to express their purposes and objectives in generic and vague terms. The description of objectives in general terms may not help in translating the same into concrete projects and programmes, which may be different not only from national and regional objectives but also from those of other institutions. One should not infer from this that almost all institutions serve the same purposes and pursue the same objectives. This may, however, be a misleading inference. For example, exclusively girls, boys and coeducational institutions will seek to promote education of different clientele groups. The difference is confined not only to the gender or the gender mix but it extends to socio-economic backgrounds, academic achievements, career objectives, values and outlook. This is true about the differences between the objectives of institutions of professional and general education on the one hand, and the rural and urban institutions on the other. Despite the generalities and vagueness of objectives, pursuance of distinct goals and different styles of functioning do make institutions differ in reputation, efficiency and quality of education imparted. But the objectives have to be converted into targets and tasks which may be further broken down into subtargets and subtasks in order to facilitate the identification of the steps to be undertaken at the implementation stage.

Historical Review of Institutional Performance

Development objectives will have to be translated into concrete goals. Targets will have to be set in concrete terms for the realisation of the chosen objectives. But the choice of objectives, and hence, the determination of goals and the target setting for their realisation cannot be performed in a vacuum. It requires an indepth evaluation and analysis of (i) national objectives of educational development, and (ii) performance of the system as a whole in general and the given institution in particular in the historical perspectives in order to identify (a) successes and failures of the system, and hence, its inherited strengths and weaknesses. It is with reference to this that individual institutions may plan to carve operational areas and space for themselves, and mark the turning-points in the life of the institution, and (b) achievements and failures of the institution in the past, and hence, strengths and weaknesses that characterized its functioning. Special attention has to be paid to its functioning in recent past, since remote history may not be much relevant to present and future problems. A careful examination and evaluation of the basic objectives and felt societal needs at the local, regional, and national levels in response to which the institution had originally been established in the first instance, an exhaustive and critical evaluation of the styles and patterns of its historical growth, conventions and traditions that have been evolved and nurtured by it through time, nature and extent of impacts and the efficacy and effectiveness of its actual working with reference to the societal and institutional needs and requirements. The shifts in emphasis on different objectives at different points of time may also be called for.

In case of extremely old institutions, critical analysis of most of the above aspects of the actual functioning of the institution during distinctly different phases of its historical growth may be specially rewarding in identifying and analysing the changing patterns, reorientations of its aims and objectives in response to the temporally changing nature of socio-economic development and nature of changes and developments in knowledge, including educational technology. Such review may facilitate the determination of relevance and degree of responsiveness of the institution to the perceived needs and objectives of the society which the institution seeks to serve on the one hand, and it will place the achievements and failures of the institution both in narrow and wider perspectives on the other. It will also help in knowing how far the institution has succeeded in keeping pace with the new developments in educational field and the extent to which it has realised its chosen objectives in the past.

Historical review will also serve the purpose of identifying the problems that the institution face and solutions are found both in remote and recent past. This may instil confidence to solve the current problems and may also shed light on possible solutions of future problems. It will have to critically examine the physical, financial, and other constraints subject to which it had been functioning, specific operational areas in which it has had failed to fulfil its own aspirations, live up to community's expectations and needs of the educational system which it belongs to. It may facilitate the delineation of broad contours of the directions of changes in future development of the institution. For purposes of planning, all these aspects are required to be translated into precise information and data. These data themselves will help in identifying the future objectives of institutional development.

> *If the institution under consideration happens to be operating sub-optimally, then current enrolments and the pattern of their past growth may highlight the causes of sluggishness of growth of enrolments and/or rigidity of structure, obstructing proper responses to community's needs and expectations, shortcomings in operational designs, that impinge upon the goodwill, and hence, reputation of the institution as causes of malfunctioning.*

Several institutions, both schools and colleges, have extremely high unit costs in India due to their sub-optimal size (Prakash, 1995, 1996). If the institution under consideration happens to be operating sub-optimally in the past, raising its unit cost above the optimum, then current enrolments and the pattern of their past growth may highlight the major factors of sluggishness of growth of enrolments, and/or rigidity of structure, obstructing proper responses to community's needs and expectations, shortcomings in operational designs, that impinge upon the goodwill, and hence, reputation of the institution as causes of malfunctioning. Different policy packages may furnish solutions of different problems. If the sluggish growth of enrolments is due to the servicing of purely science stream, which operates within capacity limitations warranted by the constraints of laboratory facilities, or even otherwise due to requirement of costly equipment and disposable materials for the conduct of practicals, diversification of courses by the introduction of arts and humanity streams may augment enrolment size. But the application of norms of the optimal size of a purely Arts institution may not hold good, though addition of the Arts stream will mitigate the problem of sub-optimality to a great extent. Therefore, the objective of expansion of size by the introduction of Arts subjects will become highly desirable so as to exploit the economies of scale for reducing the unit costs.

But the introduction of any new subject or stream of subjects should be evaluated with reference to the pattern of demand in education and employment markets on the one hand, and socio-economic relevance on the other. If, however, the given institution's internal efficiency, as reflected by success rates in examinations and proportion of first divisioners among the successful candidates, or the proportion of students of this institution among the successful candidates in the competitive tests for JRF, IAS, etc., is low relative to those from the competing institutions in the command area, then the objective of selection of programmes for the improvement of internal efficiency will be warranted. The institutions may attempt to improve the quality of teaching by greater motivation of teachers and higher facilitation of their professional development and by efforts to attract better students. Some institutions may strive to build reputation in extra mural activities in order to attract talented students.

If below optimum size is due to indifferent reputation of the institution, which induces and prompts parents in the command area of the school/college to enrol their wards elsewhere, institutional planning should focus on building reputation through improvements in quality. Often examination results and number of alumni qualifying in admission/employment tests serve as indicators of internal efficiency of an institution. If enrolments are low due to mainly poor results in examinations, following quantitative and qualitative aspects will have to be examined: (i) are the results poor relative to what the institution considers as satisfactory performance level for itself? (ii) are the results below the overall average for all institutions? (iii) are the results low in relation to those of competing institutions? (iv) are the results low due to poor infrastructure? (v) are the results low due to mainly poor quality of instructions, discipline, and overall academic environment? This may itself be due to lower qualifications and learning levels of teachers, or (vi) does the open door admission policy account for the predominance of poor calibre students in the institution? Any specific policy of planning will follow from the specific nature of the answer to above type of questions.

Specific objectives, policy thrusts, and directions of institutional planning will follow from the specific nature of the answer to specific problems that the particular institution faces in its operations. Planning for increasing the efficiency is warranted so as to expand the command area itself by offering competition to the institutions located beyond its own command area. Programmes of good-will generation and image building will also be desirable in order to sharpen the competitive edge of the given institution. Such institutions will have to acquire the traits of a firm offering non-price competition to its rivals.

If low population of the command area is the cause of under-utilisation of intake capacity, then also the planning for increasing the internal efficiency will be warranted so as to expand the command area itself by offering competition to the institutions located beyond its own command area. The programmes of goodwill generation and image-building will be desirable in order to sharpen the competitive edge of the given institution. Such institutions will have to acquire the traits of a firm which offers non-price competition to its rivals to raise its share in the market. The determination of the planning and policy packages will depend upon the nature of specific problems that an institution faces and their diagnostic causes.

Appropriate planning for an institution requires that (i) problems are defined precisely so as to choose the objectives and specific programmes properly; (ii) a definite strategy of problem solving has to be designed and implemented. For example, internal efficiency may be raised through supplementing lectures by tutorials or extra coaching both to extremely dull and extremely intelligent students in order to improve their performance both in quantitative and qualitative terms. If the performance of students reflects only the lower academic qualifications possessed by teachers, their poor motivation and inadequacies of professional competence, teachers may be sent for in-service programmes of improvement in their qualifications and professional competence. This will also mitigate poor motivation and want of commitment. If, however, inefficiency reflects the poor quality of students admitted into the institution, it will call for different remedial measures; (iii) operational methods and instruments for translation of programmes into actions have to be devised for activating chosen programmes, projects and schemes; (iv) a definite time frame has to be fixed for the operationalisation of the plan programmes and projects; (v) a plan for monitoring and evaluation of progress and the mechanism of evaluation should be formulated and adopted in advance in order to avoid slippages in execution. Machinery and methods of monitoring and evaluation will also have to be established; (vi) the conceptualisation and implementation of various steps for qualitative improvements require that the comparative advantages are exploited, strengths are further enhanced and weaknesses and loopholes are removed and plugged at the earliest possible through implementation of well-designed programmes of qualitative improvements in the functioning of the institution; (vi) specific programmes of expansion and diversification should be properly formulated and expeditiously executed.

> *Various steps involved in institutional planning for improvement require the enhancing of the strengths and exploitation of comparative advantages and the plugging of areas of weaknesses through the implementation of well-designed programmes of qualitative improvement. Adoption and the attainment of objectives depend upon the adequacy of available resources, though implementation of certain programmes may be feasible even with currently available resources.*

Adoption and the attainment of objectives depend upon the adequacy of available resources, though implementation of certain programmes may be feasible even with currently available resources. Adequacy or otherwise of the available resources also depends, to a large extent, upon the nature, extent and the pattern of utilisation of available resources. An empirical study of elementary education in India has highlighted that available resources are suboptimally utilised (Prakash, 1995). Hence, a part if not the whole of the resource crunch in education may easily be mitigated if allocative and utilisation efficiencies of resources are raised. After ensuring optimal resource utilisation, alternative sources and modes of resource mobilisation may be explored both at institutional and macro levels.

Special care should be taken of poor maintenance and under-utilisation of infrastructural facilities in general and equipment in particular. The poor after sales service tends to make this task extremely complex, difficult and even an expensive proposition. Inadequately trained or qualified personnel, especially teaching staff, poses even more serious problems than this. In-service learning and training may be encouraged as retrenchment in Indian conditions is not feasible. Knowledge explosion warrants the continuous upgradation of the skills of even the best and most qualified teachers through refresher and/or reorientation courses and in-service training programmes. It is of the greatest importance since quality of teaching, and hence, learning depends, a great deal, upon teachers' (a) competence as determined by their own academic qualifications at the time of recruitment and subsequent improvement thereafter, (b) motivation and professional commitment, (c) opportunities for professional development through in-service training and enhancement in academic qualifications, (d) energy and time devoted by teachers to self-learning and time spent in preparations for teaching, (e) promotional avenues and their relationship with efficiency and academic attainments, and (f) quality of leadership at institutional level provided by the principal or head of the institution.

Knowledge explosion warrants continuous upgradation of the skills of even the best and most qualified teachers through refresher and/or reorientation courses and in-service training programmes.

Whenever the resources permit and it is warranted by the needs, technological base of the institution should be upgraded. If other institutions at accessible distances have better facilities, their use may also be acquired on payment basis or otherwise. Interlibrary loans, purchase of computer time, utilisation of regional instrumentation centres furnish examples of this type of interinstitutional cooperation. It is of paramount importance in a resource scarce country like India, where infrastructural facilities in most of the institutions fall short of requirements. It avoids unnecessary duplication of costly facilities without affecting functional efficiency adversely on the one hand, and it also facilitates the mitigation of difficulty of such institutions which do not possess such facilities on the other.

Democratic and Decentralised Structure of Planning

Head of the institution plays a pivotal role in institutional planning. Therefore, his style and mode of functioning will have a direct bearing upon the quality of institutional planning. The head of the institution cannot afford to be autocratic, arrogant and arbitrary. Success of planning warrants democratic functioning and decentralised power structure, where both rights and responsibilities have to be shared in a transparent operational environment. Principal or head of the institution is the first among equals. Involvement of all teachers in plan formulation, its implementation, monitoring and evaluation of the progress is to be ensured through participatory management. This objective may be realised by (i) devolution of power and decentralisation of responsibilities of decision making, plan formulation and its implementation, (ii) periodic consultations either through meetings or individually both during the plan formulation and implementation phases. Both collective and individual consultations are warranted even for routine administrative functions. Head of the institution has to work as the first among equals but he/she has to furnish leads and guidance through practice rather than through precept. He has to lead from the front rather than bringing the team from the rear. If community participation is also ensured, it shall impart realism, augment support base, and dynamise institutional development. Teacher-parents associations and their frequent meetings and students-teachers groups should also be formed for involving all the transacters in educational processes. But such meetings should neither be ceremonial nor should these be throttled by hierarchy. There should be free exchange of views and opinions among all transacters in order to bring below-surface problems to the fore and to derive benefit of a variety of experiences, views and insights. It may be noted that the need for cooperation is that of the head of the institution rather than that of teachers. Among all stakeholders, it is the head of institution who is expected to manage the show. Others are there only to help him/her. They are not accountable for successes and failures. Of course, once responsibilities are shared among all, both transparency and accountability will be ensured.

Interinstitutional Interaction

It shall be highly rewarding, if heads of different institutions interact among themselves periodically in order to exchange views and experiences. It shall throw light on problem solving through alternative routes.

Monitoring and Evaluation

Progress of institutional plan implementation should be concurrently monitored and evaluated. But the responsibility of monitoring and evaluation should be collective rather than individual. For one person, howsoever powerful and intuitive he/she may be, it will not be feasible to know each and every detail and keep track of what happens in classrooms daily. An elaborate machinery for the purpose should also be established and norms should be evolved, indicators of development be conceptualised and methods of their measurement identified in order to carry the task of monitoring and evaluation in a meaningful manner.

Advantages and Disadvantages of Institutional Planning

Planning at micro level in general and institutional level in particular, irrespective of spatial or behavioural nature of planning unit, is relatively more difficult than planning at the macro level. Following are the main factors making the task of micro and institutional planning relatively more difficult than that of macro planning:

(a) It is relatively easy to close the society/economy at the national level in order to control the disturbing and distorting influences of external forces on the endogenous working of the system. Closing of the system at the level of states/districts is extremely difficult, if not impossible. Failure of the policy of restricting interstate/district movements of cereals during the early seventies is a testimony to this. Population movements, especially those of students among institutions and among different geographical areas, are neither feasible nor desirable to control. Up to seventies, University of Saugor attracted students practically from the entire country. Large number of students from southern states of Andhra Pradesh and Kerala used to join this university. First, the introduction of Hindi as the compulsory medium of instruction at postgraduate level, and secondly the demand by the government of M.P. that governments of Kerala and A.P. should shoulder some financial burden for providing higher education to their students eliminated this inflow. It impaired the standards of teaching and research in that university. Movement of students and teachers among regions and institutions, especially at higher levels, is sought to be encouraged under the New Policy of Education. Occupational mobility of teachers and higher administrative staff on the one hand, and that of students on the other, mitigate the problems of in-breeding, indiscipline, and politicking. Some states have adopted the policy of making the services of Registrars and Deputy Registrars of universities transferable among the universities of the state in order to cope up with last two problems. Interstate migration for education accounts for a sizeable proportion of total migrants in India (Prakash et.al. 1991, Prakash & Mohanty, 1995).

(b) Educational planner at macro level is free to modify and even change policy packages, whenever warranted by newly emerging patterns and problems. As against this, several parameters and overall policy frame is externally fixed for micro planning, especially at the level of institutions. Hence, micro planner in general and institutional planner in particular is required to operate within the fixed macro policy frame and parameters. Scope for innovations and experimentation becomes narrower. But within the given frame, micro planner is free to operate provided that micro objectives and operations do not move in directions that are contrary to the national/state objectives.

(c) Resource crunch is much more severe at the institutional than the macro level, though the former is, by and large, a mirror image or reflection of the latter. The problem gets compounded by the fact that education is considered to be partly a public and partly a private goods, partly a social service and welfare promoting goods and partly an investment or merit or capital good, (Prakash, 1998). This restricts the scope of raising additional resources for education by certain measures, say by the raising of tuition fees, lest it may run counter to the realisation of the goals of welfare and equity on the one hand, and the objective of socio-economic development on the other. Notwithstanding the above, the Government of India had been silently withdrawing support to higher education under the thrust of new economic policy. In its White Paper on Subsidies, Government of India has gone to the extent of even defining

Higher Education to be a 'Non-Merit Good' (Cf. Prakash, 1998). This has already started eliminating the poor from higher education in general and technical and professional education in particular. Its adverse effects are likely to be experienced in the medium run both in terms of the availability of high level manpower and the accentuation of income and occupational inequalities.

But there are distinct advantages of planning at micro institutional level. The advantages of micro and institutional planning are as follows: (i) there exists firsthand knowledge and experience of problems at the grass roots; (ii) teachers and students on the one hand, and local community and its resources on the other, may easily be involved both in plan formulation and its implementation. Willing and enthusiastic participation in the planning, implementation and monitoring and evaluation of progress by teachers, students and parents can ensure a fair measure of success in the realisation of the cherished goals and objectives; and (iii) face to face situation in institutional planning makes the plan formulation, its monitoring and evaluation relatively more realistic and meaningful.

Success or failure of macro, micro or institutional planning education depends ultimately on its implementation at the level of individual institutions. Institutional planning is, therefore, of utmost importance in the present context.

References

Prakash, S. (1977), *Educational System of India— An Econometric Study,* Concept, New Delhi.

Prakash, S., Chowdhury, S. & T.J. Buragohain (1991), Demographic Pressures and Migration: A Case Study of Meghalaya. Published in *Manpower Journal,* Vol. XXV, Nos. 1 & 2.

Prakash, S. (1995), Optimisation of Resource Use in Elementary Education in India. Published In Koti, R.K. and Hashim, S.R. *et.al.*(Eds.), *Studies in Indian Economy,* Himalaya Publishing House, Delhi.

Prakash, S. and Mohanty, N.K.(1995), *Migration as Source of Human Capital Formation and Measurement of Its Economic Value.* Presented to the Twelfth International Conference on Input Output Techniques, New Delhi.

Prakash, S. (1997), *Cost of Education:Theoretical Explorations and Empirical Prognostication,* Anamika, New Delhi.

Prakash, S. (1998), Is Higher Education a Non-Merit Good? Published in, *University News,* Special Issue June.

7

Resume and Conclusions

This chapter presents a resume of the study and its major findings.

An important aspect of this study is that it delves deep into the philosophical and theoretical foundations of planning in general, and educational planning in particular. It incisively and penetratively discusses both the materialistic and non-materialistic, that is, spiritualistic views of determinism, which rules out any space for state interventionism, and hence, planning. The intellectual explorations of the spiritual determinism lead to a new interpretation of *Karma Yoga.* This interpretation propounds the thesis that the *karmafal* or outcome(s) of an action depends upon (a) nature and direction of relationship between the cause *(karma)* and its effect(*fal*). Hence, expectation of any result that is contrary to the nature of this relationship will lead to disillusionment. One should not entertain expectations of this type from his activities, (b) circumstances under which the action has been undertaken have a great bearing upon the nature of the result, that is, success or failure. The timing of the action is an important facet of the consequences of human actions. Hence, the time and place of activities have to be kept in view when one expects any result from his actions, (c) mode of performance and the strength of motivation, perseverence of efforts and dedication to the cause one upholds dear also make an impact upon the fruits one reaps. Therefore, one has to give a careful thought to these factors in forming expectations from the actions, (d) above all, *Daiv Yog*, or God's Will, or in scientific language, the random factors often affect the consequences of human endeavours. One should always leave a margin for this factor while expecting any particular fruit or reward. Hence, success or failure should lead to a careful evaluation of these facets of human activities and their results both before and after the completion of an act. Good causes have to be upheld and one should never be indifferent to the factors that are designed to achieve desired results. Causes of failures or deficiencies in efforts should be identified and removed in subsequent attempts to achieve the desired objectives and goals. Duty or *Karma* can be performed better if all above aspects of human actions and their likely consequences are systematically evaluated both before and after the performance of the act. This does not warrant an indifference towards the *karmafal* or outcomes of the performance of duty. If Arjun was defeated in *Mahabharat*, that would have been the victory of deceit, dishonesty and treachery which would have been a disaster not only for *Pandavas* but for the society as a whole. That is why Lord Krishna himself devised all sorts of strategies for *Pandavas* to win the war. Besides, Lord Krishna himself told Arjun that if he won the war, he would enjoy the fruits of kingdom. If he died fighting, he will be remembered as a great warrior. But if he flinched from his duty of fighting the war, he will be known as a coward and betrayer of duty. Thus, there is no question of indifference to results. This interpretation makes *karma yoga* plausible to be practised as the way of life.

Theoretical explorations of the roots of planning lead the study to propound a refreshingly innovative concept of planning. It defines planning as the deliberate and conscious choice of technically feasible and economically viable policy package out of the available options with a view to realise the a *priori* chosen goals and objectives. The study discusses the ideological nature of the choice of objectives, goals and priorities, while it emphasises the technical feasibility and economic viability for listing and prioritising of the options from which choices are to be made. The role of strategy of plan implementation, administrative set-up and institutional organisation are duly emphasised as essential prerequisites of successful planning. The general concept of planning has been elaborated with reference to education in order to present such an intricate concept of educational planning as is in consonance with the concept of economic planning and as is appropriate for educational development.

The study discusses exhaustively the various approaches to planning and offers a concrete concept of *educational demand*. The concept of educational demand has never been propounded, though analysts and policy makers have often talked about it. The study highlights the subtle differences between the 'aggregate private demand for education' and 'social demand for education'. The two concepts have been treated as synonymous in literature both explicitly and implicitly. The confusion and the cobwebs woven around the concept of 'social demand for education' have thus been removed.

Besides, an attempt has been made to take an integrated view of different approaches to educational planning by highlighting the common features of seemingly different approaches in order to emphasise the fact that returns on educational investment, manpower requirements and social demand approaches to educational planning represent the same basic facets of resource allocation for investment in various sectors of the economy, including education, and the developmental phenomena. The study highlights the commonality in the ultimate pattern of resource allocation and final shape of development plans and the outcomes of planned development, irrespective of approach adopted for educational planning. Consideration of this nature of different approaches to educational planning is emphasised.

The applicability of 'Materials Balances Approach' to education has been explained with practical illustrations and experiences. The importance of consistency in planning has been explained. Consequences of inconsistency in economic and educational planning have been highlighted with the resultant difficulties, bottlenecks and constraints encountered both by Indian economy and education. Such problems as the time slippages, cost and time over runs involved in the execution of plan projects have been traced to inconsistency in planning and halting and faulty manner of plan implementation. Adverse consequences of such facets of planning have been brought into sharp focus.

The study has pinpointed the bidirectionality of education-economy interrelations on the one hand, and sequentiality and laggedness of the nature of income-educational investment interface on the other. It is explicitly recognised that correlation and regression analysis do not help in identifying and choosing the explained and explanatory variables on their own. This is the function of theory. Besides, the coefficient of correlation may be interpreted to identify either of the two variables as the cause. Therefore, on the basis of correlation coefficient, one cannot say whether income is the cause of educational development or education is the cause of the growth of income. Empirical reality and a *priori* logic prompts us to argue that current educational investment is financed out of current income and past savings, whereas those currently receiving education are not a part of labour force, and hence, their education does not contribute to the generation of current income. But the current educational investment will facilitate future growth of income when the current students join the labour force after completing their education. Therefore, the cause and effect relationship can be detected from the coefficient of correlation or regression if the current or lagged nature of the variables is examined in the context of above theorising. Correlation analysis needs to be supplemented by regression analysis in accordance with the proper theoretical paradigms.

The study elaborately explains the objective criteria of classification of planning into different typologies and extends the application of these criteria to delineate and differentiate between different types of educational planning. The study also highlights the overlapping nature of the classification of educational planning into different types. It is explained that differences in the typologies of planning arise from the differential nature of (a) resources involved in planned allocation, (b) tools and instruments used in plan formulation and plan implementation, (c) structure and mechanisms that constitute the base of plan formulation and plan implementation, (d) nature and size of spatial or other units of planning, (e) hierarchical interrelationships between the planners at different layers, plan implementers and planning units, (f) nature and degree of power and authority exercised by actors involved in planning at different layers of the hierarchy.

The study very elaborately discusses the concept, process, actors, products, mechanisms of plan formulation and its implementation. The congruence and coherence of various elements and facets of educational planning as the prerequisites of success of planning have been elaborately explained in full details.

The study detours the factors and circumstances that made planning universally acceptable and popular in the second half of the present century. Success of the Keynesian prescription of state intervention to remove the deficiency of demand in order to eliminate recession or depression and its subsequent extension and popularisation not only as the means to macro economic stabilisation but also as the policy to initiate and nurture economic growth in developing countries, spectacular success of planning in the former USSR to put it economically on par with the developed countries of the West in a period of only three decades, success of wartime controls and state interventions in managing the needs and facilitating the achievement of desired goals in the West, and lastly, the want of physical capital, private enterprise and other types of human capital in developing countries needed for their development made planning universally acceptable and popular in the post Second World War period.

Findings of the empirical researches of the author have been used extensively to substantiate the theses and viewpoints analysed in different contexts.

The study highlights the wide-ranging differences in opinions among planners regarding a seemingly factual facet of the historical origins of educational planning. The time gap between the postulated dates of the origins of educational planning ranges from three decades to the vaguely dated point of origin of the state system of education, whereas the place(s) of origin of educational planning is postulated in the former USSR on the one hand, and all the countries of the Third World on the other.

The study very painstakingly marshalls historical evidences from the UK, Tanzania, Kenya, Japan and India in order to settle the issue of dating and spatially locating the historical origins of educational planning quite decisively. The study, in this process, highlights such little known facts that 20 per cent Indians were highly educated in 1870s, when only one in 15 and 17 Americans, Britishers, and Australians were literate or had the benefit of some education. This raises doubts about the factuality of literacy rate being only five per cent in India in 1901 as has been reported by the alien rulers of those days in the second census of India. The study implicitly propounds the thesis that educational planning was developed in India with manpower requirements approach being its driving force. But the system focused almost exclusively on manpower requirements for white-collar jobs in general and the manpower needs of the British administration in particular. The study also highlights the envisagement of the Western education as an instrument of cultural colonisation through brain-washing for enlisting support for British rule .

The study combines historical, analytical and quantitative methods of research in educational planning. Purely theoretical speculations and intuitive insights supplement the analysis of the facts and their interpretations.

The study concludes with the chapter on institutional planning, which offers not only an explanation of the theory and method of institutional planning but it also explains the sequential steps needed for the practice of institutional planning. The study throws light on the roles, functions and rights of different transacters involved in educational processes and the nature of the transactions that take place among these transacters. The study emphasises the constraints and important parameters that should inform and define institutional planning in a democratic set-up. Thus, the study attempts to fill up the gap in literature by furnishing material on institutional planning.

Index